THE
CARTOON HISTORY
OF
THE AMERICAN REVOLUTION

THE
CARTOON HISTORY
OF
THE AMERICAN REVOLUTION

Michael Wynn Jones

G. P. Putnam's Sons
New York

ACKNOWLEDGMENTS

I am deeply indebted, for the help given me personally and for permission to reproduce prints in their collections, to:

AMERICAN ANTIQUARIAN SOCIETY

BOSTON PUBLIC LIBRARY

BRITISH MUSEUM, DEPARTMENT OF PRINTS & DRAWINGS

JOHN CARTER BROWN LIBRARY, PROVIDENCE

LIBRARY OF CONGRESS, WASHINGTON DC

LIBRARY COMPANY OF PHILADELPHIA

NEW YORK PUBLIC LIBRARY

WESTMINSTER CITY ART LIBRARY

MASSACHUSETTS HISTORICAL SOCIETY

CONTENTS

ARTISTS

ANON. By far the greatest contributor to this book. Until the arrival of such virtuoso engravers like Gillray, it was extremely rare for the author of a print to append his name. Indeed in many cases a print was not designed and engraved by the same hand. Designs (often by amateurs) were bought up wholesale by print-sellers, if not actually pirated, and then handed on to the engraver. Although he may well have been responsible for giving the production any style it possessed, in the early days he was regarded as little more than a hack-craftsman.

BUNBURY, William Henry (1750–1811) was the son of a clergyman and was educated at Cambridge University. He was accustomed to moving in fashionable circles, becoming equerry to the Duke of York in 1787. He is said to have studied drawing in Rome, though he never achieved a status greater than that of gifted amateur. He was also an accomplished performer in private theatricals. (*p. 152*)

COPLEY, John Singleton, was born in Boston in 1737. As a young man his paintings attracted sufficient attention for him to be elected a fellow of the Society of Artists in Britain. On the outbreak of the war he departed on a Continental Tour of Europe and later settled in London, where he worked successfully as a portrait painter and composed large scale patriotic canvasses. The only evidence that he ever drew a cartoon is a hand-written annotation on the back of a variant on *The Deplorable State of America.*

COLLEY, Thomas. Examples of this caricaturist's work survive from the period 1780–83. He is known to have published many of his own cartoons from various addresses. (*p. 174*)

CORBUT. I have found no trace of anyone of this name, French or American, working in Boston or Philadelphia. CORBUTT, however, had been a widely-known pseudonym in the 1760s of one Richard Purcell, a mezzotint engraver and notorious wag. He had died bankrupt in 1765, but is

it possible that someone had remembered and resurrected his disguise? (*pp. 114, 118*)

DARLY, Matthew, was originally a drawing-master. He later became a prolific printseller who, in 1773, held London's first exhibition of cartoons. His own specialities were caricatured variations on contemporary fashions such as the extravagant ladies' coiffures of the day and the ludicrous 'macaroni' styles for men). He ceased work—or died—in 1778, but his influence lived on in the freer styles and interpretations of his successors. (*pp. 64, 108, 134*)

DAWES, Philip, was the natural son of a merchant in the City of London. He worked under Hogarth as an engraver around 1760, and in 1761 exhibited his own humorous prints at the Society of Artists. He was also a painter—in 1768 he was represented at the Royal Academy—but is best known for his mezzotints. He died shortly after 1780. (*pp. 48, 52, 60, 62, 64*)

DAWKINS, Henry, was an American engraver and silversmith, who worked in New York in the mid-1750s then moved to Philadelphia. His specialities were titlepages and bookplates—and apparently counterfeiting. He was arrested in 1776 for engraving counterfeit Continental paper money. He confessed, implicating the Tory printer Rivington, and was imprisoned. (*p. 22*)

DIXON, John, was born in 1740 in Dublin where he practised as a silver engraver. He migrated to London and eventually became a member of the Incorporated Society of Artists, and worked as an engraver for Gainsborough, Zoffany and Stubbs among others. He appears to have neglected his art after marrying a wealthy lady, and died in 1780. (*p. 52*)

DU SIMITIÈRE, Pierre, was born in Paris in 1736 but by 1768 had turned up in America. He was best known as a painter, but also contributed frontis-

pieces to the Pennsylvania Magazine and the United States Magazine. He died in Philadelphia in 1784. (*p. 36*)

FRANKLIN, Benjamin (1706–1790) was, among his many accomplishments, a printer and publisher, but it is doubtful whether he was a cartoonist. He admits to 'inventing' (that is to say, designing) *Magna Britannia—Her Colonies Reduced,* for propaganda purposes. But there is no evidence to show that he also engraved it.

GILLRAY, James (1757–1815) was the outstanding cartoonist of his day. He studied engraving at the Royal Academy where he was taught by the great Bartolozzi. His most memorable prints date from the period of the Napoleonic Wars, after he had begun his association with the famous printseller Hannah Humphrey. The earliest attribution to him is in 1769, with several dating from 1775. But none can be made with total certainty until some years later. Most of his earliest work was published by William Humphrey (Hannah's brother) and is notable—like the majority of his work—for its political independence. In his later years he grew insane and it is said (with little evidence) that he finally committed suicide. (*pp. 94, 122, 124, 138, 142, 154, 156, 164, 170*)

PELHAM, Henry, was born in Boston in 1749 and was drowned in Ireland in 1806. He was the half-brother of J. S. Copley and a fellow-engraver to Paul Revere. His only claim to inclusion in this index is that he disputed, most virulently, with Revere over the authorship of *The Boston Massacre.* Since some superior watercolour copies of the print have been preserved, he may well have had a point. (*see p. 34*)

REVERE, Paul (1735–1818). Apart from his fame as a patriot and mid-night rider, Revere was a noted silversmith and engraver in Boston. Occasionally he applied his talents to producing propaganda prints for the patriot cause, usually by adapting an English design (though Clarence

Brigham has identified a couple as being all Revere's own work). (*p. 34*)

ROWLANDSON, Thomas (1756–1827) attained fame as much as a water-colour artist as a caricaturist. Much of his satire was socially orientated, for instance his famous series on Dr. Styx (which may be called, with some justice, the forerunner of the modern strip-cartoon). His first published work dates from after the end of the American War. (*p. 182*)

SAYERS, James (1748–1809) was by profession an attorney who practised at Yarmouth. His political cartoons were very often officially inspired—he was known to have been in the pay of the Treasury and was awarded a sinecure in 1786 for his somewhat un-critical support of Pitt. His earliest work dates from 1781. (*p. 56*)

TERRY, G. Little is known of this mezzotint engraver, except for the fact that he was a member of the St. Martin's Lane Academy and was chiefly employed in engraving portraits. (*p. 58*)

TISDALE, Elkanah, was born in Connecticut in 1771. He is known to have worked for part of his career as an engraver and miniature painter in New York, and to have returned to Hartford as a designer of vignettes. His illustrations for Trumbull's epic *M'Fingal* (1795) are his earliest recorded productions. (*p. 176*)

TOWNSHEND, George (1724–1807). More properly, the 1st Marquis Townshend. He was an active politician and Lord Lieutenant of Ireland, as well as being one of the leading amateur caricaturists in Britain. None of his work is represented in this book, though there are several in his style included. (*See p. 166*)

VERNEY, no record of anyone working as an engraver in London under this name can be found. (*p. 106*)

WILKINSON, the only mention of an American artist of this name and at this period is of a landscape painter in Tuckerman's American Artists' Life. So he, too, must remain a mystery. (*p. 24*)

WILSON, Benjamin (1721–88) was, in his day, a distinguished scientist and painter who rose to the post of Sergent-Painter to the King (in which he succeeded Hogarth). He was apparently adept at faking Rembrandts, and achieved immense popularity with his occasional satirical prints, produced, so he said, 'to please Lord Rockingham'. (*p. 26*)

WRIGHT, Inigo, was a mezzotint engraver born in London in about 1740. He is known to have engraved a series of country scenes in the style of Morland in the 1770s. (*p. 120*)

CHAPTER

I

CARTOONS AS HISTORY

To start with a hypothetical question. Suppose one were documenting the 1970s through the whims and doodlings of our political cartoonists (rather than, let's say, the deathless prose of Hansard or the Congressional records), what kind of impression would our administrators make on posterity? A generation of unscrupulous, war-mongering, self-seeking, irresponsible politicians? Probably. Then again, if the only records to survive a universal holocaust happened to be Cabinet minutes or Pentagon reports, how would they look then? Misunderstood, ill-used, public-spirited almost to a fault? Perhaps they are, of course, but I doubt it. I feel obliged to put forward these thoughts here, at the very beginning, only to underline the pitfalls of compiling history from partisan and provocative sources (which is what cartoons are)—and at the same time to reject the idea that purely objective sources exist anyway.

Consider, for a moment, the newspaper cartoons of today as documentary material. They are prejudiced, for a start, being either the results of personal pre-occupations or a reflection of editorial policy. They are selective; they focus only on issues of topical interest and then only on those aspects of them which are controversial; they don't pretend to be fair nor do they need to justify themselves. They are obsessive (very often), ambiguous and conventional. On the other hand they can, and fortunately do, speak for minorities as well as silent majorities. They are infused with a healthy disrespect for pomposity and double-talk, indeed they thrive on them. They have an immediate impact and occasionally a shrewd political insight.

All these foibles and flaws are inherent in the eighteenth century cartoons in this book. They, too, were drawn to amuse or to propagandize or to draw blood, without a thought of being enshrined in a collection two hundred years later. The vast majority of them were thrown away probably within weeks. The few that have survived, survived by accident or as carefully husbanded curiosities. We owe it, therefore, to the largely anonymous authors of these cartoons to judge their productions as the ephemeral things they were intended to be. They were published, if not with the speed, then at least with the urgency of our newspapers today. In the absence of a wide range of reading-matter, they fulfilled much the same sort of function. No eighteenth century gentleman-about-town would consider himself politically fortified for the day without a visit to the print-shops. Nor would he have considered going out to dinner without an intimate acquaintance with Mr. Gillray's latest offering.

The American War provided an enormous impetus to the engravers and print-sellers of London, both artistically and politically. The inexorable decline of the country's prestige, the wastefulness of the war, North's edifice of power founded on privilege and royal patronage all combined, slowly but positively, to crystallize a Parliamentary Opposition more articulate and vehement than any since Walpole's fall from office. And since cartoonists, by their very nature, tended to be anti-Ministerial, the more single-minded the Opposition the more vigorous the satires. Satire was the language of the eighteenth century, the century of Swift and Gay, Pope and Fielding. It was the age when open insolence was requited by duelling-pistols and a rendezvous at dawn, but caricature (to use the word that quite indiscriminately covered all kinds of graphic satire) whatever else it involved, carried no dishonour.

The cartoonists had, in fact, by the middle of the century, won for themselves a remarkable degree of immunity. Walpole had objected to disrespect on the stage and slapped a censorship on the theatres—which lasted almost to the present day. George III resented the insults of Wilkes, and had him tried for seditious libel. Yet the cartoonists continued to ridicule and lampoon with ever-increasing ferocity, but without ever suffering any attempts at official suppression.

It was as if the parliamentary privilege of the politicians they satirized embraced them as well. In a sense it did. Walpole, the first to suffer a concerted barrage of satirical abuse at their hands, might have suppressed them, but he left it too late. The cartoons (no doubt) had helped to speed his downfall. After that satirical prints became accepted weapons in the armoury of political propaganda. The only answer to satire was satire; litigation only made the victim look more foolish, brute force branded him as boorish. (Let it be said, though, that by no means every cartoonist pierced his target with the delicacy and precision of a rapier-thrust. The eighteenth century was a lusty and vulgar period, as well, as is only too apparent from a great many forgettable efforts.)

THE CARTOON TRADITION IN ENGLAND

The prints of the revolutionary period were themselves going through a significant change.

The engravers of the 1760s were the inheritors of Hogarth's tradition. They rarely if ever equalled him, never excelled him; but his influence was profound and enduring. While still a bookseller's assistant he had burst upon the scene at a most propitious moment, in 1721 while that orgy of greed and commercial lunacy known as the South Sea Bubble was still afloat. Dutch prints on the subject had flooded the market, and their success had encouraged English engravers first to copy them, then to create their own designs. The popularity of these 'bubble prints' confirmed the market for regular and organized print-publishing—largely, to begin with, of social conceits and passing fancies, but soon (as a parliamentary Opposition consolidated against Robert Walpole) of specifically political satire.

Many diverse influences were absorbed by these early cartoonists: from Germany the reformation imagery of Lutheran propaganda prints (fork-tailed devils were still popping up within Lord North's Ministry), from Holland the boisterous fantasies of Bosch and the comic art of Brueghel, from Italy complicated Renaissance symbolism and the fashionable new art of Caracatura (the gross exaggeration of features for satirical effect), from medallions and folk-art the stereotypes which were to serve them so long and so well (John Bull, though, made his first unambiguous appearance in 1779—see page 133). In the second half of the century they began to break free of these conventions, to discard their hieroglyphics, their heavy allegorical and emblematic creations, their elaborate explanations—some artists with more abandon than others. (Even in the last year of the war the flowing lines of Gillray's *Thunderer* (page 155) were still in commercial competition with the old-fashioned symbolism of *America Triumphant*.) But Hogarth had taught them to dramatize and to characterize—after his savage engraving of John Wilkes Esqr. *no one* thought of omitting the poor man's squint—and, above all, to experiment.

They were also more organized as a profession. Since 1735 they had enjoyed the erratic protection of the Copyright Act, known as Hogarth's Act (this is the act referred to on the imprint to be found at the bottom of many examples in this book, though it by no means stamped out the pirating of successful prints as Benjamin Wilson discovered to his cost—see page 26). By the 1770s they had a far greater profusion of outlets as new periodicals, such as the *Political Register* 1767 and the *Oxford Magazine* 1768, started the practice of running regular engravings, and older-established ones like the *London Magazine* followed suit. Print-shops, too were proliferating and successful partnerships between artist and publisher were springing up (between Townshend and Darly, for instance, and later between Gillray and William Humphrey). Many of the old school of engravers remained enshrouded in their anonymity—though they may well have been engraving someone else's design, a common practice throughout the century. But as confidence grew and sales increased, cartoonists began to take on a public identity and to reveal themselves by their signatures or their individual styles, amateurs like Viscount Townshend and Henry Bunbury and professionals like Matthew Darly, Thomas Colley, John Dixon and William Dawe (of whom more later). The print-shops began to establish themselves as social centres, almost rivalling the coffee-houses. The grander ones offered morning lounges where gentlemen could browse, gossip or catch up on the latest follies of Parliament or dispatches from abroad. Among the most important of the period were Messrs Bowles' establishments, one in Cornhill, the other in St. Paul's Churchyard. In the Strand stood William Humphrey's, and Darly's nearby; in Bond Street Hannah Humphrey's. Shortly after the end of the war others became fashionable, as well, like Holland's in Drury Lane and Fores' in Piccadilly. By then the golden age of cartoons had arrived.

THE CARTOONISTS OF THE AMERICAN WAR

The most striking thing about the satires of the revolutionary era is that the overwhelming majority of them are pro-American, to a degree which at first sight might seem disgracefully unpatriotic. But, of course, opponents of the war refused to think of the colonists even as rebels, let alone foreigners; they were Englishmen fighting against tyranny in the cause of freedom. When real foreigners, like the French and Spanish, began to meddle in the war the cartoonists—without exception—attacked them from the bottom of their hearts. But at all times it was the war itself the prints attacked (in the same way that present-day cartoons attack the Vietnam war), and therefore by extension the policies and motives of the men who had instigated it and the conduct of the men who ran it. At first the barbs are directed at the Ministers Grenville, Townshend and North; later they embrace the generals and admirals, Howe and

Germain, Gage and Burgoyne. Finally when all else fails, the King himself.

To be sure, there are isolated prints which come to the support of the Ministry, despising the fighting qualities of the Continentals or disparaging the English 'patriots' for obstructing the war-effort. But, as I observed earlier, it was not in the nature of a cartoonist to glorify the virtues of the Establishment or to support an administration. Satire is an offensive weapon, and there was much to attack, from departmental inefficiency to downright corruption. How far the Opposition actively patronized individual cartoonists or commissioned particular prints cannot be known for certain. That this was a regular, and accepted, practice is beyond question (James Sayers was awarded a sinecure by Pitt for services rendered and Gillray himself, much later on, obtained a state pension). Wilson is known, for instance, to have produced *The Repeal* at the request of Edmund Burke, in order to please Lord Rockingham. Cartoonists who were published in magazines were obviously influenced by the political colour of the magazine in question—though that could be unpredictable at times: in 1776 the pro-American *Westminster Magazine* suddenly turned on the patriots with *The Parricide* (see page 77). Nor can the cartoonists be dismissed as a breed of slavish political hacks; once in office, Chatham, Fox and many other patriots were meted out the same kind of punishment as their opponents.

Equally, it is impossible from this distance to be certain just how far cartoons influenced events or policies. Years later Charles Fox complained that the cartoons of Sayers had cost him more votes in the House of Commons than all the speeches of his opponents—but that was at the end of a long-drawn-out personal vendetta between himself and Pitt. The *Morning Herald* in 1782 claimed that seeing a copy of *The Royal Hunt* (page 169) had persuaded the King finally to dismiss North's Ministry. This is to be doubted (even North had trouble persuading the King to dismiss him). Britain's enemies, to be sure, were quick to seize on any print which could be used for propaganda purposes—and there was no lack of them— most notoriously, *A Picturesque View of the State of the Nation*, which went into countless editions abroad (page 109).

A number of prints were specially designed as anti-recruiting posters and might, arguably, have persuaded numbers of men not to enlist. But here again, service in America was unpopular at any stage in the war and most of the recruiting was done in Scotland and Ireland, beyond the reach of sophisticated London satires. However it is not an unreasonable conclusion that, since the print-shops were in business to sell their prints and since, during the war, these pro-American satires must have represented a significant percentage of their stock, they must have found a degree of favour with the public. Even satirical publishers cannot afford to flout public opinion too blatantly. There was one instance (quoted by Trevelyan) of an army officer marching into one shop, grabbing a print of Putnam from the window, tearing it to pieces and paying for it over the counter. And another of a group of soldiers neatly removing the head of Charles Lee from a print on display with the point of a sword (they didn't pay for that one). But, on the whole the print-sellers do not seem to have suffered unduly from official or unofficial reprisals.

OBSESSIONS AND INHERITED PREJUDICES

There are two sub-themes running through the satires of this period which, on the face of it, are totally irrelevant to the American conflict: the encroachment of Popery over the land, and the insidious influence of Scotsmen over all policy-making. The two were, of course, connected. In 1715 and again in 1745 swarms of Highlanders had invaded England to try to instate a Catholic King. On the second occasion they had penetrated as far south as Derby, inspired a counter-avalanche of ferocious Protestant prints, and frightened London severely. Just as our generation is inclined to see Reds under the bed, so Protestant Londoners saw Scotsmen behind every door. Then when the young King George had the nerve to appoint a Scotsman (Lord Bute) as his first Minister— that was the last straw. The satirical attacks grew merciless. Bute became Boot, a tribute to the symmetry of his legs, which (so his enemies put about) he passed many hours of the day contemplating. It is certain that Bute had once had an important influence on the King, but his Ministry survived barely ten unmemorable months and his association with the King not very much longer. Yet a dozen years later there were many people who remained unshaken in their belief that Bute still held sway over the King's decisions, and newspapers (without a shred of evidence) shamelessly reported the proceedings of an 'inner cabinet' over which Bute supposedly presided. The cartoonists fos-

tered this belief and introduced Bute or his proxies, a boot and a thistle (the Scottish emblem), into satires castigating unpopular measures. From their prints one might have believed that the entire war was being conducted for the benefit of Scotsmen—a myth widely accepted by the colonists themselves, and even by the Dutch artists who inserted Lord Bute into their own productions (surely without the foggiest idea of his significance).

So far as the other Ministers were concerned as well, the cartoonists showed they had long and tenacious memories. Lord George Germain, the American Secretary from 1775, was never allowed to forget that as George Sackville he had been found guilty of cowardice at the battle of Minden. The First Lord of the Admiralty, Lord Sandwich, was frequently portrayed as the rake, libertine and composer of dirty ditties he had been in his youth—nor was he ever forgiven for turning on his fellow-rake, John Wilkes, and producing a copy of a pornographic poem attributed to him at the crucial moment during his trial for seditious libel. Lord North, who had unfortunately for them lived a life of the utmost probity, was simply indicted for his flabbiness and short-sightedness.

But their very special hate was reserved for France, who in the three wars between the beginning of the century and the American war had been on the opposing side to Britain. In their entire output of the war there is not one kind word for Louis Baboon (or Monsieur Frog)—nor for that matter for Don, his Spanish Bourbon brother. Holland is traditionally treated with the contempt owing to a former ally; he is a knickerbockered, gin-and-herring merchant as often as not, grubbing around for trade. America, on the other hand, is rarely represented as other than a dignified Indian (female if being put upon, male if taking the initiative) —a handy and easily-recognized personification since the exotic parade of Chief Joseph Brant before fashionable society. Occasionally America contributes to the satirical menagerie as a mosse-deer, a zebra and a horse. Britain, depending on the degree of passivity she was required to display, is variously a cow, a bull and a lion.

CARTOONS IN AMERICA

Home-grown satires of the colonial and revolutionary era are rare in the extreme. William Murrell has tracked down a cartoon of Hercules in Franklin's publication *Plain Truth* (1747) and counts that as the first example. Then if one discounts the broken snake motif which first appeared during the trouble with the French, there is nothing until an isolated batch of them sprang out of the maelstrom of Philadelphian politics in 1764 (see page 23). During the Stamp Act crisis a number of British prints were copied or adapted (an example, said to be by John Singleton Copley, appears on page 25), and this practice continued for as long as there were communications between Britain and America. In Boston Paul Revere re-engraved several British originals and adapted them for propaganda purposes; he also is credited with designing his own, though only two examples can convincingly be attributed to him, *View of the Year 1765* and one on the Rescinders (see page 32). His famous engraving of the Boston Massacre was almost certainly lifted from a design by a fellow engraver.

Several others like the du Simitière drawing on page 37 and the *Representation of Figures* (page 147) are unquestionably American, and a few more may have been American in origin, even though re-published later in Britain: *America Triumphant* (page 159) feels as if it ought to be American and there are details about *Liberty Triumphant* which have an American ring to them (but would a colonist have depicted his country as an Indian woman?). All the same, the fact remains that until the work of William Charles during the War of 1812 there was no more than an embryonic tradition of American cartoons. During the war a number of French productions were engraved and designed in Boston or Philadelphia and, to judge from the number still extant in the United States, massive imports of stately, symbolical Dutch prints must have been received on every boat that put into port.

It may seem a little surprising that the colonists did not make more use of pictorial propaganda, at least during the years of civil disobedience. The radical newspapers were shrill and influential in their opposition to Britain's 'tyranny', but their weapons were words and apart from the occasional use of simple motifs they almost totally ignored graphic satire (perhaps their impossible profit margins simply could not accommodate it). Almanacs, certainly, made use of pictures but scarcely of cartoons. However, the danger is of judging mid-century colonial towns by the cultural standards of London. In 1763 Boston had a population of only about 22,000, Philadelphia slightly more, New York rather less. Attention in these towns was centred on local affairs rather than on collective issues; any demand there might have been for satirical attacks on the Ministry in London was no doubt satisfied by the regular supply of prints from the centre of the Empire anyway. When the war began there was very little need—and less time—for making drawings of an enemy who was already on one's doorstep.

THE CARTOON HISTORY OF THE AMERICAN REVOLUTION

There have been certain obvious drawbacks in trying to present a consecutive commentary on the Revolution through the eyes of the contemporary cartoonists, the most serious being that some notable events were ignored completely by them. The Declaration of Independence, for example, inspired not one single gloating swipe at Lord North or Parliament nor even a howl of indignation. I find this significant, if no-one else does: either everybody was expecting it to happen or the Ministry deliberately underplayed the news of it. And other events were inconveniently overlooked. The expedition against Canada, though much discussed in Parliament and the press, is not portrayed in any extant cartoons. Likewise Cornwallis's advance through North Carolina (on which many British hopes were pinned) was overshadowed by more domestic preoccupations. However, given reservations of this kind, the cartoonists obviously took a very keen —if not always well-informed—interest in the American situation. It is clear from the maps of America they insisted on introducing into their cartoons that they had about as hazy an idea of the geography of North America as the administrators in Whitehall. They were not even always quite certain which of the colonies across the Atlantic had revolted. (These criticisms, to be fair, only apply to a few of the cartoons; the author of *The Alternative of Williamsburg* and others in that series, for one, clearly was perfectly *au fait* with the colonial situation.)

I shouldn't, I appreciate, refer to either the designers or engravers of eighteenth century prints as cartoonists, nor to their work as cartoons. The word only came into vogue, in its modern sense, after John Leech (*Punch*'s political cartoonist) used it to describe the frescoes in the Houses of Parliament in 1863. Its original meaning was a design for a painting, and that is the sense in which it was used in *The Political Cartoon for the Year 1775* (page 67). But the Georgian print-sellers were notoriously sloppy about their descriptions, calling any remotely humorous print a caricature (which it strictly wasn't). So that's my excuse.

CHAPTER

2

AN EMPIRE AT ODDS

Peace of Paris to the
Boston Tea Party

1763-1774

1763	February 10	*Peace of Paris ends Seven Years War*
	March 31	*Cider Act*
	April 7	*Fall of the Earl of Bute's Ministry, succeeded by George Grenville (16th)*
	April 23	*Issue number 45 of John Wilkes's newspaper* The North Briton: *Wilkes arrested (30th)*
	May 7	*Pontiac's rebellion starts*
	October 7	*British Proclamation for new colonies frontier and Indian trade regulations*
	December	*Patrick Henry's speech on Two-penny Act*
1764	January 19	*Wilkes expelled from Commons*
	April 5	*Sugar Act (Revenue Act)*
	April 19	*Currency Act March of the Paxton Boys on Philadelphia*
1765	March 22	*Stamp Act*
	May 29	*Patrick Henry's speech in the House of Burgesses challenges Britain's right to tax colonies.*
	July 16	*Grenville resigns; Rockingham forms Ministry*
	October 7	*Stamp Act Congress meets in New York*
1766	March 18	*Stamp Act repealed, Declaratory Act passed*
	July 12	*Rockingham's Ministry dismissed: Chatham's administration*
1767	June 29	*Townshend taxes, on imports of tea, glass, paper and dyes*
	December 2	*Publication of first of* Farmers Letters
1768	February 11	*Circular letter from Massachusetts Assembly*
	June	*Wilkes sentenced for seditious libel*
	June 28	*Rescinders vote in Mass. Assembly: Assembly dissolved*
1769	May 17	*House of Burgesses dissolved*
	June 10	*Customs commissioners seize Hancock's sloop 'Liberty'*
1770	January 28	*Lord North's Ministry, on resignation of Grafton*
	March 5	*Boston massacre*
	April 12	*Repeal of Townshend duties, except tea duty*
	February 8	*Imprisonment of Alexander McDougall in New York*
1772	June 10	*Burning of the Gaspée in Rhode Island*
	November	*Committees of Correspondence formed in Massachusetts*

Until it dawned on cartoonists in the months preceding the outbreak of the Seven Years War that Britain was having bother with the French near a place called Fort Duquesne somewhere in the backwoods of America, they had totally ignored the colonists. From time to time the word America had cropped up in their prints, to be sure, but only as yet another of the many British territories corrupt politicians seemed prepared to auction off or lamely relinquish to the enemy. The country had no special interest, its inhabitants no identity. It was a very long way away, after all, and it obediently provided its tobacco and timber, furs, fish and rice for English markets, without complaint. Parliament had no consistent policy on the colonies and plantations (as America was referred to) which could be attacked or defended; it rarely debated about them, and never with bitterness or rancour. For the most part, it was thought of (if it was thought of at all) as the place to which dissenters removed their undesirable presence or where convicts were sent for a spell of indentured service (and few of them seemed to come back).

The territorial ambitions of the imperial arch-enemy France changed all that. If she was trying to extend her empire in North America, it had to be important. In 1755 several prints appeared on the subject of the Ohio Valley dispute, one of them *The American Moose-deer* (page 21) giving the colonies an explicit, though not yet a human, form. The stirring events of the war, the early disasters, the execution of Admiral Byng, the triumphs of Pitt, the inauspicious debut of Bute all overshadowed any satirical interest in the colonies after that, though no less stirring events were taking place there too. Not until the Stamp Act crisis is attention specifically focused again on America —and then in a positive flurry of denunciations. The first was advertised in October 1765 (*The Great Financier*, page 29) by which time London would have had its first intimations of the rising tide of protest in the colonies; it probably reflects the early concern of the City merchants for their Atlantic trade.

From that moment all developments on the American question were watched closely. Succeeding Ministries rarely saw the need to resort to graphic propaganda in defence of their policies—perhaps they sensed that the bulk of politicians shared their inherent belief in Parliament's sovereignty (as even many opposition members still did in these pre-war years) or else they considered that an exposition of the true constitutional issues was more suited to the pen of a pamphleteer like Dr. Johnson rather than the engravery of frivolous cartoonists. A few unsympathetic prints did appear (like *The Triumph of America*) but generally it was only the radicals and dissenters, the traders and colonial agents who saw fit to add fuel to the fires of the cartoonists' obliging indignation. From the numbers of these pro-American prints still in collections in the United States, it would seem that most of the relevant cartoons were seen (and no doubt circulated) across the Atlantic; some were copied or freely adapted by native engravers, notably Wilkinson and Revere. But since the colonists' grievances at this stage rested mainly on delicate points of political theory and constitutional law, it is not difficult to see that the oratory of lawyers like Otis and Henry or the writings of thinkers like Dickinson might prove more appropriate revolutionary weapons.

Hogarth had died in 1764, while the Stamp Act was still a notion in George Grenville's mind. It would have been interesting to see what contribution he would have made to the crisis it precipitated. Probably none, strange to say. For most of his life he had assiduously avoided factional entanglements, until 1762 when he blundered to the support of Bute with two misconceived plates attacking Pitt. They brought a torrent of abuse down on his head, particularly from fellow artists. He became known as 'the butefyer' and Wilkes devoted a whole issue of his newspaper to attacking him. When he died, it was in bitterness and disillusion.

BRITAIN'S COLONIES AND PLANTATIONS

The war in which the two great imperial powers of Europe, Britain and France, had belaboured each other on four continents for seven years ground to a halt in 1762. The last few years had been intoxicating ones for the British public, with West Indian islands falling like ninepins, French sovereignty in Canada extinguished by Wolfe and tottering in India in the face of Clive, its fleet battered into impotence by Hawke and Boscawen. It seemed at times that not a ship could put into harbour without bearing news of some great victory from a remote quarter of the world. It had been Pitt's war, and Pitt's ambition had been to crush French commercial power beyond all hope of recovery; and when the antagonists sat down at Fontainebleau in the autumn to juggle with their conquests, it looked as if nothing could stand in the way of his ambition. But at the moment of triumph it was not Pitt (who would have extended the war to Spain) in the seat of power but the Earl of Bute, whose critics claimed had less interest in the shaping of foreign policy than in the shape of his legs of which he was inordinately proud.

Coming to the throne in 1760, young and self-conscious, George III brought with him an irrational dislike of his grandfather's Minister and a genuine distrust of his policies. Where else would they lead if not to an ungovernable national debt and isolation against every major power in Europe? The King wanted peace, whatever it cost. In 1761 Pitt fell and with him dissolved the country's warlike tendencies. In vain he railed in Parliament at the terms of the peace which restored to France her rich sugar islands, her gum trade, her fishing rights on the Grand Banks. He understood—as the merchants of the City also understood—that Britain had ransacked the French Empire sufficiently to humiliate her, but not enough to prostrate her for ever. What was more, the King was lamely handing back to her the means of recovery.

Nevertheless Britain emerged from the war poorer by thousands of pounds but richer by untold thousands of miles of new territory. French presence on the continent of North America was obliterated utterly and, as it turned out, permanently. They had been driven out of the frontier posts in the interior (where the bloody business of the last seven years had started), they had surrendered Quebec and Montreal, and abandoned Louisiana to the Spanish. To be sure, their Indian allies—concerned that there was now no further check to the insatiable land-grabbing of the American colonists—were fighting on in 1763 and wreaking havoc and terror throughout the back-settlements. All the same there was no reason to suppose that, under paternal guidance of Britain, the colonies could not look forward to an era of peaceful development and prosperity. For in London winning the war had brought more than the consolidation of Empire; it had helped also to crystallize an imperial consciousness, a pride appropriate to the sheer extent of its dependent territories. The old *laissez-faire* attitudes were not good enough any longer.

Before the war responsibility for and administration of the colonies had been diverse and haphazard. To varying degrees the Secretary of State for the Southern Department, the Treasury, the Board of Trade and Plantations, the Admiralty, the Commissioner of Customs and a dozen other officials (including the Bishop of London) were all involved. Parliament rarely concerned itself with American affairs—unless it was to introduce some measure to regulate and protect imperial trade as a whole. The Privy Council's most demanding function was the approving or vetoing of legislation by the colonial assemblies, which in any case had already been filtered through the royal governors on the spot. Even the governors had varying influence from one colony to another. In the charter colonies of Connecticut and Rhode Island they were annually elected by the people and therefore subject to local opinion. In the proprietary colonies, Maryland, Pennsylvania and Delaware they were the delegates of the Proprietor; in the others they were commissioned by letters patent from the King directly, but in any event none of them could afford to stand entirely aloof from the popular will —if only because their salaries were voted annually by their respective legislatures.

To Ministers in Whitehall the war appeared to have confirmed rather than diminished the colonies' dependence on Britain. Accordingly in the years that immediately followed George Grenville's new Ministry (Bute's having crumbled in April 1763 beneath the weight of his incompetence) embarked on a series of measures which touched nervelessly on all the areas of colonial contention; on the frontier question (the Proclamation of October 1763), on trade restrictions and revenue (the so-called Sugar Act), on currency (Currency Act), on defence (Quartering Act) and internal taxation (the notorious Stamp Act). At no time did Parliament consider it was acting against the colonists' interests; the tragedy is that it acted without the slightest inkling of their true political temper.

TOP RIGHT
The American Moose-Deer, or away to the River Ohio. *Anon: This print was published in June 1755, at a time when an obscure tract of land to the south of Pennsylvania was occupying the attentions of no less than four European monarchs, the King of France (feeding the moose-deer with hay), the King of Portugal (peering between its horns), the King of Spain (mounted on its back) and George II (lifting its tail). Apprehensive of the activities of British speculating companies around the Ohio, France had begun constructing a chain of forts along the Western frontier and arrested a number of British traders. Ministers in Paris seemed surprised at Britain's remonstrances on this score, however. Portugal was wavering as to whether to support the French in their claims; Spain had decided to remain neutral —in spite of the capture of one of its bullion ships by Lord Anson (kneeling). The cleric standing behind the animal is probably intended to be Bishop Secker (for whose interest in the colonies see page 38). The squabbles of the European powers bent on 'ruining our rich country' were to be resolved in the war which followed almost immediately.*

BOTTOM RIGHT
An Exciseman. *Anon: This emblematic gentleman is a concoction of all the articles on which the people of Britain were obliged to pay taxes to pay for the government's costly wars. His shoulders are a bottle of cider (2),*

The American Moofe-Deer, or away to the River Ohio.

his arms are candles (3), his body a barrel of beer (4), his sword a gage (5), his breeches leather (6), his legs soap (7), his feet chocolate (8); he points to cartons of coffee and tea (9 & 10); behind him the sun rises, indicating light (11, windows above a certain number per house were taxed at this time), and he stands on land (12). The whole is ostensibly an attack on Lord Bute, who introduced the Cider Tax in March 1763, but it incidentally explains in some measure why the Ministry was so anxious to make the colonists pay in part for their own defence.

An EXCISEMAN made out of ỹ Neceſsaries of Life now Tax'd in Great Britain except the head which is a Knaves taken from ỹ Court Cards.

When Fame first the Olive Branch held o'er the Land

THE COLONIES AND PLANTATIONS

While the war might have convinced the government three thousand miles away of the need for firmer, more coordinated policies in America, at home it had a very different effect. In the first place it had emphasized the internal disunity of the thirteen colonies. Virginia and New Jersey had declined to turn up at the Albany Congress, assembled in 1754 to attempt to formulate a unified policy against the French threat; its proceedings had been hamstrung by border disputes and commercial rivalries, its proposals jealously vetoed by the local assemblies. Even after war broke out colonial militia often refused to serve under any but its own provincial commanders or to march beyond its own borders; assemblies (with the conspicuous exception of the New England colonies) were reluctant to vote men and money for the collective defence unless they saw others doing so—some neglected any form of requisition at all. Men with the vision of Benjamin Franklin warned of the short-sightedness of it all: his Philadelphia newspaper first ran the famous disjointed snake emblem with the motto 'join or die'. Yet, still in 1765 no less a patriot than James Otis could declare quite truthfully 'were these colonies left to themselves tomorrow, America would be a mere shambles of blood and confusion'.

At the same time the war and Grenville's subsequent bout of legislation served to highlight those issues of conflict between Britain and the colonies which, though they had existed before, had remained largely dormant or had been tacitly circumvented. To the disgust of Ministers in London a number of assemblies had quite unscrupulously used the war-emergency to hold governors to ransom; military quotas were withheld until some point of political independence were granted or some inroad on proprietorial privilege made. For its own part the Ministry replied with periodic attempts to have the governor's royal 'instructions' rigidly enforced and the judicial superstructure kept firmly in British control—with the result that minor but acrimonious battles were waged on such technicalities as the 'writs of assistance'

for customs officers in Massachusetts, 'suspending clauses' and electoral procedures in South Carolina, and judges' tenure of office in New York.

These were the early rumblings of the constitutional volcano which was to erupt finally with the passing of the Stamp Act in 1765. To the colonists a disturbing pattern of active Parliamentary sovereignty seemed to be emerging, an ominous threat to the freedom of their own assemblies which, in their eyes, owed ultimate allegiance only to the Crown. On the other hand, while there were those in Parliament who urged that Parliamentary authority over the colonies ought to be applied with tact and discretion if at all, there was almost no one who denied that Parliament possessed that authority. And there were, regrettably, few British politicians in 1763 who saw the over-riding need for tact either, in their dealings with what were not infrequently referred to as 'our subjects'. Debtor colonies had attempted to pay their debts in depreciated currency (especially in states where the planter interests predominated in the assembly); very well, colonial currencies must be more tightly controlled. Yankee merchants had flagrantly traded with the enemy during the war; so, customs regulations must be implacably enforced—to the distress of many a corrupt British official who had grown comfortable in his sinecure, and to the severe inconvenience of the rum distillers who had ceased to object to an unenforced 6d duty on a gallon of foreign molasses but now found themselves actually having to pay a reduced duty of 3d (under the Sugar Act).

But perhaps what irritated the Ministry most of all was the colonists' reluctance to shoulder any part of the burden of defence. Pontiac and his warriors were even then ravaging the forts up and down the western frontier, yet only four colonies came forward to offer aid of any sort. At a conservative estimate the defence budget for America required some £200,000, and unless the Indians were pacified and their hunting-grounds assured it would soon be considerably higher. A limit, therefore, to westwards expansion was set by the Proclamation Line of October 1763. No land-purchases beyond it were to be authorized, for

the time being. No trade was to be conducted with the Indians under British auspices; to ensure this Indian superintendents were appointed and garrisons posted throughout the interior. Britain's frontier policy upset not only pioneers and speculators hungry for land (who, it soon transpired, were not at all inhibited by any such arbitrary demarcation lines) but the colonial legislatures also who felt their natural western territorial claims had been summarily clipped. What was worse, British regulars now appeared to be employed in the task of containing the colonists themselves. These were the very troops for whose maintenance Parliament was bent on extracting money. With the French menace removed, it smacked too much of a peacetime standing army; viewed in the context of the government's growing authoritarianism, it boded very ill indeed for the colonists.

The German bleeds and bears ye furs. Attrib. to Henry Dawkins: This print was one of a spate of satires inspired by the highly partisan nature of Philadelphia politics in 1764. This particular example (on the March of the Paxton Boys) epitomizes both the tensions on the frontier and the factious rivalries within Pennsylvania. The pacific Quaker element within the Assembly, with its pro-Indian sentiments, conflicted with the violent and independent nature of the Scotch-Irish and German frontiersmen (who alarmed by the activities of Pontiac had massacred twenty friendly Indians in 1763). Demanding representation in the Assembly 200 of them from the interior marched on Philadelphia, with the declared intention of murdering any Indians they found there. They were only propitiated through the admirable exertions of Benjamin Franklin, who is attacked (left) here as a lackey of the Quaker proprietary family. The Irish and German settlers are represented as being no better than beasts of burden for Quakers and Indians, even being sacrificed on their behalf. The Indian seated on one Protestant settler (right) carries a consignment of furs for I.P. (Israel Pemberton, a Quaker merchant). In reality, Franklin was not ill-disposed to the Quakers.

The German bleeds & bears y Furs | Th Hibernian frets with new Disaster | But help at hand Resolves to hold down
Of Quaker Lords & Savage Curs | And kicks to fleng his broad brimd Master | Th Hibernians Head or tumble all don'n

MR. GRENVILLE'S STAMP ACT

There had been a stamp duty in England since 1694; it had worked tolerably well and was currently enriching the Exchequer to the tune of well over a quarter of a million pounds. A similar levy on the colonists would produce at least £50,000, with luck a great deal more. There was little reason to think in England that the Americans would consider it a less equitable means of raising revenue than any other. Yet could George Grenville himself have entertained a shadow of doubt on that score which, instead of including it as one of the wholesale provisions of the Sugar Act as had been intended, he postponed it until the spring of 1765? This was, he said, to give the Americans a chance to come up with something better.

There was no lack of suggestions. 'Why not assign a quota for each colony which it would make up in its own way?' enquired Franklin. But neither the Government nor anyone else had the faintest notion of what constituted a fair and acceptable quota for colonies that varied so greatly in population and resources. Then, what about an American Bank which could issue its own currency? There is no evidence that Grenville gave any serious consideration to this, or any other proposal. Besides, it was evident from the spate of petitions and protests that flooded into London from America that it was not alternatives the colonial assemblies were concerned with, but the very question of their constitutional rights. From New York and Connecticut, Rhode Island, Virginia and Massachusetts, Pennsylvania and South Carolina came howls of indignation at this quite unprecedented form of taxation. As indeed it was; it was the first time Parliament had proposed to impose a direct and internal tax upon them without the consent of their assemblies; it was also an attempt to raise revenue, unlike the traditionally-accepted (if largely evaded) external duties which were primarily for the regulation of trade. It violated their freedom as Englishmen for, in the words of the Connecticut remonstrance 'if the Privilege of not being taxed without their Consent be taken from them, Liberty and Freedom are certainly gone with

it'. Englishmen at home could signify their consent through their members of Parliament; the colonists had no representatives at Westminster (nor ever showed any great universal desire for any).

The torrent of complaints delayed the passage of the bill by not one day. It was carried through both Houses at speed and by overwhelming majorities; few voices were heard in support of Colonel Isaac Barré who warned that they were prodding the Americans into revolt. On March 22 the Act—which by levying heavy duties on all newspapers, legal and commercial documents, playing-cards, pamphlets, even dice, affected colonists of every station—became law. No insuperable obstacles to the application of the Act were foreseen, since Vice-Admiralty courts were empowered to lean heavily on violators. Even several of the colonial agents in London, by accepting appointments as the Government's official stamp distributors, appeared to accept this conclusion. Only when they returned to America to take up their lucrative posts did they discover their painful and embarrassing mistake.

TOP RIGHT

Untitled. Wilkinson: This American copy differs from the original in a number of interesting aspects. America, significantly, is represented not as an Indian but as a daughter; here she is positively refusing to accept the Act. Minerva still counsels rejection and Mercury is still on the point of departing. A French maiden, rather than the King, offers her bribe to the meteoric Boot, while the Scotch thistle is far more luxuriant (it still harbours a serpent). The figure leaning on the Liberty Tree is quite explicitly labelled Loyalty in this production and she is supporting a crown. The date on the tree (Aug. 14 1765) commemorates the first public demonstration in Boston against the Stamp Act; that morning an effigy of Andrew Oliver, the new stamp distributor, was found hanging on a tree in the High Street (see next spread). It is clear from events on the left that intimidation against the Stamp men had progressed far by the time this satire was published: one has been buried alive (according to the Pennsylvania Gazette of October 31 this incident occurred in New Providence in the Bahamas). Other small interpolations

are the dog whose collar proclaims him to be William Pitt's dog, and Magna Carta in tatters (right), which whenever liberty of the subject was the theme of a print, popped up as a convenient and readily-understood symbol. (A note on this print says 'The Original Print Done in Boston by Jo. S. C-pl-y'. Copley had yet to achieve fame as a portrait painter, nor was he ever regarded as an ardent patriot. Before the outbreak of the war he travelled to Europe to study art, and remained in England thereafter.)

BOTTOM RIGHT

The Deplorable State of America or Sc---h Government. Anon: This print, though unquestionably of English origin, appears to have been first advertised in Boston (in November 1765). By the following January it was certainly also on sale in London. Resting on her shield Britannia offers Pandora's Box (representing the Stamp Act) to America, here in the guise of an Indian (but see below). Minerva's advice is not to accept it; she emphasizes her point by indicating the figure of Liberty prostrate on the ground. Other figures involved in this tableau are Mercury with his winged helmet (playing the role of Commerce); he has decided he must 'reluctantly' leave, his wand obviously under the harmful influence of a phantom Boot (Lord Bute's ministry and his supposed anti-American policies were still fresh in propagandists' minds; he was to crop up as a symbol of the Court's secret power for many years to come, though his influence on events even at this juncture is to be doubted). Such miserable legislation, it is assumed, had to be the work of enemies so the French King (right) is introduced presenting a bribe to the Boot— though where he was able to raise money at that time isn't clear. A harsh wind is blowing the Tree of Liberty so fiercely that a regal figure (perhaps Loyalty, see below) fears it may fall over. On the left in the background stand a group of Stamp Men, looking aghast at the gallows prepared for them and concluding they would sooner rob or starve before risking their necks. Nearby ships are for sale (shown by the broom attached to the mast) and sailors stand idle on the shore.

THE DEPLORABLE STATE of AMERICA or SC—H GOVERNMENT.

THE STAMP ACT: RIOT AND RESISTANCE

From Massachusetts to South Carolina not one solitary stamp was sold. They reached America safely, by the ton in neat little packages. Some were delivered to the local garrison; others were transferred to the holds of armed frigates. And there they stayed, for there was not a stamp-merchant to be found in all America (with the exception of Georgia) to collect them. Several months had passed since news of the Act becoming law had reached the colonies, but those months had utterly transformed the political situation. The first outburst had come on May 29 in the Virginia House of Burgesses from a young, oratorical lawyer Patrick Henry. With his inflammable (there were those there who called it treasonable) rhetoric he pressed on the House a number of resolutions—including two which invested in the legislature the exclusive right to taxation and which branded any dissenter 'an Enemy to this His Majesty's Colony'. Most of the burgesses had gone home, so they missed his remarkable performance. When they discovered the next day what had been resolved in their name, they promptly expunged the offending utterances from the record.

It made no difference. The newspapers had got hold of the story and published all of Henry's resolutions as official. On June 8 the Massachusetts Assembly issued a circular letter inviting all the other assemblies to send representatives to a Congress in New York to present a united all-American front. What the elected spokesmen had begun in their deliberate, bureaucratic way, the less articulate took up in their own forthright, practical manner. In Boston a mob began to make life a misery for the newly-appointed stamp distributor. They levelled the brand-new Stamp Office he was erecting; they paraded his effigy around the town, beheaded it and burnt it on a bonfire; they then went off in search of the real thing, and broke into his house only to find him prudently not at home. He was found the next day and strongly advised to resign 'or his house would be immediately destroyed and his life in continual danger'. Andrew Oliver resigned on the spot, as did

his fellow-distributors over the following weeks, for much the same reasons. When the 'Sons of Liberty' had dealt with the stamp-merchants, they went off in search of the stamps (some of which they found and destroyed). Then they went off in search of customs officers, law officials, or if all else failed friends of British authority. Houses were ransacked, their contents burnt, their wine-cellars drunk dry. Only the good, solid American workmanship of Lieutenant Governor Hutchinson's mansion prevented it from being pulled down by solid American workmen.

Not all the Stamp Act demonstrations were violent, or any less effective for that. In Philadelphia the arrival of the stamps was marked by flags at half-mast and church bells tolling throughout the day. Newspapers continued to publish without a stamp, some of them cheekily printing their own made up of a skull-and-crossbones or a space pointedly inscribed 'this is the place to affix the stamp'. The majority of delegates, too, to the Stamp Act Congress when it met on October 7 were moderates. Yet in their Addresses to King, Lords, and Commons—beneath the effusive expressions of loyalty to 'the best of Kings' and the 'most perfect form of government'—there was apparent their unequivocal resolve to regain two of their most cherished privileges: taxation only by consent and trial by jury.

TOP RIGHT

The Repeal or the Funeral of Miss Ame-Stamp. *After Benjamin Wilson: This is in fact a pirated version of Wilson's famous print (published, he claimed, within minutes of the Stamp Act being repealed). The success of the original (see page 16)—it sold over 2,000 in four days—inspired several copies such as this which were on the streets within 10 days. This one differs from the original mainly only in the wording over the vault (left) and in the care taken over the background. A funeral procession is on its way to bury Miss Ame-Stamp (Stamp Act) in a vault reserved for similar infringements on freedom such as ship mon(ey), gen(eral) warrants etc. 'hop'd never to rise again'. At the head of the group is Dr. Scott, Lord Sandwich's chaplain and an eager pamphleteer on behalf of the Stamp*

Act. Next, bearing standards on which the white rose of the Jacobites and the Scotch thistle are intertwined, come two pillars of the law, Wedderburn and Fletcher Norton, Solicitor-General and Attorney-General respectively. Then comes Grenville himself bearing the coffin, closely followed by a lacrimose Earl of Bute. Other responsible ministers trail behind, the Lords Bedford, Temple, Halifax and Sandwich (who frivolously fails to have caught the spirit of the solemn occasion). Two unidentified bishops make up the procession. To emphasize the 'Jacobite' spectre haunting this particular piece of legislation, two skulls are mounted over the tomb inscribed with the dates of the two Jacobite risings (1715 and 1745). In contrast to this mournful troupe, the wharves in the background are bustling once again with activity; a statue to Mr. Pitt is being loaded for America; the good ships Conway, Rockingham and Grafton (the administration which had effected repeal) stand proudly ready to sail.

BOTTOM RIGHT

Goody Bull or the Second Part of the Repeal. *Anon: A sequel of sorts to the above: Mr Pitt's statue has arrived in America to be hailed by cherubs and protestations of affection for such assorted characters as King George, Pitt and Wilkes. Across the water, however, Mrs. Bull (Britain) is apparently still peevish at the success of her daughter America, who claims she would have prostituted herself if the treatment meted out by the Stamp Act had been applied. Pitt, in spite of his crutch (he was seriously disabled by what was diagnosed in those days as 'suppressed gout') berates the mother for wanting to 'turn her daughter adrift' from the straight and narrow path of loyalty.*

THE REPEAL: PARLIAMENT IN RETREAT

The Addresses of the Stamp Act Congress, when they arrived in England, landed not on the desk of George Grenville, who had been dismissed by the King the previous July for his inconsiderate attitude towards the Royal Mother, but on that of the Marquess of Rockingham. The new and inexperienced First Minister was cruelly soon to be made aware that he and his Ministry were landed with a crisis not of their own making—as much through the anguished supplications of their own countrymen as through the ominous murmurings from America. It was clear by the fall of 1765 that Britain's own trade was suffering sorely. All commerce between the colonies and the mother country was paralysed. Many American debtors joyfully postponed fulfilling their obligations to British merchants, because colonial judges denied the legality of unstamped documents. By the new year Parliament was swamped with petitions from all the major ports and boroughs in the country. 'We have no remittances' was the universal cry. 'We are at our wits' end for want of money to fulfil our engagements with our tradesmen.'

To the Rockingham Ministry pondering the situation over the Christmas recess, there appeared to be no honourable compromise between armed suppression, for which they had no stomach, and abnegation of sovereignty, which they could not countenance. They did what they could. They summoned Benjamin Franklin to the bar of the House to give evidence. Yes, he declared, the colonists made a fundamental distinction between internal and external taxes, adding ominously that they might not continue to do so. The Ministry also called for the American correspondence and gave notice of debate for February 3. No one awaited the day more apprehensively than the King, to see how his Ministry would fare. On the morning of the debate he wrote 'This day . . . I believe will prove a fatal day to them; this hour is perhaps one of the most critical ever known in this country'. And added 'My headache is not abated'.

Parliament's was just beginning. Grenville was there, unrepentant and unmoved by 'the desperate doctrines' of the Americans. On the 7th he called on the House to put down 'the rebellion' by force, but the House was not ready for such extreme measures. True to his declared intention to speak his heart and mind on the state of America 'if I can crawl, or be carried', William Pitt was also there. He expressed his satisfaction that the colonists had resisted and his opinion that 'the Stamp Act be repealed absolutely, totally, and immediately'. There were many other members who were now prepared to do so, if they could be sure that it would in no way diminish Parliament's authority over the colonies. So that there should be no misunderstanding on that account, the Ministry framed a Declaratory Act to reaffirm that authority and to invalidate all colonial resolutions which had questioned it. The Act was carried with almost total unanimity in both Chambers. Only Lord Camden noted that it begged the fundamental point at issue: 'taxation and representation are inseparably united; God hath joined them, no British Parliament can separate them'. But their Lordships clearly were not unduly worried that the Almighty would intervene on that score.

The way was now open for an orderly withdrawal on the Stamp issue. But Rockingham found it still an uphill journey. An embarrassing number of peers spoke out vehemently against repeal. Waverers in the Commons looked to the King (especially those who owed their places to his patronage). He was little help to his Minister. 'I told him I had on *Friday* given him permission to say I preferred repealing to enforcing the Stamp Act; but that modification I had ever thought more consistent with the honour of this country.' It was more than his Majesty believed the Americans could justly hope for, but on February 22 repeal of the Stamp Act was voted in the Commons by 275 to 167. On March 11 it scraped through the Lords by thirty-four votes.

TOP RIGHT
The Statue, or the Adoration of the Wise-Men of the West. *Anon: a further sequel to the Repeal (see previous spread). Miss Ame-Stamp is safely interred in the vault (left) and the members of her funeral procession have now raised their own statue to rival that to Mr. Pitt. They have chosen an equally outspoken—albeit less worthy—champion: Dr. Scott, whose writing campaigned ceaselessly for a Stamp Act. His nickname 'Anti-Sejanus' recalls the unscrupulous ex-slave who was the trusted and disastrous advisor to the Emperor Tiberius.*

BOTTOM RIGHT
The Great Financier. *Anon: The great financier is, of course, Grenville (centre) who is attempting to balance the national debt of £140,000,000 with idiotic economies. His assistant (right) is trying to do this—much to the disgust of a cat—by paring the ends of candles. Pitt (centre, left), points out that 'conquests will ballance it' but all the richest possessions, Guadaloupe, Martinique, etc. have been allowed to slip out of the Chancellor's hat. America (left) kneels beneath the yoke of 'taxation without representation', clutches a bag of dollars and cries out that 'commerce will outweigh it'. Behind her tax-collectors dig in to the money-bags, in spite of one of their companion's suggesting they pillage the French instead (the French and Spanish, top right, are delighted by what they see). Britannia's spear, meanwhile, is broken and her throne dismantled by Grenville's monkey.*

Detail from The Great Financier (*alternative version*)

The STATUE, or the ADORATION of the WISE-MEN of the-WEST.

THE TOWNSHEND TAXES

Six months after the people of America had celebrated the news of the Stamp Act's repeal in a delirious cacophony of bells, guns and drums, John Adams was able to write 'The people are as quiet and submissive to Government as any people under the sun; as little inclined to tumults, riots, seditions as they were ever known to be'. All was forgiven; the streets were safe to walk at night, even for the most assiduous customs official. Flowers adorned the Liberty Trees in place of crude effigies. But if the Government at home imagined it had won a constitutional battle, it was sadly mistaken. There were signs that even the truce was uneasy. In New York the Assembly had been holding out since 1765 against the provisions of a revised Mutiny Act (under which it was required to contribute to the quartering of the British soldiery in its midst) and continued to do so. In Boston a radical element under the eloquent James Otis had gained control of the Assembly and was dragging its feet over a somewhat tactlessly worded requisition from Parliament *demanding* compensation for those who had suffered in the Stamp Act riots. Both these local impasses, in Boston and New York, were ultimately resolved by both sides sternly maintaining their histrionic stances but allowing the implications of them to go by default. For in June 1767 a new offensive—of national importance—originated from London, beside which all local skirmishes paled into insignificance.

That this blow should have been struck at the colonies by a Ministry of which William Pitt—the friend of America—was the nominal head made the effect of it all the more shattering. Not four months after it had performed its parliamentary somersaults over the Stamp Act, Rockingham's Ministry tumbled out for good. The King had never liked the Marquess nor held him in high esteem. He liked Pitt not much better but unquestionably esteemed him as the only man who commanded sufficient respect to hold together a Ministry. As Ministries went, Pitt's was a scratch affair, 'a tessalated pavement without cement' as Burke dubbed it. The major paving-stones were the exceedingly young Duke of Grafton (as titular head), the Earl of Shelbourne, General Conway (one of Rockingham's former officers) and Charles Townshend (as Chancellor of the Exchequer). The cement was intended to be Pitt himself, who accepted a peerage and appointed himself Lord Privy Seal—a job without responsibilities which would allow him to direct the government. For Lord Chatham (as Pitt must from now on be dignified) was severely sick with the gout, a complaint which removed him for long periods to Bath (to take the waters) where he was seldom even inclined to answer his letters. In March 1767 it removed him permanently from London.

Into the vacuum created by Chatham's enforced absence stepped Charles Townshend, a reckless and contradictory politician who had argued against repeal of the Stamp Act but reputedly voted for it. As Chancellor of the Exchequer it was his job urgently to raise the revenue lost by the recent shilling reduction in the land tax. He had not wanted to reduce it, but the landed interests on the back benches in Parliament had flatly refused to go on paying the war rate of 4s in the pound. He had exhausted all the possibilities he could think of in Britain so he looked, with no sign of reluctance, to the colonies. 'I do not know any distinction' he declared 'between internal and external taxes . . . if we have a right to impose one, we have the other'. But now he claimed 'since Americans were pleased to make that distinction, he was willing to indulge them'. His indulgence embraced a duty on all imports into America of glass, dye, paper and tea. The proceeds would go to paying the salaries of certain governors and other royal officials, and to paying the troops whom he intended to concentrate on the western seaboard. Townshend's Act became law on July 2. Not one member spoke up to ask if the colonists would consider the duties harsh, nor wondered what might be the implications of Mr. Townshend's legacy. Legacy, quite literally, for within three months he was dead of a fever.

TOP RIGHT
The Triumph of America. *Anon: Whipping on his ill-matched ministry Chatham drives America in an ornate carriage down a precipitous slope. Britannia has already toppled over the edge. The accompanying text assesses the qualities of each of the post-horses: Royal Oak (Grafton) is young and spirited . . . and willing to draw in a dung cart; Crafty (Shelburne) is full of tricks but obedient and tractible; Surly (Northington) broken-winded and much given to snorting, kicking and plunging; Weathercock (Townshend) is apt to look one way while drawing the other; Prudence (Conway) lately purchased out of another set, and Prerogative (Camden) very tame and obedient. Another Indian is effectively leading the team on the postilion horse. This parody on the new Ministry was published before Chatham's absence and Townshend's proposals for new taxes. But it is interesting to note that of all the horses it is Townshend who has reared up beneath the lash of the whip.*

BOTTOM RIGHT
The Colossus. *Anon: This unfriendly print was but one of many that were to greet Pitt on his taking office after Rockingham's dismissal in July 1766 (see next spread). His colonial sympathies were not popular with the Court and large sections of the Tory faction. His hand was espied in the resistance in America to the Stamp Act; his respect for the commercial rather than the landed classes made him a dangerous radical. Accordingly he is here depicted with one foot (or rather stilt) in the colonists' camp in New York, the other in the City merchants', one spreading sedition, the other espousing popularity. With one crutch he assaults the seat of Parliament; the other is firmly esconced amid places and pensions. The gentleman apparently blowing public-spirited bubbles in the clouds is Lord Temple, Pitt's brother-in-law but an entrenched opponent of his policies (he had warned that the repeal of the Stamp Act 'would make the authority of Great Britain in America contemptible thereafter'). There is a prophetic touch in this print, with the inclusion of an Irishman (centre) bellowing out for his independence too.*

THE TOWNSHEND TAXES: PROTEST AND PROPAGANDA

At first it looked as if Townshend had aimed his Act at the very spot the colonists had left themselves vulnerable. They could not logically object, in principle, to paying a duty on paper and other commodities when they had passively accepted a prohibitive tax on molasses since 1733. The newspapers initially confined their protests to the harmful effects of the Act on an economy struggling to lift itself out of a post-war depression; the radicals urged only that this new economic burden be countered by legal economic means, by a boycott of the offending articles. But then in the *Pennsylvania Chronicle* of December 2 there appeared the first of a series of articles from 'A Pennsylvania Farmer'. These 'Letters' (after the wildest speculation found to be the work of John Dickinson) calmly and objectively denounced the political motives behind the Townshend duties and firmly dumped the issue back into the constitutional arena.

What Dickinson was saying, in effect, was that there were two kinds of external taxation: that for the purposes of regulating trade (as the original Molasses Act had done), and that for the raising of revenue (as these duties were intended to do). The colonies had cheerfully submitted to the first, but had never consented to the second. The same arguments applied, therefore, to the new duties as to the Stamp Act. This distinction did not accord with that offered by Franklin in his evidence in 1766. And there were those who found it paradoxical that the stiff 1733 Molasses Act should be acceptable because it effectively suppressed trade, but that a revised 1764 Molasses Act (reducing the levy from 6d to 3d) should suddenly become unconstitutional because it virtually encouraged the trade— and was thereby revenue-raising. Nevertheless Dickinson's arguments were seized upon eagerly; they were re-published in newspapers in every colony and reprinted in pamphlets. They became the spearhead of the new crusade.

Dickinson had called for the non-importation agreements to be revived, and the merchants of Boston were quick to take the lead, in March 1768. New York followed in August and Philadelphia the next year after nothing had been accomplished by petitioning. Another effort to precipitate concerted, inter-colonial action was contained in the Circular Letter of February 11 from the Massachusetts legislature to all other assemblies calling for a general congress. It struck deep into the heart of the Ministry at home, who insisted that the recalcitrant body repudiate it immediately, under pain of dissolution. On June 28 in a famous and much-celebrated vote the men of Massachusetts determined not to rescind their resolution; there were only 17 dissenters. Governor Bernard was duly obliged to order a dissolution, though by that time seven colonies had already endorsed the Circular Letter.

NEAR RIGHT
A Warm Place—Hell. *Anon: The English based on Paul Revere's original propaganda print. The seventeen Rescinders in the Massachusetts Assembly are being consigned to the jaws of hell by devils. 'There puny Villians damn'd for Petty Sin' the accompanying verse exhorts 'On such distinguished* SCOUNDRELS *gaze and grin'.*

FAR RIGHT, TOP
The Colonies Reduced. *This particular example of this famous print was published in Almon's* Political Register *in August 1768, though it is known that Benjamin Franklin had made use of the original design in 1766, while lobbying for the repeal of the Stamp Act. He had had it printed on cards, which he then posted off to leading politicians with appropriate messages or else had distributed by hand. It is not clear (though often asserted) that he actually designed the cartoon himself. The moral contained in it was as appropriate to the aftermath of the Townshend duties as to the Stamp Act: that in the long run it would be Britain herself who would suffer from alienating her colonies. She would slip from her perch on top of the world and be reduced to beggary (the great Roman General Bellisarius was popularly believed to have been a cripple).*

FAR RIGHT, BOTTOM
Its Companion. *Anon: This companion print to the above appeared for the first time in the* Political Register. *It shows the ubiquitous Lord Bute (centre) exposing Britannia and inviting Spain to 'strike home'. America as an Indian has thrown herself into the arms of France, who has only been awaiting this opportunity to become 'King of the whole World'. In the middle of the fracas, a Dutchman makes off with her trade.*

THE BOSTON MASSACRE

It was not unnatural that Massachusetts, and Boston in particular, should take the initiative in the growing movement for resistance; for in that city the new Customs commissioners (created by the late Charles Townshend for the more efficient collection of his own and other duties) had set up their headquarters. For honest—and no-so-honest—merchants and seamen and workmen going about their daily business with those hateful symbols of imperial tyranny in their midst, the provocation often proved too strong. After weeks of jostling, intimidation and abuse the Commissioners began appealing for help, to the Governor, to London, to Commodore Hood with the British fleet at Halifax. It was not just a question of personal safety, they pointed out, they were being positively obstructed in their work. In two and a half years they had been able to bring only one successful prosecution for smuggling; impounded ships had been forcibly 'liberated' or simply disappeared in the night; guilty men had been acquitted through 'the Influence of the People'.

Hood responded at once by dispatching the warship Romney to Boston harbour. Its presence emboldened the commissioners to seize **John Hancock's** sloop *Liberty* (on a charge of smuggling Madeira wine) on June 10 1768. It was a bolder stroke than they knew. The violence of the mob burst instantaneously about their heads. They fled for sanctuary on the Romney, while town meetings clamoured for their removal altogether. Fearing the city to be on the brink of anarchy, the Ministry shipped two regiments from Ireland to Boston, and instructed the commander-in-chief in America, General Gage, to send two of his own without delay. Boston was to be to all intents and purposes under military occupation. The Sons of Liberty laid plans to give them a warm reception, summoning a convention of delegates from all the other towns of the province. The response from their neighbours was disappointing to the more blood-thirsty elements; they were persuaded not to take up arms. When the troops disembarked on October 1 the city was quiet, suspiciously quiet.

Suspicion was heightened by the general belief that the troops were sent not just to maintain order but also to flush out the ring-leaders of the disturbances. Rumour had it that the Ministry in England were exhuming a treason statute from the reign of Henry VIII with a view to bringing the conspirators to trial in Britain. And so they were, though it was a threat they wisely forbore from applying. For eighteen months the inhabitants put up an irritating but passive front; the troops drilled on in a state of unrelieved tension. Two military commanders applied for new posts. The Governor was relieved of his. But by July 1769 General Gage was confident enough to pull out two of the regiments, and would have withdrawn the other two but for the entreaties of the new Governor, Thomas Hutchinson. The General might have stuck to his guns had he foreseen the slow fuse of bitterness which was to begin with a coffeehouse brawl on September 5 and to end in an explosion in King Street the following March.

On that day in September James Otis was severely beaten up by a commissioner in reprisal for one of the lawyer's swinging attacks in print. It was said Otis never properly recovered his faculties from that day on. In any event it was the signal for the mobs to go once more on the rampage. In the weeks that followed soldiers and friends of the government were abused, mauled, even tarred and feathered. On February 22 a young boy was accidentally killed. On March 5 a mob confronted the customs house in King Street and the seven British soldiers who were sent to protect it. There was a scuffle; the soldiers fired, killing five and wounding six others. The Boston 'massacre' had finally taken place, and the city was in an uproar. Hutchinson did the only thing he could do: he evacuated the city of all troops and put the seven nervous redcoats and their captain under lock and key to await trial. He thus averted temporarily a great deal of bloodshed even if, as John Adams later concluded 'on that night the foundation of American Independence was laid'. It was also, ironically, the same day that Lord North introduced the repeal of most of the Townshend duties into Parliament.

AFTERMATH

The radicals now had their martyrs, even if no one was entirely clear how many of them were innocent bystanders. But instead of getting worse from that moment, they got relatively better. The army, the immediate cause of friction, was removed from the nearest Bostonian by at least three miles of sea and stayed there by General Gage's orders. Captain Preston and his men, the perpetrators of the massacre, were accorded an exemplary defence by John Adams and Josiah Quincey (ardent patriots both of them), a conspicuously fair trial, and were acquitted of murder. A better advertisement of American goodwill could not have been conceived of. It was to be regretted, then, that Parliament's gesture should have been so back-handed.

At the end of April news arrived that the Townshend duties on paper, dyes and glass had been repealed. The duty on tea remained, as a matter of principle. It was reported that many members of the Cabinet, which had been considering this measure since May 1769, were in favour of total repeal but that the King, through the man who was soon to become his First Minister, Lord North, had insisted on the retention of the tea duty simply for 'the unprofitable exertion of a speculative right' (as the anonymous pamphleteer Junius put it). So what could have been a settlement emerged as a half-baked compromise. For the truth of it was that Parliament repealed the duties not out of a superabundance of loving kindness towards the colonists, but because they were highly unprofitable. It was estimated at the beginning of 1769 that the Townshend taxes in toto had extracted only £3,500; the resulting non-importation agreements had cost Britain in the region of £7,250,000.

The instinctive and widely-felt reaction of the American merchants, on hearing that the tea duty was retained, was to pursue their non-importation policy with renewed vigour. But as the months wore on and the balance-sheets spelled out their intractible message, gaps began to appear in the ranks. First the merchants of New York, then of Philadelphia, finally of Boston began filing their orders to England.

Prosperity returned and with it a degree of reconciliation. The fact that throughout the years 1771–3 there was no parliamentary debate on any colonial controversy must speak for itself.

Controversy did not cease in America, exactly, during these years. In New York the imprisonment of Alexander McDougall for seditious libel (see below) stirred the patriot press to a rare frenzy and won him the glorious title of 'the Wilkes of America'. The burning of His Majesty's customs ship *The Gaspée* by Rhode Islanders in June 1772 and the wounding of her officious captain brought prompt action from the Cabinet. Huge rewards were offered, a very important Royal Commission appointed. But, remarkably, not one whisper of evidence could be obtained against the culprits, all of them highly respected citizens of Providence. A proposal in July 1772 to strengthen the position of judges in Massachusetts by taking their salaries away from colonial and into Royal control inspired a spate of public protests and denunciations of such 'a despotic administration of government'. More significantly it led to the creation of committees of correspondence in many towns within the colony as an aid to concerted, and therefore more effective, action. The next year Virginia adopted this useful system of communication; and before long a network of committees was established throughout the continent, though as yet Lord North had not provided them with a universally abhorrent issue with which to test them. For it may not have been a period of 'profound tranquillity' as General Gage would have had it, but in retrospect it was a much-needed breathing-space, if only in preparation for the storm that was to come.

McDougall's Imprisonment (*untitled*) *du Simitière: This pen-and-ink drawing celebrates primarily the notorious imprisonment of Alexander McDougall, but it is also packed with patriot symbolism. Friction between the townspeople and the redcoats quartered in New York was never far below the surface: on January 18 1770 it exploded in the so-called Battle of Golden Hill, where there were casualties on both sides. Some weeks*

before that, however, a highly inflammatory broadside entitled 'To the Betrayed Inhabitants of the City and Colony of New York' had appeared on the streets. The Assembly, already nervous of impending violence, made strenuous efforts to uncover the author. McDougall was betrayed by one of the apprentices who had printed the piece, and he was thrown into jail on February 8 1770 (left). At once he became a focus for patriotic demonstrations, 'converting Chains into Laurels and transforming a Gaol into a Paradise' as he put it himself. The Assembly's attempts to secure a conviction were frustrated by the untimely decease of their only witness, the printer's apprentice: they nonetheless committed McDougall to prison till March the following year. He soon acquired—and revelled in—the title of the Wilkes of America. Wilkes himself is remembered by the number 45 at the top of the Liberty Pole and by his disembodied voice from prison (he had courted a prosecution for seditious libel in 1763 by attacking both the King and the terms of the peace in issue no. 45 of his newspaper The North Briton). The number 45 took on an almost mystical significance for patriots throughout the colonies (as did 92, the number of Massachusetts delegates who refused to rescind their circular letter in 1768). It was reported that on the 45th day of 1770 45 New York patriots ate 45 pounds of beefsteak from a bullock 45 months old. This is the incident depicted here (right) inside the building (Libel Hall) which displays the sign 'Beef Stake Hot & Hot'. From the door of the Hall the 'road to liberty' winds round the stocks to the liberty pole, past a recumbent animal which bears an uncommon resemblance to a sheep.

The Mother and Child. Anon: The King entreats his harrassed 'mother' for yet more supplies to pursue his designs upon the colonies. The policy of garrisoning so many troops in America, as the Opposition were never slow to point out, was a constant drain on the country's resources. Yet this print is not entirely accurate in its implication of George III's wastefulness. It was true that the national debt had risen from £70 million before the war with France to £130 million in 1763. However, it had not increased in the next ten years (indeed nearly £6 million had been paid off).

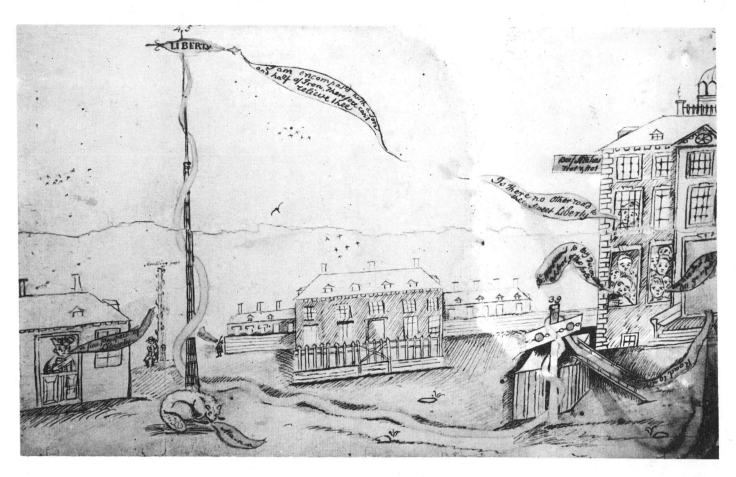

Privy Purse in 1753.   Privy Purse in 1773.

GR III

The Mother and the Child

THE RELIGIOUS QUESTION

Of those settlers who had travelled to America to escape religious persecution and worship the Almighty in whatever way they saw fit, by no means all of them attained this ideal if they had the misfortune to disembark in the wrong colony. A Baptist arriving in Massachusetts or Connecticut, where Congregationalism reigned supreme, would be more likely to find himself in a prison than near a pulpit. A Roman Catholic settling anywhere did so in the knowledge that he would be disbarred from holding office, even in Maryland which sprung up out of that faith. In Virginia and North and South Carolina the Anglican Church was established, and all denominations were obliged to contribute to its upkeep. In Pennsylvania the Quakers wielded an influence far beyond their numbers; in New York it was the Dutch Church. Even Rhode Island which had been founded on exemplary principles of religious toleration did not interpret this to mean religious equality.

To the Churchmen of England this state of affairs in the colonies was as sackcloth and ashes. No opportunity, however unpromising, to impose an Anglican establishment over a wayward colony was overlooked. Some notable advances towards that end had indeed been made; since 1742, for instance, Anglican clergy in Massachusetts had been permitted to collect their share of church taxes instead of watching the entire revenue disappear into Congregationalist coffers. In New York and New Jersey a status equivalent to establishment had been appropriated over the years as surely as if it had been legally instituted. Equally there had been stumbling-blocks. The Anglican clergy of Virginia had been confounded by the Twopenny Act of 1758, in which year they had been obliged to take their stipends in hard cash—rather than the infinitely more profitable currency of tobacco. The Act was disallowed in London, but litigation over back-pay rumbled on until Patrick Henry silenced it in court in 1763 by denouncing the priesthood as 'rapacious harpies who would snatch from the hearth of their honest parishioner his last hoe-cake!'

After the return of peace in 1763 the Anglican hierarchy in England renewed its efforts, in particular Archbishop Secker of Canterbury whose ambition it had long been to import a bishop into America (for much the same reasons as Parliament later wished to import tea). The Anglican congregations of America, too, desired one—not just to facilitate the laying on of hands but also to check the follies and vagaries of the profession. At the end of the year Secker began his lobbying for an American Bishop; in May 1764 he admitted that the question was in suspense but optimistically did not see 'how Protestant Bishops can decently be refused us' with the proviso that the whole affair must be 'managed in a quiet and private manner'. How right he was. When wind of the project reached dissenting ears in Boston, there was an outcry. The pastor of West Church, Jonathon Mayhew, burst furiously into print: 'Will they never let us rest in peace? What other new world remains as a sanctuary for us from their oppressions in case of need? Where is the Columbus to explore one for us and pilot us to it, before we are deluged in a flood of episcopacy?' But the Archbishop had been too sanguine. The government was wary of the religious tumult such a bishopric would provoke, and it had no desire to add gratuitously to the troubles which overtook it after the Stamp Act and later the Townshend duties. The plan went into abeyance, and Secker died in July 1768. But his ideas lived, partly in an ancient tract of his 'Concerning Bishops in America' published posthumously (probably at his request), and fervently in the hearts of many a colonial churchman.

RIGHT
An attempt to land a Bishop in America. *Anon: This satire was published in the* Political Register *in 1768. In that year, Franklin wrote in a letter to an American correspondent, the bishops 'were very desirous of effecting the enlargement of the Church of England in America, by sending one of their number thither'. The government having enough political problems on its hands after the Townshend taxes judiciously declined to give in to their pressure. In this speculative print, one optimistic prelate has arrived in America on board* The Hilsborough *(after the first holder of the recently-created Secretaryship of State for America). He has been met by an angry reception-committee of dissenters and forced to flee for safety up the rigging. The ship is being pushed back out to sea, followed by a volley of philosophical and non-conformist tomes (the inclusion of Sydney on Government recalls John Adams' retrospective opinion that the bishop question, as much as anything, caused ordinary people to question the constitutional authority of parliament over the colonies). The departing bishop has—empirically—discovered a new twist to the Nunc Dimittis.*

Poor old England endeavouring to reclaim his wicked American Children: *Anon.*

CHAPTER

3

THE COLONIES ALIGHT

The Boston Tea Party to the
Declaration of Independence

1773-1776

1773	March 12	*House of Burgesses appoints Provincial Committee of Correspondence*
	May 10	*Tea Act*
	December 16	*Boston Tea Party*
1774	March 31	*Massachusetts petition refused*
	May 20	*Coercive Acts*
	May 27	*House of Burgesses calls for a Continental Congress*
	June 16	*Quebec Act*
	October	*General election*
	October 26	*First Continental Congress*
	December 1	*Non-importation resolution comes into force*
1775	February 1	*Chatham's Conciliatory proposals*
	April 19	*Lexington and Concord*
	May 10	*Capture of Fort Ticonderoga and Crown Point (12th) Second Continental Congress meets*
	June 15	*George Washington appointed Commander-in-Chief of American forces*
	June 17	*Bunker Hill*
	July 6	*Declaration of Congress sets out war aims*
	August 28	*Expedition against Quebec*
	November	*Lord George Germain becomes American Secretary*
1776	January 10	*Publication of Paine's* Common Sense
	February	*Prohibitory Act through Commons*
	February 27	*Moore's Creek Bridge*
	March 17	*Evacuation of Boston*
	June 7	*Richard Henry Lee's resolution for Independence*
	June 12	*Virginia Bill of Rights*
	June 28	*Assault on Charleston*
	July 2	*Independence resolution adopted by Congress*
	July 4	*Declaration of Independence*

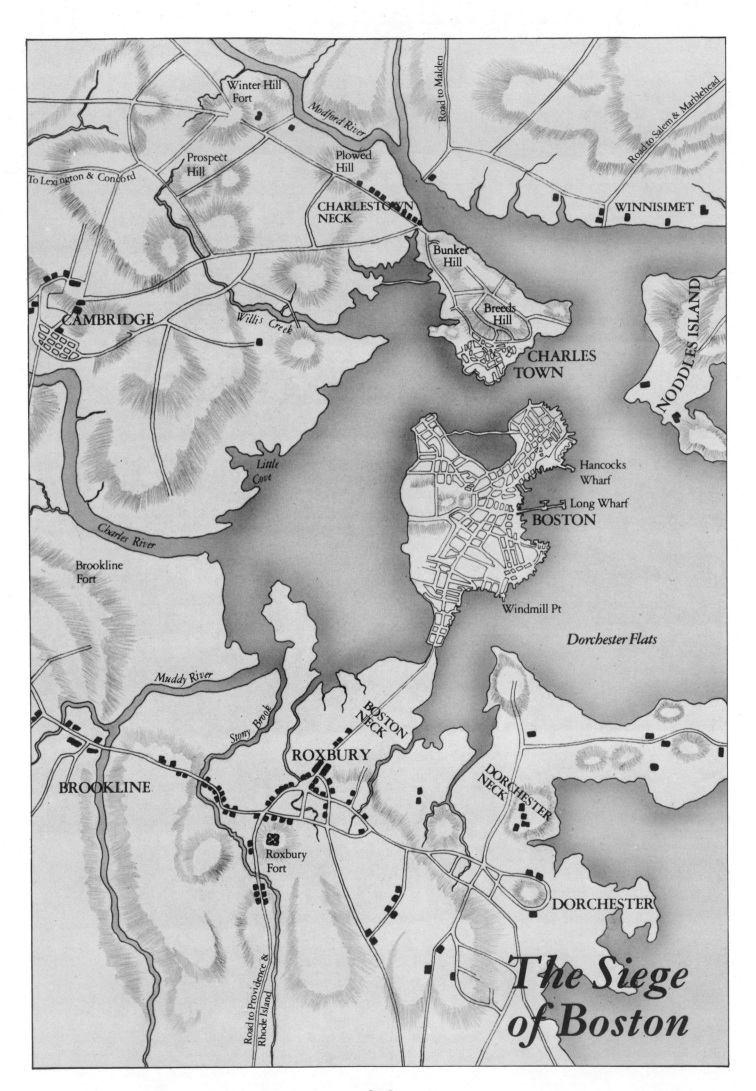

Winter Hill
Fort

Prospect
Hill

Mystford River

Plowed
Hill

Road to Malden

Road to Salem & Marblehead

To Lexington & Concord

CHARLESTOWN
NECK

WINNISIMET

Bunker
Hill

NODDLES ISLAND

CAMBRIDGE

Willis Creek

Breeds
Hill

CHARLES
TOWN

Little
Cove

Hancocks
Wharf

Long Wharf

BOSTON

Charles River

Brookline
Fort

Windmill Pt

Dorchester Flats

Muddy River

BOSTON
NECK

Stony Brook

ROXBURY

DORCHESTER
NECK

BROOKLINE

Roxbury
Fort

DORCHESTER

Road to Providence & Rhode Island

The Siege
of Boston

With Parliament's repeal of most of the contentious Townshend duties, a measure of tranquillity returned to the colonies and further efforts of extreme patriots to fan the flames of revolution were, for the time being, doomed to failure. Surprisingly, even the storm of protest against the taxes themselves had made little impact on the cartoonists, who in their own volatile fashion had become pre-occupied with a different struggle between freedom and tyranny, the Wilkes affair. America was not entirely removed from their thoughts, of course, for a close parallel was observed between Wilkes' struggles with Parliament and America's; the colonists themselves recognized this identity of interests, sending him gifts, naming townships after him and drinking his health on every conceivable occasion. In the torrent of Wilkite satires which poured forth in 1769 and 1770 America is mentioned occasionally, makes a personal appearance in several in a minor role, and in one (*Political Electricity*, page 35) the inhabitants of Boston are portrayed quite specifically. But in 1771 interest in Wilkes declined, and with it the general concern with the colonies which had now resumed their right and proper position of an obedient and lucrative annexe of Britain (or so the Ministry hoped).

When it revived, suddenly and explosively early in 1774 after news of the Boston Tea Party, there were fresher and equally satisfying targets to hand: Lord North (who, when Grafton, unable to carry the Cabinet on the repeal of the tea duty had eventually resigned, took over as First Minister) and his equally immovable colleagues Mansfield and Sandwich. These men were the 'King's Friends' and embodied everything the cartoonists rejoiced to attack, autocracy and despotism, patronage and privilege. Months of coercive legislation against the colonies sharpened their claws and, as the news from America grew blacker and blacker, they scoured the radical newspapers (which still arrived on every packet) from the colonies for details of provoking incidents (see *The Patriotic Barber, Paying the Exciseman,* etc.). The general election at the end of the year raised them to a crescendo of invective, but without any apparent effect. Lord North and friends returned with a massive majority.

At the outbreak of hostilities the attitudes in many prints become more extraordinary. Patriot triumphs were greeted with salvoes of derision for the Ministry, idealized (sometimes imaginary) portraits of patriot generals were displayed in print-shops, the characters of leading proponents of the war systematically demolished. A few artless efforts to discredit the Continental armies (see *Yankie Doodle Intrenchment*, page 79) appeared also, but the general tenor of the cartoons is one of violence against the Ministry which mounted with every year of the war. No effort seems to have been made to suppress this treachery. The Ministry remained remarkably aloof from these satirical attacks (as it could well afford to). In Parliament, where the Opposition called almost daily for surrender, ministers responded often with warmth, even asperity. Against pamphleteering American sympathizers, like Dr. Price, they employed whole armies of hacks; against the Reverend Horne Tooke (an erstwhile friend of Wilkes) who advertised in the press that he was opening a fund for the oppressed colonists, they contemplated a prosecution (and then rejected the idea). But against the barbs of the cartoonists they suffered—so far as we can tell—in silence, as a politician was required to do.

Many of the satires in these years are taken from polemical magazines, whose columns were often filled with tirades against the Ministry as withering as the engravings which accompanied them. Many of them had a very uncertain lease of life, and soon died; but in fostering the cartoonists they played an important part in the development of graphic satire which was to bear fruit in the next two decades. One peculiarity of this short period was the outbreak of humorous mezzotints by such competent artists as John Dixon and Philip Dawe (a pupil of Hogarth). Clearly there was some sort of popular craze for them, short-lived and more informative than savage (but none the worse for that). The leading caricaturist of the day was Matthew Darly who in 1773 advertised one of the first exhibitions of caricatures in London. He had once been the leading publisher of political satires, but though there are occasional examples of purely political prints from his pen at this time, his most famous work was the pillorying of extravagant fashion (*Noddle Island* etc.) into which political references intrude more by whim than by design.

THE TROUBLE WITH TEA

In the early months of 1773 it became clear in London that the East India Company was in financial trouble. Its Indian warehouses were stuffed with tea it couldn't sell; with the threepence-a-pound Townshend tax on top of the costs of auctioning it in London and the profits of American middlemen, it was cheaper—and ideologically sounder—for the Americans to buy the smuggled Dutch variety. In March and April consequently North was besieged by directors of the company lobbying him to bail them out. He agreed, and if at the time he had an inkling of the explosion he was brewing he strenuously denied it later.

The remedy seemed simple: relieve the Company of all import duties on tea shipped to England for re-export to America, and permit the Company to use its own agents and ships for conveying the beverage across the Atlantic. But it was, as Benjamin Franklin readily perceived, an expedient fraught with dangerous implications. In June he wrote incredulously 'They believe that 3d in a pound of tea, of which one does not drink perhaps ten lb. in a year, is sufficient to overcome all the patriotism of an American'. In the event this patriotism was not put to the test, for not one leaf of the new cheaper consignments ever reached an American teapot. Rather than expose their fellow-countrymen to the temptations of cheap British tea (and thus condone the principle of Parliament's right to tax the colonies), the radicals determined to prevent any of it being landed on American soil.

The East India Company's first ships reached Boston in November. For several weeks three of them moored in the harbour afraid to offload their cargoes—four customs commissioners and five Company agents had been attacked by a mob just before their arrival. On December 16 bands of Bostonian radicals, disguised as Mohawk Indians, boarded the vessels and emptied more than £7,500 worth of tea into the harbour. On December 22, 257 chests of tea were unofficially impounded at Charleston. On the 25th at Philadelphia a Company ship was unceremoniously sent packing back to England. Throughout the following year 'tea parties' were conducted up and down the coast—except where caution got the better of commercial instincts and captains retired with their cargoes intact.

RIGHT

Liberty triumphant, or the downfall of Oppression. Anon: Across the Atlantic Ocean the antagonists square up to each other. On the left, Lords North and Bute (1 & 2) confer with an East India Company director (3) and the King in the grip of the Devil. Behind them stand a gaggle of Company directors, including the Duke of Richmond (9) whose involvement in the Company's affairs directly conflicted with his association with the Rockingham Whigs, and perhaps partly explains why the Opposition allowed North's legislation to pass through the Commons with scarcely a murmur of dissent. On the right, the spirit of colonial resistance is once again personified by warlike Indian ladies, whose militancy contrasts strongly with the group of disappointed American traders (18) who had been granted a monopoly to distribute the Company's tea. More than any other measure, it was this monopoly which alienated the majority of American merchants who might otherwise have remained loyal. John Hancock was only one of many whose exclusion from the monopoly finally threw them into the arms of the Radicals. The parlous state of British shipping is epitomized by the ships lying idle in Boston harbour (16), wrecked on Cape Cod (17) and returning with their wares from New York and Philadelphia. This print was probably published in England in April or May 1774, when the full extent of American resistance had dawned on the Administration.

HARSH REMEDIES: THE COERCIVE ACTS

News of the Boston Tea Party reached London in the middle of January 1774. The mood of the House was ill-disposed to receiving a bombshell of these proportions; it was already considering an impudent petition from the people of Massachusetts for the removal of Governor Hutchinson for expressing anti-American sentiments in his private correspondence (he was not to know, of course, that his mail would be intercepted by Benjamin Franklin and returned to Boston for publication). Inevitably the hearing of the petition in Privy Council on January 29 turned into what Burke denounced as a 'public trial' of the Americans in general and Franklin in particular. According to the *Public Advertiser* the Solicitor General excelled himself 'decking his harangues with the choicest flowers of Billingsgate'.

The end of January marked the disappearance of any vestiges of a compromise policy with the colonists for the time being. Anyone inclined to moderation was now swept away on the tide of righteous indignation: Parliament's sovereignty in Massachusetts *must* be asserted. Throughout February while the law officers pondered with infuriating deliberation over prosecutions for high treason and the King scribbled off impatient memos to his Ministers, North and his rather more hard-line colleagues in the Cabinet formulated their coercive measures. The Port of Boston was to be closed until such time as its unruly inhabitants came to heel, and the Constitution of Massachusetts was to be amended to increase British authority in the rebellious colony. For once the factions seemed reasonably united, for during March the Boston Port Bill swept through Parliament with few dissenting voices. Later the Opposition was to denounce the Bill for its discrimination against Boston, but declined at the time to demonstrate its weakness by forcing too many humiliating divisions.

There remained simply the task of dispatching General Gage off to Boston as Hutchinson's successor (he had requested leave to return to Britain the previous summer) and to give official notice of the Bill to amend the Massachusetts Charter, before Parliament retired. When it reassembled members discovered that two more coercive measures had been drummed up: the Impartial Administration of Justice Act (the 'Murder Bill' as the colonists were more inclined to call it) which would permit the Governor to have offenders removed and tried elsewhere, in Britain if necessary; and the Quartering Act, which extended the obligations already laid on the colonists to provide quarters for the army in their midst. The last of the four Intolerable Acts passed largely ignored, but on the other two the Opposition did contrive to muster some sound and fury (if not many votes). Colonel Barré warned, as he had done so before on another memorable occasion, that they would stir the Americans to war. Dunning and Burke inveighed against them; Rockingham made a speech which was in itself an unusual occurrence. His herculean effort was of no avail. By the end of the third week in May both Bills had passed with handsome majorities and received the King's assent.

TOP RIGHT

The Whitehall Pump. *Anon: From a pump adorned with the head of George III Lord North pours cold water over Britannia, whose fall has dashed America (an Indian brave) to the ground. On the right, two members of the Opposition, Lord Camden and Wilkes, are protesting; on the left various ministerialists are highly approving—in the judges' robes are Lord Chancellor Apsley and Lord Mansfield, behind them a posturing Lord Sandwich and in the window Fox (not Charles James who had yet to make his mark in cartoons on the American controversy, but his father Henry Fox, Lord Holland, who was to die later in the year).*

BOTTOM LEFT

The able Doctor or America swallowing the Bitter Draught. *Anon: This print was published in May 1744 when the Opposition had been informed of the true extent of the Government's Coercive legislation. It was later copied by Paul Revere for an American publication. North forces his coercive remedies down the throat of a prostrate America—appropriately enough from a tea-pot. Lord Chief Justice Mansfield pinions her arms; Lord Sandwich, First Lord of the Admiralty and a notorious womanizer, peeks up her skirt. Lord Bute, wielding his sword, is as out of place as usual having had no say in the framing of the measures but continues a handy symbol of the King's favouritism. Britannia weeps and the Kings of France and Spain look on with interest (as well they might). The Boston petition (for the removal of Hutchinson) lies in shreds on the ground; in the background the city itself, we are informed, being cannonaded—an ominous prediction rather than a statement of fact.*

BOTTOM RIGHT

The Way of the World, things as they are, or a Toutch at all Parties. *Anon: During the debates in May on the Coercive Act, Lord North also introduced his Quebec Act—Canada Bill as it is called here—(see page 50). The ease with which the Ministry got its repressive laws through all their stages in Parliament is reflected here. An irradiated King sits sublimely at the apex of power; North with his familiar lorgnettes and Mansfield with his legalistic Bills hold the next rungs of influence, untroubled by the efforts of clerics and political opponents (including Chatham with his crutches and Wilkes, right) to clamber up or shoot them down.*

The Whitehall Pump.

Westminster Mag. Ap. 1774

The able Doctor, or America Swallowing the Bitter Draught.

BOSTON: PATRIOTS AND PLACEMEN

By virtue of their adventures on the night of December 16 Sam Adams' Mohawks had committed the rest of their fellow-citizens to an unpalatable decision. Boston was now a renegade city; was it going to see this thing through to the bitter end, or was it going to submit humbly and apologetically to the King's will? It was soon apparent that there were plenty of respected citizens who wished it to do the latter. When Gage arrived to take up his post as Governor in May, civic courtesies had not been so far suspended as to deny him his traditional welcoming banquet. Over a hundred inhabitants even indicated to him that they were prepared to open a subscription to compensate the East India Company for the loss of its tealeaves. Gage clutched eagerly at these incipient signs of remorse, but he was to be disappointed. One town-meeting after another declared it would have nothing to do with it, and the project was still-born. Throughout the province the various committees of correspondence went still further by calling for an embargo on British goods and issuing a convenant for all and sundry to sign.

The time had come for all Massachusetts men to stand up and be counted as a King's man—or a patriot. Those who had served the Crown and continued to do so were the first to find their loyalty tested in the face of manhandling (if they were lucky) or that familiar partisan art of tarring and feathering. To publicly express, or even to be suspected of, an attachment to King George, was attended by serious danger. Peter Oliver (himself a prominent Tory who suffered for his beliefs) later enumerated some of 'the many, very innocent Frolicks of Rebellion': the houses of royalists were fired into, their horses poisoned or mutilated; one unfortunate drover who had bought an ox from a King's friend was covered in its offal and paraded through the countryside; one indiscreet doctor was stripped, tarred and thrown into hog's dung. Many Tories were allegedly confined prisoners down the Simsbury mines, others were ducked in convenient rivers or ostracized. The Anglican Church was found to be a rich repository of loyalism: one cleric found his pulpit nailed up, another was removed to the village pond and showered with herrings, yet another was treated to a naked, night-time horse ride. From all corners of the colony persecuted loyalists streamed into Boston where, as more and more troops arrived, Gage shrewdly determined to establish a strong haven for his men and his supporters.

FAR RIGHT

The Bostonian's Paying the Exciseman or Tarring and Feathering. *Philip Dawes: This mezzotint, published in London in October 1774, depicts the rough justice meted out to one John Malcolm on January 29. Malcolm was an exciseman at Boston of an officious and universally unpopular variety. The news of his treatment reached London at a time when feeling against the Bostonians was still running very high, and his case was brought up in Parliament as a justification for the necessity of restoring royal government by force. The patriots claimed he had brought the punishment upon himself: in the* New York Journal *February 17 1774 it was asserted that he had been found 'standing over a small boy, damning, threatening and shaking a very large cane' and that when accosted he 'had pricked Mr. Waddel in the breast, the bone stopping the (sword's) course, which would otherwise have reached his vitals'. His general unpopularity appears to have sprung from his habit of 'seizing vessels on account of the sailors having a bottle of gin or two on board'. For which he was obliged, as the print shows, to swallow a large bowl of tea 'with orders to drink the King's health'. Unfortunately for Malcolm his patriotism was not required to stop there—the patriots made him also to drink the health of the Queen, the Prince of Wales and the rest of the Royal Family right down to the Bishop of Osnaburg (the King's second son). In the background stands a Liberty Tree with a noose hanging from it—a reference to the second part of Malcolm's punishment, a mock lynching. On the left, chests of tea are being symbolically dumped into the harbour. In the forefront, even more symbolically there lie the cap and staff of liberty.*

NEAR RIGHT TOP

A New Method of Macarony Making as Practised at Boston. *Philip Dawes: This is a later reference to the same event, inspired by the news (confirmed in the* London Chronicle *of December 15 1774) that John Malcolm was to be given a pension of £200 p.a. for his pains. The number 45 on the patriot's hat (left) refers to issue no. 45 of Wilkes's anti-ministerial newspaper the* North Briton *(see page 56). A Macarony was a class of foppish, over-dressed man-about-town currently to be seen on the streets of London. (Note: this illustration is taken from a 19th-century copy of Dawes's original.)*

NEAR RIGHT BOTTOM

Hancock's Warehouse for Tarring & Feathering. *Anon: Unlike the other two examples, this print is clearly unsympathetic to the patriots. There is no evidence to show that Hancock was ever directly involved in such enterprises, although his name was well known in Britain as one of the Boston radicals since the seizure of his ship the* Liberty *(see page 34). The lady on the left is undergoing her preliminary ducking in a barrel of tar; the lady in the centre acquires her feathers; the lady on the right displays the finished effect. The print is pure propaganda as was Peter Oliver's assertion that '. . . they continued their laudable Custom of Tar & Feathers, even the fair sex threw off their Delicacy, and adopted this New Fashion. Had it been imported from France it might have been indulged to them, but as it was imported from a Region where Delicacy is not much encouraged, it was a great Pity they did not consult their own Characters . . .'*

THE LOYALTY OF CANADA

The problem of reconciling Protestant British rule and Catholic French majority in the Canadian territories had dogged the heels of successive Ministries since 1763, when Quebec and the Indian reservations to the south had been ceded to Britain at Paris. Suddenly, in the spring of 1774, it assumed the proportions of an emergency: if the loyalty of Canada were not assured there would be dire prospects for any British operation in the Northern colonies, should it come to war. The velocity with which the Administration bull-dozed its Quebec Bill through all its readings aroused the suspicions of the Opposition. Dunning imagined he perceived 'something in its breast that squints and looks dangerous to the other inhabitants of that country, our own colonies'.

And so thought the colonists. In particular they objected to the clause that incorporated all the Indian lands north of the Ohio into the province of Quebec. They objected to it as an attempt to attach the Indians to the British cause—which it partially succeeded in doing; and they objected to it as an effort to curb the colonists' inexorable westwards expansion—which it patently failed to do. In May the proprietors of Pennsylvania presented a petition protesting at the new proposed boundaries, and a week later Burke (on behalf of New York) obtained some concessions in Committee for the colonists. The Opposition fought the Bill tooth and nail at every stage. Under its provisions Roman Catholics were free to practice their religion and their clergy to collect their tithes, and all citizens were to be governed by a Governor and Council and be subject to an amalgam of Old French and English Criminal laws. It was, so one newspaper claimed, 'the only statute which has been passed these 200 years to establish Popery and arbitrary power in the British Dominions'. Yet the Opposition was not entirely consistent in its attacks, since much of the spadework had been done by Rockingham's own Ministry of 1766. It was not the measures themselves, perhaps, which they reviled, so much as their inclusion within the context of the Government's total American policy. To colonists and Opposition alike, the Quebec Act became the fifth Coercive Act.

BELOW
The Mitr'd Minuet. *Anon: To the music of Bute and the Devil and the approval of Lord North, bishops dance at the passing of the Quebec Act. The Act's provision for extending the freedom of religion in Canada was predictably reviled by the Opposition as a stage in the further encroachment of Popery (it was to be only four years before Parliament was to take the first tentative steps towards such freedom for Catholics in Britain as well). In practice only the Methodists (who felt themselves discriminated against in the thirteen colonies) protested volubly against this clause. This print appeared in July, a few days before the King gave his assent to the Act.*

RIGHT
This Sr. is the Meaning of the Quebec Act. *Anon: In this mezzotint, a Frenchman, an uncouth Scotsman and a prostitute gleefully mull over the implications of the latest piece of legislation—leaving no doubt in anyone's mind just what the author of this print thought the Act was good for.*

The Mitred Minuet.

THIS Sⁱ IS THE MEANING OF THE QUEBEC ACT.

BOSTON: THE REVOLUTIONARY REGIME

General Gage's efforts to restore civil government to his colony were doomed from the start. He had removed the legislature north from Boston to Salem and the customshouse to Marblehead. He might as well have removed them to the Arctic wastes for all the good it did him. The men of Marblehead proved to have no more respect for the chests of tea that arrived in their port than the men of Boston. The twenty-four tried and true Tories whom Gage had sworn on to his new royal Council were soon browbeaten by the patriots into total quiescence or chased back to Boston. The Assembly, meeting in Salem in June, locked its doors and resolved to call for a Continental Congress. Gage dissolved it on the spot; but he was too slow to curtail town-meetings, which continued on the specious argument that each one was in fact the same meeting adjourned from a date preceding the ban. Even his local courts were paralyzed for want of juries to sit in them.

Desperate, Gage called for a new Assembly to be elected for early October. Then he changed his mind —irrelevantly, as it turned out, for a new Assembly turned up at Salem on October 5 regardless. Since the Governor declined to have anything to do with this extra-legal body, it turned itself into a Provincial Congress and, quite inappropriately, adjourned with its thoughts of war from the town of peace (Salem) to the village of Concord. In secret and under the presidency of John Hancock, the Congress prepared itself for armed resistance; it purchased muskets and mortars, bayonets and grape-shot; it appointed a committee of public safety with authority to call out local militias (minutemen) at a minute's notice; it laid down Rules and Regulations for its fledgling army. It may not have been a terrifying prospect to a nation which had lately taken on the combined might of France and Spain, but Gage by November had the sense to see that he would need no less than 20,000 men to stamp out the spark of insurrection then being ignited.

RIGHT

A Political Lesson. *John Dixon: This mezzotint—more like an epic painting than a political satire— catches General Gage being thrown from his horse en route to Salem, whither he had abortively summoned the Massachusetts Assembly to meet instead of Boston. For a similar reference to the colonies (the horse) throwing their rider (Britain) see page 135.*

FAR RIGHT

The Bostonians in Distress. *Philip Dawe: This mezzotint, published in London towards the end of 1774, was aimed at enlisting British sympathy for the sufferings of the people of Boston under blockade by the Navy. It probably had its effect, for at least one member of the Opposition, the Rev. Horne Tooke opened a subscription for their aid. The Bostonians are depicted as suffering the fate of slaves who had been convicted of capital offences (i.e. starvation by incarceration in a cage). They are being fed by the fishermen of Marblehead who donated '207 quintals of codfish' (just one of the many offers of assistance that poured into the city from their fellow-colonists). In the harbour stand the 'four or five frigates' Lord North believed would be necessary to enforce the Boston Port Bill, together with the four regiments then stationed on Boston Common, the one at Castle William, the one on the new fortification on the Neck and the six supposedly on their way from Europe.*

The BOSTONIANS in DISTRESS

THE FIRST MINISTER

It was the misfortune of Frederick Lord North—as skilful a Parliamentarian and as conscientious a Minister as any eighteenth-century government could have hoped for in peacetime—to have found himself in charge of a war. An amiable man, he was not badly-disposed towards the colonists, indeed by inclination (as he demonstrated with his proposals in February 1775) would have preferred to conciliate them rather than crush them. He lacked the single-mindedness to direct a war, the will to channel the motley passions of his war Cabinet and the nerve to temper his King's intransigence. 'A pliant tool' he was called by Horace Walpole—rarely disposed to charitableness in his assessments, of course. But so he was. Driven to the edge of despair by political reverses time and again he begged the King to be allowed to resign. But without fail he was always cajoled back into harness by the King who, while noting 'many things about him I wish were changed' couldn't conceive 'of any who would do so well'.

In a sense the King was right: there was no one else capable of sustaining the semblance of a stable Ministry. Chatham was riddled with gout, Rockingham's party racked by dissention. It was no mean achievement for North, in the tangled skein of Georgian politics, to have nursed an Administration through twelve gruelling years and to have retained the confidence of the independent country gentlemen. The support of these well-intentioned men, which barely faltered through thick and thin until faced with the stone-cold inevitable in 1781, goes far to explain the British conduct of the war. They held the balance of power between the Court party in Parliament (the members whose votes were, in effect, paid for in sinecures or expectations of sinecures) and the Opposition. For seven years the independents voted solidly in the Government lobby allowing North to direct the course of the war as he willed. North, in turn, left it to Germain and Sandwich (in charge of the army and navy respectively)—indeed during those seven years he proved extremely reluctant to answer any questions or criticisms in the House

which were not concerned with what he regarded as his domain, the Treasury. But it was his personal qualities which attracted the country gentlemen. He might have the disconcerting habit of dozing off during a crucial debate; but that they could forgive, because he was himself a gentleman in every respect, cultured and witty (some said he was the equal of Burke in his day).

The fact remains that the history of North's ministry is the story of cumulating disaster and the progressive decline in the standing of Parliament. For this historians have blamed his utter dependence on the King—who was said to have paid North's debts in return for his unflinching loyalty—and his willingness to allow his monarch to meddle in and influence Parliament's affairs. That may be so; it is significant that the nadir of George III's popularity coincided with the lowest point in his Minister's Administration. After North's removal, the King's fortunes revived immeasurably. It was the combination of the King's will and the premier's acquiescence which hastened the onset of the American conflict. But who would dare say it could have been prevented had there been a Pitt or a Walpole then instead of a Lord North?

TOP RIGHT

The Colossus of the North; or the Striding Boreas. Anon: An Opposition tribute to the influence, if not the political integrity, of the First Minister. Brandishing pensions and places, North stands aloft two pedestals enscribed Tyranny and Venality, while the 'stream of corruption' flows beneath his legs. Britannia appeals to a workmanlike Wilkes (in his Mayor's robes—he had finally been elected Mayor of London in 1774) for protection from her destroyers.

BOTTOM RIGHT

Boreas. Anon: Boreas (North Wind) was a favourite epithet for Lord North by pamphleteers and cartoonists. Here he is propelled by Aeolus, the God of wind, and credited with uttering a threat (for which there is no evidence) which he was ultimately quite unable to carry out. Published in September 1774 this print appears to be a contribution to the Opposition's propaganda on the eve of the elections. No better caption for it could be found

than Walpole's description of North in his Memoirs: 'Nothing could be more coarse or clumsy or ungracious than his outside. Two large prominent eyes that rolled about to no purpose (for he was utterly short-sighted), a wide mouth, thick lips and inflated visage, gave him the air of a blind trumpeter. A deep untuneful voice which, instead of modulating, he enforced with unnecessary pomp, a total neglect of his person, and ignorance of every civil attention, disgusted all who judge by appearance, or without their approbation until it is courted. But within that rude casket were enclosed many useful talents. He had much wit, strong natural sense, assurance and promptness. What he did, he did without a mask, and was not delicate in choosing his means.'

The Colossus of the North: or The Striding Boreas.

I Promise to reduce the Americans.

WILKES, LIBERTY AND THE ELECTION

The first intimations of just how critical the situation in America was reached London with General Gage's dispatches at the beginning of August. They were in sad contrast to the bravado with which he had embarked on April 18. The Americans would be 'lions whilst we are lambs' he had told the King, 'but if we take the resolute part they will undoubtedly prove very meek'. Now he knew otherwise, not least from his sorry experiences with the recalcitrant Assembly. It had proved impossible for him to punish any of the tea rioters, and he had got wind of plans for energetic resistance to the Coercive Acts when they arrived. This—and the news that the colonists were brewing up a Congress in Philadelphia for September—hardened the King's resolve. There must be a new Parliament 'to fill the House with more gentlemen of landed property' (he told North) 'as the Nabobs, Planters and other Volunteers are not ready for the battle'.

It went against the grain with the First Minister to dissolve his Parliament six months before it had run its appointed course. It hadn't been done since 1747, and he had the uncomfortable feeling that the lack of preparation would cost him not a few seats. But the King was adamant, and his colleagues in the Cabinet preferred not to have their American business in the spring interrupted by elections. So on September 30 an immediate dissolution was announced, to the chagrin of the Opposition who complained bitterly at the Ministry's underhand manoeuvres. No one really expected the American troubles to be an issue in the election, nor were they. Under local patronage, many constituencies were a foregone conclusion. Others were shuffled like a pack of cards by the Administration and dealt out to supporters. Where there was a contest it was more likely to revolve around personalities and local issues than national controversies. Only in ports like Bristol (where Burke was asked to stand on his anti-coercion platform) and in constituencies where Wilkes and his radicals were active was the American Question raised as a specific issue.

For John Wilkes this was the chance of a parliamentary comeback, having four times been denied entry to the 1768 Parliament, and he was not the man to waste it. On September 26 he produced his Radical Declaration which, among other such vital issues as parliamentary reform and lowering the price of beer, called for the repeal of the Coercive Acts. A number of other radicals signed the Wilkes Declaration, though outside the home counties (where they made a clean sweep of the seats in Middlesex, the City of London and Southwark) it availed them little with the electors of whom Burke remarked that 'any remarkable highway robbery on Hounslow Heath would make more conversation than all the disturbances in America'. When the results were declared on November 14, the Government had 321 seats, the 'doubtfuls' and the Opposition 237. Lord North was safe for another seven—or as it turned out—another six years.

John Wilkes Esq. *Sayers: Since 1763 when Wilkes had attacked the King in issue number 45 of his newspaper* The North Briton *and had survived the resulting charges of seditious libel, his name had been identified by the common people with the cause of Liberty. Expelled from the Commons, he had fled to France and returned to contest the 1768 election. Four times elected by the voters of Middlesex, he was four times disbarred from Parliament—a scandal which served only to enhance his reputation and carry it to the remotest corners of America. The colonists saw in Wilkes a victim of the same brand of tyranny as oppressed them, and adopted him as a hero (far beyond the influence he ever could, or ever did, wield). They sent him food and tobacco in prison; South Carolina even voted him £1,500 to pay his debts. In 1774, as Lord Mayor of London and now as the unopposed Member for Middlesex, he was in a position at last to justify in some measure their confidence in him.*

The Parl'nt dissolv'd, or the Devil turn'd Fortune Teller. *Anon: To the horror of Lord North and an unidentified minister, the devil summons up a vision of America, triumphing over the body of a prostrate British soldier, and shaking Parliament free of its puny inhabitants. The picture on the wall ominously portrays Temple Bar where the heads of executed traitors were displayed to the people.*

The Dissolution of P*********t. *Anon: A wry comment from the* London Magazine *on both parties at the election (with leanings towards the Opposition). The Honourable Members are being driven off by one of Mr. Wilkes's post-chaises, the ministers in the post seats inside, the patriots (the radical opposition) on top, where the common people were usually accommodated, and the placemen (supposedly 'honest though poor') in the rear extension. They have left behind them a great deal of 'litter' which includes the Coercive Acts, General Warrants (under which Wilkes had been arrested) and Inclosures, a reference to the current policy of enclosing common land for agricultural purposes (which had destituted many poor labourers). The populace—many of whom would not have qualified anyway for a vote—look on in derision.*

The Parl^{mt} dissolv'd, or,

The DEVIL turn'd FORTUNE TELLER.

The Dissolution of P——t.

THE NEW PARLIAMENT

By the time the new Parliament re-assembled on November 30 to hear the King's Speech, the Ministry was aware that the American crisis was rapidly reaching the point of no return. General Gage had written again, abject letters complaining that 'civil government is near its end' and warning Britain to prepare for the worst since 'by all appearances these provinces must be first totally subdued before they will obey and a powerful force must in that case be employed'. Nor was Lord North's private observer in Philadelphia sending any happier news of the proceedings of the Continental Congress. The King's Speech may have made no mention of war with the colonists, but there was plenty of talk of it about. Even in September, on receiving a cool letter from the Pennsylvania Quakers, the King had written: 'The die is now cast, the colonies must either submit or triumph'. On November 19 he grew more specific: 'I return the private letters received from Lieut.-General Gage (to Lord North); his idea of suspending the Acts appears to me the most absurd that can be suggested. The people are ripe for mischief . . . we must either master them or totally leave them to themselves and treat them as aliens'. Lord North could be in no doubt as to which course he would be expected to follow.

Already there was considerable pressure on him to replace Gage (on which the Cabinet was inclined to temporize) and to prevent the trade in gun-running from the Continent to Boston (on which the Cabinet acted with remarkable energy). The Opposition was cautious. On its first test of strength (the Address of Thanks to the King, supporting him in any actions he felt compelled to take in the colonies) it had mustered only 79 votes. But when, on December 13, a report arrived that Congress was proposing to boycott British trade, it demanded that all American papers be laid before the House. North could not refuse, but he could buy time. He promised to do so the moment Parliament met after Christmas—more than a month's time—and went off home to Banbury for the festivities.

Minority

Majority

TOYS, for untoward Children

Terry del, et sculp.

Pater noster Row

The STATE PEDLARS, Or, the NATIONAL CONTRAST.

North America

THE FIRST CONTINENTAL CONGRESS

It might have appeared to the uninformed in England, from the excess of energy being expended in exacting retribution from the people of Boston and Massachusetts, that the New Englanders were the single source of disaffection in the colonies. This was anything but the case. But, in the circumstances, the other colonies could only wait upon events in Boston and do what they could to alleviate the sufferings of its inhabitants. South Carolina sent rice, North Carolina money, Connecticut walked huge flocks of sheep across the border. Copies of the Boston Port Act were printed on mourning cards and circulated the length of America. June 1 was observed as a fast day, when muffled bells rang out and flags hung at half-mast. The Governor of Virginia, Lord Dunmore, was obliged to dissolve his House of Burgesses for that very reason, but he failed to stifle them: they retired to Williamsburg and issued a general invitation to a Continental Congress (anticipating the appeal from Massachusetts by several weeks in fact).

Twelve out of the thirteen colonies showed no hesitation in electing delegates to the Congress, which was convened for September 5 in Philadelphia. Only Georgia failed to turn up—and that through the intervention of the royal Governor. Feted in every city and town on their route, the five Massachusetts delegates set out on August 10, a journey which turned into a triumphal progress as they neared Philadelphia. There they met others whose contribution to the destiny of America had been no less than their own (or was soon to prove so): John Dickinson from Pennsylvania, Christopher Gadsden and the Routledges from South Carolina. Patrick Henry and Richard Henry Lee from Virginia. And George Washington.

For nearly two months—to John Adams so far from home it seemed an eternity—this august assembly declared and debated, amended and resolved, and came up with a document, a Declaration of Rights and Resolutions, which impressed Chatham more than any other political manifesto he had read. They appealed to the laws of nature, to the English constitution and to their own provincial charters; they condemned the recent Intolerable Acts as unconstitutional as well as a great many others which had found their way into the statute book since 1763; they demanded the removal of 'the standing army' from their shores. They then moved on to the formulation of their economic strategy, which was laid down in the terms of the Association. This sombre agreement forbade the importation of any kind of British merchandise and (after the lapse of one year) the export of American goods to Britain. It also discouraged any form of 'extravagance and dissipation' which included horse-racing, cock-fighting, plays and the wearing of gloves at funerals. Under article 2, the slave trade was to be discontinued.

The delegates returned home on October 26, agreeing to reconvene in May 1775. But before they left, they drafted a petition to the King and an address to the people of Britain. They pointedly omitted to communicate anything to Parliament. Their days of treating with that body were past.

RIGHT

The Patriotick Barber of New York. *Philip Dawe: New York, though it failed to achieve the same unanimity of purpose as either Boston or Virginia, had its active and radical element. Its 'mohawks' succeeded in preventing two shiploads of tea being landed in the harbour, conducting one of the offending captains 'with music, through the multitude, to the end of Murray's Wharf . . . and wished him a safe passage'. This print portrays a well-authenticated incident at the hairdressing establishment of a Mr. Jacob Vredenburgh. On discovering the identity of his client the 'firm-spirited and patriotic' barber refused to finish the shave of Captain John Crozier, whose only offence was that he happened to be the commander of His Majesty's ship* The Empress of Russia. *On the walls are portraits and speeches of traditional heroes, Lords Chatham and Camden. The names on the wig-boxes (an intentional pun?) refer to prominent New York Whigs. John Lamb and Isaac Sears were well known as patriot leaders; Abraham Livington was later appointed Commissary by the Provincial Congress; Jacobus Zandt, Cpt. (Samuel) Broome and Welle (Walter) Franklin were merchants of distinct patriotic sympathies; Bleck Johnno is identified as John Blagge, the town's coroner, Cornelius the Big as Cornelius P. Low who was known to have fitted out privateers during the war with the French; Anthony Griffiths and Francis Van-Dyke were known for their energy whenever 'any policy of intimidation was required'; William Lugg, if related to Charles Lugg, is presumed to be a rigger and therefore an ardent patriot; for Alexander McDougall see page 36.*

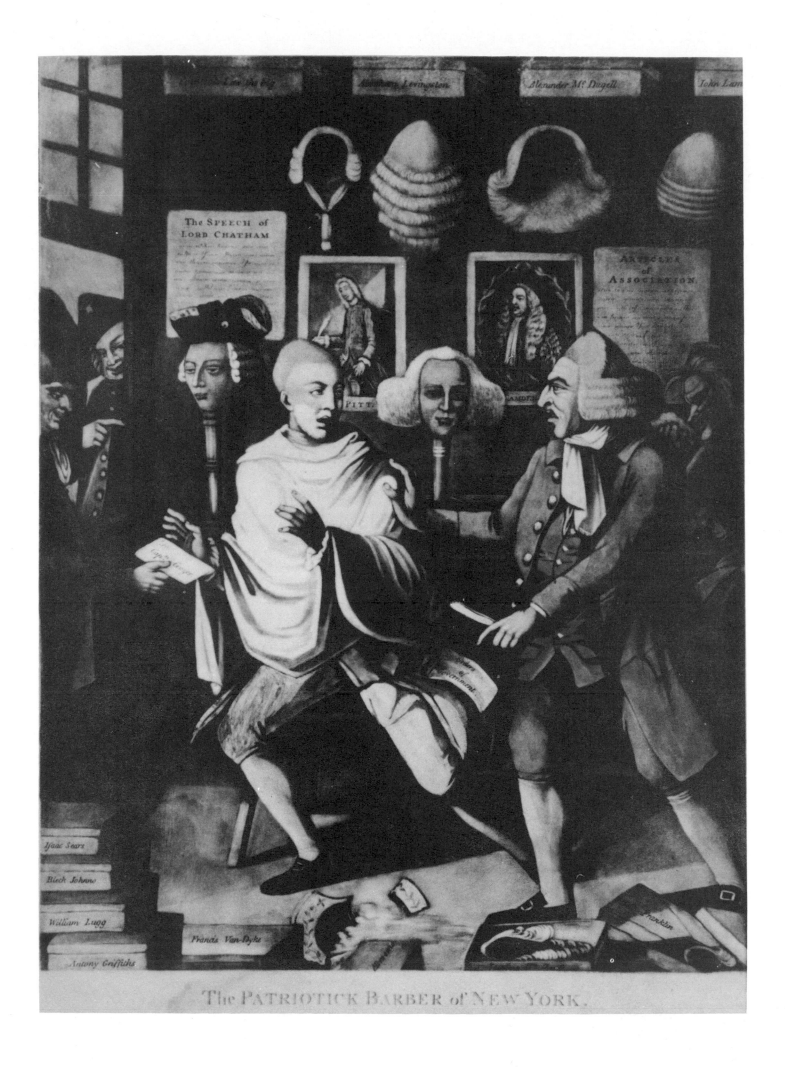

The PATRIOTICK BARBER of NEW YORK.

THE FIRST CONTINENTAL CONGRESS (continued)

RIGHT

Jean Hancock. *Anon; An idealistic French portrayal of John Hancock as President of the Continental Congress —'King' Hancock as his more enthusiastic New England supporters wont to call him at this time.*

FAR RIGHT

The Alternative of Williams-Burg *Philip Dawe: Throughout the thirteen colonies there were a great many conservative merchants who declared themselves unwilling to break off commercial ties with Britain in accordance with Congress's Non-Importation agreement. In such cases the patriots were obliged to secure their co-operation by intimidation—as in this episode at Williamsburg, Virginia. It was reported in the* London Chronicle *for January 26 1774 that 'they at last fell upon an expedient at Williamsburg, the provincial capital, to remedy this backwardness. They erected at the principal avenue to the town a very high gibbet, upon the one side of which they hung a barrel of tar and on the other side a bag of feathers, and on each of them the following inscription:* A Cure for the Refractory. *In a very short time the deed bore testimony that there was not one who had not experienced the salutary effect of so healing a medicine.'*

Under the aggressive scrutiny of an armed mob two merchants (centre front) reluctantly sign a declaration of non-importation; their finely-cut coats contrast unpatriotically with the home-made clothes of the others. On the left a clergyman is being manhandled by a couple of roughnecks—a reference to the antipathy which had existed in Virginia to the establishment of the Anglican Church since the Parson's Cause in 1763 (see page 38). The House of Burgesses was officially opposed to any attempt to introduce an Anglican Bishop into America 'a measure by which' they had resolved, much Disturbance, great Anxiety and Apprehension would certainly take place among his Majesty's faithful American subjects'.

The whole proceedings are being conducted beneath the approving gaze of a statue of Lord Botetourt, a former Royal Governor whose colonial sympathies were repeatedly compared with the present Governor's (Lord Dunmore) officiousness in imposing Parliament's will on the province. The

present of tobacco for John Wilkes (referred to on the barrel) recalls the public subscription opened for that champion of American Liberties in 1770. It is very doubtful if he ever received it, however, since the treasurer of the fund appears to have absconded with the money.

THE ALTERNATIVE OF WILLIAMS-BURG.

THE FIRST CONTINENTAL CONGRESS (continued)

BELOW

The Congress of The Necessary Politicians. *Anon: Two unidentified politicians are here seated on the lavatory (in 18th century parlance 'a necessary house'). They are clearly government supporters, as the fantasy of W(illiam) P(itt) tarred and feathered on the wall emphasizes. The gentleman on the right is perusing a pamphlet entitled 'An Answer to Taxation No Tyranny' which was the Opposition's reply to Dr. Johnson's government-sponsored pamphlet justifying the Ministry's fiscal policy, an unexceptional piece of work from so august a pen. The gentleman on the left is showing considerable disrespect to a copy of Congress's Resolutions which were first printed in the English Press on December 15. In peremptory fashion he had dismissed the Americans' claims that (1) they are entitled to life, liberty and property . . . and that (3) they, by emigrating, had not forfeited any of the rights (of natural-born subjects within the realm of England) that (4) the foundation of English liberty is a right to participate in their legislative council, and that (8) they have a right peaceably to assemble, consider of their grievances and petition the King . . . etc.*

RIGHT

A Society of Patriotic Ladies at Edenton in North Carolina. *Philip Dawe: Congress's Non-Importation agreement was rigidly enforced throughout the colonies. Even the ladies in the management of their households entered into the spirit of the thing. London newspapers reported that many women had 'unanimously agreed to lay aside the use of ribbons for which there had been so great a resort to the milliner in times past' and were appearing at dances 'in homespun gowns'. In the place of British tea they were offering up such concoctions as 'Hyperion' and 'Labrador' tea or (according to Peter Oliver) substituting chocolate and coffee 'except in Case of Sickness'. The Daughters of Liberty of Boston even came up with the following spirited Resolves:*

(1) that the Destruction of the East India tea, imported amongst us, is absolutely necessary for the Happiness of America,

(2) that the Said Tea ought to be looked upon as a Traitor to the Majesty of the People,

(3) . . . We are determined constantly to assemble at each others' House to Hang the Tea-kettle, Draw the Tea and Quarter the toast.

It is clear from this print that the ladies of Edenton had the same strength of character when it came to tea, whatever their weaknesses for the male sex.

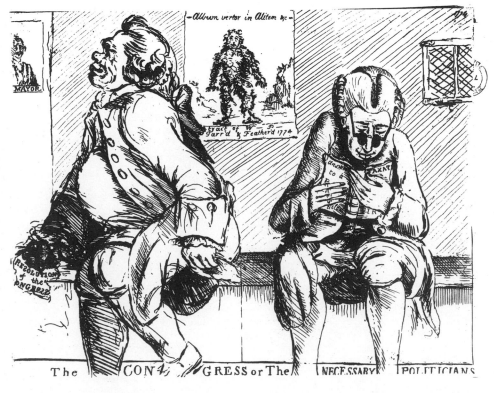

LAST HOPE FOR PEACE

Through Christmas of 1774 and the new year, against the prevailing tide of aggressive policies there ran a strong undercurrent of hope for conciliation. Even the Ministry, brandishing its cudgels in one hand, contemplated extending the olive branch in the other. The American Secretary, Lord Dartmouth (consistently the most pacific member of the Cabinet) now proposed sending commissioners to America for eleventh-hour negotiations. He got little support, but he was encouraged by North to pursue secret discussions with Benjamin Franklin which had been going on since November. Yet Franklin, even in his unofficial capacity, was unable to make noises that sounded to the Cabinet any different from the resolutions of the Continental Congress; there was no basis for settlement until the Acts were repealed. On March 2 Franklin set sail from England and by the time he arrived in America the war had begun.

Somewhat dramatically towards the end of January Lord Chatham returned to the arena from his country house at Hayes, whither he had retired from politics in 1768 to nurse his grievances and his gout. He proposed, he told their Lordships, to present a Provisional Act for settling the troubles in America. It caught the other factions of the Opposition on the hop, particularly the Rockingham Whigs who (though they hadn't come up themselves with as comprehensive a policy) plaintively suggested Chatham might have informed them first what he had in mind. What he did have in mind, it transpired on February 1, was almost total concession to the Americans: official recognition of the Philadelphia Congress, suspension of the Coercive Acts and others, no taxation without consent but the granting by the colonists of a 'perpetual revenue' to the King, the removal of troops from Boston and half a dozen other bones of dissention. The House listened respectfully to the venerable statesman's sweeping suggestions, and voted them out of sight.

Meanwhile the Ministry persisted in its attempt to break the deadlock. On February 20 North unveiled his Conciliatory Propositions, which indirectly offered exemption from taxation to any colony which would voluntarily raise the money itself. But it was a policy of too little too late and, for Franklin's taste, too double-tongued. From a Government which at that very moment had a packet at Falmouth standing by to deliver war instructions to Gage, was even then formulating further restraints on colonial trade and fishing rights and was hastily recruiting re-inforcements, it was he said 'the language of a highwayman'.

Also too late—if not so little—were Edmund Burke's impassioned Resolutions on March 22. They displayed both the strengths and weaknesses of the Opposition's stance. His speech showed a profounder understanding of the American spirit than had hitherto been articulated in the Commons. 'Do not dream' he warned 'that your letters of commerce, and your instructions and your suspending clauses are the things that hold together the great contexture of this mysterious whole. These things do not make your government. Dead instruments, passive tools as they are, it is the spirit of the English communion that gives all their life and efficacy to them.' But on the practical question of Parliament's sovereignty and right to tax, he was as evasive as only a great orator can be. It was, arguably, his greatest speech, yet had his Resolutions been passed (which they resoundingly were not), no boat on earth could have prevented that fateful march to Concord.

TOP RIGHT

The Political Cartoon for the Year 1775. *Anon: Watched by North and a motley of bishops, Lord Mansfield drives his nags Obstinacy and Pride into the abyss. Beside him the King is indifferent to his imminent fate and to the trampling of the Constitution underfoot. Bute rides as footman brandishing Pensions and Places; the populace shows more concern with its payola and gossip than with the explosion of America and the dissipation of National Credit. The only two who are attempting to stop the coach's headlong rush are Lord Chatham (right, on crutches) and Lord Camden, who had led in Opposition in support of Chatham's peace proposals.*

BOTTOM RIGHT

America in Flames. *Anon: America, in the unusual and totally inappropriate guise of an old woman, has been set alight by the repressive measures of Lord North, who contemplates his handiwork through his familiar lorgnette. The ever-present Bute (top left) and Mansfield in his Chancellor's robes continue to fan the flames. The Quebec Bill was denounced in some quarters as the encroachment of Popery and is therefore laid at the door of a Scot and a Catholic; the Massachusetts Bay Regulating Bill was indicted as a lawyer's attempt to tamper with a time-honoured constitution. A group of patriots (still a dignified title for members of the Opposition) vainly attempt to extinguish the conflagration. The Boston Tea Party, the spark which ignited it, is symbolized by the tea-pot cascading its contents.*

TO CONCORD AND BACK

So long as his superiors in London dismissed the rebels as 'a rude rabble' General Gage was forced to spend the first frustrating months of 1775 keeping his army bottled up in the vicinity of Boston. He had not 4,000 men under his command, and there was no knowing what the effective strength of the Yankees might be. 20,000 men, he guessed for Lord Dartmouth's benefit, would be needed to pacify the colony if it came to war. Bands of militia men were being organized into units, military stockpiles were being prepared at Concord and Worcester, there were reports of gun-smuggling up the Salem, and the illegal Provincial Congress continued to flout his authority by meeting out of his reach. Why, in March it had even issued an official call to arms.

In the middle of April Gage received word that four regiments were on their way to him (they weren't, they were on their way to New York) and not one, but three, generals. The letters also contained a 'secret' dispatch from Dartmouth ordering him to take punitive action since 'it will surely be better that the conflict should be brought on, upon such a ground, than in a riper state of rebellion'. Samuel Adams and John Hancock and the principal leaders of the Provincial Congress, he learnt, had now been declared guilty of treason. Gage could not hope to catch up with Hancock and Adams, but he did determine to destroy the suspected arsenal at Concord.

On the night of April 18 Gage attempted to smuggle 700 troops out of Boston by ferrying them across the harbour, but it was a manoeuvre which Paul Revere, Dr. Warren and the other revolutionaries in Boston had anticipated: two lamps were lit in North Church tower and Revere set out on horse to raise the alarm. En route for Lexington the British were left in no doubt that they were discovered; lights, church bells, drums, an occasional gunshot all bore witness to the rebels' activity. They sent back to Boston for re-inforcements, and soldiered on. In the morning they reached Lexington where they were confronted by a few dozen but determined Americans led by John Parker. The engagement detained the redcoats only a few minutes. They marched on to Concord leaving behind eight dead militiamen; but they carried with them the unnerving knowledge that a war had begun.

There was a harrowing morning spent at Concord as more and more minutemen converged on the village and watched the British destroy what little they could find (a few entrenching tools). A skirmish at the North Bridge brought some casualties to both sides, but the British retired at about midday thankful and largely intact. The worst was to come, for the road to Lexington was exposed to the unremitting fire of rebels sniping from houses, trees and walls. The company, what was left of it, was saved only by the arrival of 1,200 men under Lord Percy, whom Gage had sent from Boston. The sixteen miles back to Boston were fought for bitterly every inch of the way, and only a smart detour by Percy onto the impregnable Charleston peninsula saved the retreat degenerating into a rout. That day the British lost 73 dead, 200 missing or wounded; the Americans 49 dead, 46 wounded, but they had gained an army.

RIGHT
The Retreat From Concord to Lexington of the Army of Wild Irish Asses Defeated by the Brave American Militia. *Anon: The news of Concord came first to England in an American paper brought by an American captain on May 27. The Ministry was inclined to discredit the report, but on June 10 the official dispatches confirmed its worst fears, differing from the newspaper account only in claiming that the Americans had fired the first shot. This cartoon was published eighteen days later, depicting the meeting of Col. Smith's depleted company with Lord Percy (bottom right) and his relief column. The 'Irish Asses' of the caption possibly refers to the Royal Irish regiment which was stationed at Boston, though it by no means made up the bulk of the expedition to Concord. Many houses on the route to Lexington were indeed fired by British flanking parties to flush out the rebels and destroy their cover, and a certain amount of plundering is admitted to by Frederick Mackenzie, a lieutenant in the Royal Welsh Fusiliers in this extract from his diary: 'many houses were plundered by the soldiers, not withstanding the efforts of the officers to prevent it. I have no doubt this inflamed the rebels and made many of them follow us farther than they would otherwise have done.'*

*From Concord to Lexin...
M.ʳ Beacon M.ʳ Loeings M.ʳ Mulikens...
...according to Act June 4 177...*

The Retreat

the Army of Wild Irish Asses Defeated by the Brave American Militia

's Houses and Barn all Plunder'd and Burnt on April 19th

TO QUEBEC AND BACK

Back in October 1774 the First Continental Congress had solicited the friendship of the Canadians and invited them to send delegates to their next gathering. They did not respond. Why should they? Why should they, as French Canadians, assume that their Catholic rites and institutions would be in better hands with Protestant Americans than with Protestant Englishmen, who had at least made them legal? Nevertheless Congress did not abandon its overtures—nor cease to fear that Quebec would one day provide the launching pad for a British offensive into New England. It did not contemplate an invasion, however, maintaining for many months that the war being waged in New England was a purely defensive one.

Outside Boston, Dr. Warren and his Committee of Safety thought otherwise. News of the British retreat from Concord had spread through the colony like a forest fire; militiamen from every corner hurried to Cambridge until there were 15,000 of them, not quite knowing what to do. Old Artemas Ward, the Massachusetts commander, told them what to do: dig. And they dug until all the escape roads from the city were blocked and Boston was encircled with a patchwork of trenches and redoubts. The besieging army, however, lacked the one essential requirement for a siege—artillery; this Dr. Warren proposed to purloin from the British fort at Ticonderoga, to the north on the edge of Lake Champlain, and on May 3 he commissioned a dashing young Connecticut captain by the name of Benedict Arnold with fifty men to collect it. On his way Arnold discovered that a guerilla force with the romantic title of the Green Mountain Boys under Ethan Allen had had the same idea. There was nothing romantic about Allen and the two commanders quarrelled bitterly, but they accomplished their mission by walking into the ramshackle fort and rousing the commander from his bed to surrender. Still quarrelling they contrived to take two other outposts at Crown Point and St. Johns.

So the Americans *had* taken the offensive and, what was more, in doing so had opened up the way to Quebec. On June 27 Congress re-canted. It ordered Major-General Philip Schuyler to move up to Ticonderoga and, if the French Canadians had no objection, to march to the St. Lawrence. The Canadians proved to have no objections, but neither did they flock to the American flag. The advance was dogged with mishaps: Schuyler fell ill and gave up, his deputy Richard Montgomery was detained for more than two valuable months by a stubborn little British force which had re-occupied St. Johns. By the time Montgomery reached Quebec early in December winter had set in and the British Governor, Sir Guy Carleton, had had time to put his meagre defences in order. Montgomery also discovered that the remarkable Arnold had miraculously got there before him with 600 men whose shocking condition bore witness to their near-impossible journey through the wilderness of Maine.

To have got this far and not take Quebec was unthinkable. Montgomery prayed for a snowstorm and laid plans for an assault. Meanwhile he attempted to bludgeon Carleton into surrender with words; he even shot messages to the populace into the city on arrows—to no avail. In the early morning of December 31 the Americans attacked in two columns. Leading one of them Arnold was wounded in the leg; the towering Daniel Morgan took over and pressed on deep into the city. And he might have carried the day had he not halted, as ordered, to wait for Montgomery. For Montgomery was dead, shot to pieces in an alleyway by cannon-fire. That morning the Americans sacrificed half their stoic force (including Morgan who was captured) to kill only five of the enemy. Casting a professional's eye over the patriot prisoners, one British soldier remarked that their officers included a butcher, a blacksmith and an innkeeper. He could scarcely believe it.

The SCOTCH BUTCHERY, Boston. 1775.

VIRTUAL REPRESENTATION. 1775.

April 4. 1775.   Price 6.ᵈ

1....One String Jack....Deliver your Property   5.....I will not be Robbed
2....Begar Just so en France ?....Accomplices   6.....I shall be wounded with you
3....Te Deum   7....I am Blinded
4....I give you that man's money for my use   8....The French Roman Catholick Town of Quebeck
                                                     9....The English Protestant Town of Boston

BUNKER HILL

Gage's first reinforcements from Britain on May 25 were probably the ones he could most do without: Generals William Howe, Henry Clinton and John Burgoyne. If anyone in Boston was expecting from the combined deliberations of no less than four generals a plan dazzling in its tactical audacity, they were to be disappointed. For a fortnight they conferred and decided on an obvious and apparently harmless expedient: to occupy Bunker Hill, the high position on the neck of land facing the city across the water to the north. So it was with some surprise that the generals awoke on the morning of June 17 to find that the patriots had got there first and were busily digging themselves in. Someone had talked. But by the time the British warships in the harbour had spotted the earthworks, there was nothing else to do but row General Howe across the harbour with 1,500 men to dislodge them.

No great trouble was anticipated, and the men took provisions with them for an extended stay on the hill. The rebels were still attending to their makeshift defences as the British infantry advanced up the hill, Howe against the left flank and Pigot against the advanced fortification on Breed's Hill. Nearing the enemy lines they were treated to an unprecedented sheet of gunfire that all but wiped out entire companies. They fell back, reformed, advanced again. Clinton watching the carnage from Boston hurried over with fresh troops. Burgoyne, too, was watching. Back in London he enjoyed something of a reputation as a dramatist among other accomplishments. He was not dramatizing for once when he wrote a few days later: 'Now ensued one of the greatest scenes of war that can be conceived . . . Straight before us a large and noble town (Charlestown, immediately to the south of Breed's Hill) in one great blaze. The hills around covered with spectators. The enemy all in anxious suspense. The roar of cannon, mortars and musketry, the crash of churches, ships upon the stocks, and whole streets falling together in ruins fill the ear; the storm of the redoubts with the objects above described to fill the eye, and the reflection that

perhaps a defeat was a final loss to the British Empire in America to fill the mind.'

The British Empire in America was not lost that particular afternoon, for the engagement ended in a British victory, of sorts. Without warning the rebels' fire 'went out like an old candle'. Their powder was gone, and at last the stubborn defenders retreated to safety beyond the peninsula. The British had gained an outcrop of land of dubious value and, out of a total of 2,250 committed to the attack, 1,054 casualties, including 226 dead. 140 Americans were killed including Dr. Warren, 271 wounded. Many more victories like Bunker Hill and the British would soon be out of the thirteen colonies. But beyond the appalling losses there was the shock; the shock of experiencing at first hand the spirit and determination of the patriots. To Howe it had been 'a moment I never felt before' hardened though he was on the battlegrounds of Europe. Writing to the Secretary of War, Gage admitted 'These people show a spirit and conduct against us they never showed against the French, and everybody had judged of them from their former appearance and behaviour when joined with the King's forces in the last war, which has led many into great mistakes'.

BELOW
Bunkers Hill or the Blessed Effects of Family Quarrels. *Anon: The 'effects of family quarrels' are of course 'blessed' only to Britain's enemies who were bound to capitalize on them. France stabs Britannia through the breast and Spain holds America in a noose. From their floating perch (right to left) Lords North, Bute and Mansfield—and the devil—watch with apparent unconcern.*

RIGHT
Bunkers Hill or America's Head-Dress. *Darly: Matthew Darly was a publisher of prints with a shop in the Strand, but he also produced a famous series of satires on the grandes coiffures of the day. Sometimes he incorporated topical or political references into the designs, as here he has staged the entire battle of Bunker Hill on the lady's head-piece. It shows no acquaintance with the details of the battle (no naval engagements were*

involved, nor any encampments), and his flag-emblems are chosen purely for their absurdity—a goose, a monkey, etc.

BUNKERS HILL

or America's Head Dress

THE MINISTRY'S WAR EFFORT

The sudden outbreak of hostilities at Boston had left Britain woefully ill-equipped for a major war, for all that there had been bombastic talk of it for many months. The King was in a hurry to fight, so eager indeed that he could not bring himself to read a respectful, last-ditch petition from Congress, entreating him to intervene personally in the dispute. It reached London on August 14; in lieu of a reply there appeared on the 23rd a Royal Proclamation calling on all subjects to inform on those who were conspiring or corresponding with the traitors across the sea. The King was now convinced that the colonists were striving for nothing less than independence, that it would be more humane in the long run to wage a hard and uncompromising war. He knew just the man who would do that: Lord George Germain, who had been invoking fire and brimstone on the colonists since the first shot had been fired.

That George III should turn for his avenging angel to the man whose name was inscribed in the order-books of every regiment in the army as the cowardly blackguard who had refused to charge his cavalry at Minden, was a testimonial to the dedication with which Germain had rehabilitated himself. What ever else he was, Lord George was not a coward, physically or morally. In November he was elevated to the Secretaryship of State for the Colonies in place of the soft-hearted Lord Dartmouth. Meanwhile there was a desperate shortage also of men to actually fight the war. After quotas for Ireland and the outposts of the Empire had been fulfilled, there were barely 15,000 men stationed in Britain not one of whom could justifiably be spared. Recruiting in the Highlands was going well, in Ireland very slowly, in England hardly at all—even the East India Company was doing better for its own private army and had to be asked to desist. Britain, clearly, must buy its soldiers where it could and damn the expense. Holland politely refused to send its Scots Brigade to fight in any war in America. The King wrote personally to his sister Kitty (the Empress Catherine of Russia) but was rewarded with no more than a brusque admonition to keep the peace. Only the princelings of the numerous little German states—who never refused such requests when there was money involved—rose to the occasion. From Hanover and Hesse, Brunswick and Bayreuth the mercenaries began to pour in by the thousand; by the end of the war some 30,000 of them, speaking not a word of English, had been packed off to America and to die in their thousands in an alien land. And by the end of the war the net profit of this grisly trade, which sharpened the colonists' bitterness, drained the farms of Germany and exhausted the coffers of Britain, was little more than a few fine mid-European opera-houses.

Such were the men who were to restore Britain's influence. As to the means, Lord North introduced his Prohibitory Act on November 20. What he proposed to prohibit was all American trade. Their ships were to be seized, their cargoes forfeited and their crews drummed into service with the Royal Navy. He formally recognized that a state of war existed, and was accordingly putting America under blockade. In vain the planters complained that they would be ruined, having no time to find alternatives to the American vessels at present carrying the West Indian trade. In vain it was pointed out that other nations would undoubtedly supply the Americans and that this would force Britain ultimately to clash with countries it had no quarrel against.

BELOW
The State Blacksmiths Forging fetters for the Americans. *Anon: Lord North (left) clutching a copy of his Prohibitory Act superintends his Ministerial smithies. Sandwich fashions an anchor, Mansfield beats chains into shape, Germain (? right) inspects a gun-muzzle. In the background Bute attends to the bellows, while a delighted King peers in through the window to see how it's all going.*

RIGHT
The Wise Men of Gotham and their Goose. *Anon: The village of Gotham was proverbial for the folly of its inhabitants. In this mezzotint the ministers are Gothamites, intent on slaughtering the goose (America) which has laid them so many golden eggs. Bute attends to the execution (right), observed with indifference by judges—unidentifiable, but presumably Mansfield, Bathurst and Wedderburn—ministers (a youthful-looking North leaning over the table, Sandwich and Germain, background left) and a seated bishop, probably the Archbishop of York (see page 122). A dog urinates on the map of North America; the British Lion slumbers in his frame on the wall. The fable on the wall catalogues the efforts of the 'wise men' to extract two golden eggs a day from their goose.*

THE STATE BLACKSMITHS
Forging fetters for the Americans

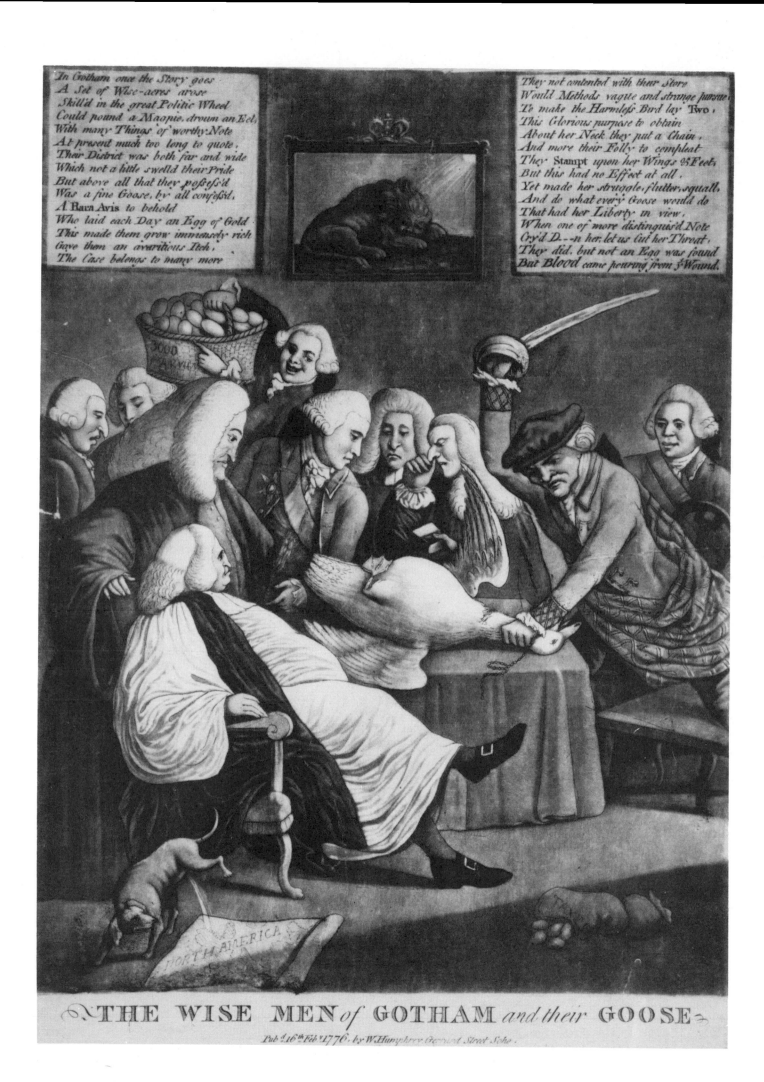

THE WISE MEN of GOTHAM and their GOOSE

Pub.d 16th Feb.y 1776. by W. Humphrey Gerrard Street Soho.

OPPOSITION TO THE WAR

In spite of the seemingly endless majorities with which Lord North was bull-dozing his anti-American legislation, coercive, prohibitory or otherwise through Parliament, the opposition to the war was deep-rooted and passionate. It was the hallmark of politics in George III's reign that, until it were unequivocably shown to be to the severe detriment of the country, policy was a reflection of the private opinion of the King and his Cabinet. But both inside and outside Parliament there were a great many eminent men whose consciences were profoundly troubled by the use of armed force against the colonists, and who interpreted the government's policies as nothing less than a declaration of civil war. Some of the country's most competent generals and admirals refused to serve in a war against fellow-Englishmen. In spite of the proffered peerage General Amherst had declined a command against the Americans 'to whom he had been so much obliged'. General Conway 'abhorred and detested the war' believing it to be unjust and unconstitutional. Admiral Keppel declared he was ready to do his duty against the French 'but not in the line of America'. Though they both later accepted commands in America —more in the hope of bringing about peace than waging an implacable war—the brothers Howe initially advised their constituents at Nottingham that they would not serve across the Atlantic. And such sentiments were to be found at every level of society: in 1775 and 1776 petitions urging compromise not war with the colonists were raised in cities and boroughs throughout the kingdom.

What the Ministry's opponents in the Commons lacked in weight they made up for in vehemence. In October 1775 Fox was able to remark (and did so) that in one campaign Lord North had lost more territory than Alexander the Great, Caesar or Lord Chatham had won in the course of all their wars. A month later Burke offered a new plan for conciliation, which included the recognition of Congress; it was defeated by two votes for every one in favour. In the Lords, the Duke of Richmond fulminated against the war: 'I do not think the people of America are in rebellion. They are resisting acts of unexampled cruelty and oppression.' And there were those who believed the war was not only wrong but unwinnable; Wilkes attempted to impeach the ministers who had started it in the first place; Fox called for a committee to enquire into the Causes of the ill Success of His Majesty's Arms in North America; the opposition newspapers arraigned the King as 'a bigoted and vindictive prince, whose administration was odious and corrupt in every part'. Even within the ministerial ranks there was not total harmony. In November 1775 the Duke of Grafton (the same one under whose premiership the Townshend taxes had been enacted) resigned in protest, and subsequently fought tooth and nail against the Prohibitory Act. Yet whatever moral value the Opposition's arguments may have had their practical effect upon the immediate course of events was minimal. As their ultimate protest in October 1776 the Rockingham Whigs were reduced to withholding their presence, and their good advice, entirely from Parliament.

One Englishman whose patriotic advice, however, was heeded in important quarrels was Thomas Paine. He had emigrated, a failure, to Pennsylvania in 1774, taken to the pen and in January 1776 issued a pamphlet entitled *Common Sense*. In racy but transparently rational prose he urged the Americans to free themselves from a monarchy to which they owed nothing and seek Independence from which they could expect everything. His arguments were devoured in every corner of the continent and received wide circulation in Europe. They made a deep impression on leading patriots, even those who hesitated to abandon all ties with Britain. They undoubtedly helped to precipitate the movement which was gathering in Congress to take this irrevocable step; and in so doing helped to make an accomplished fact that which the Opposition at home was even then warning the Ministry would be the inevitable consequence of their actions.

TOP RIGHT
Six-Pence a Day. *Anon: This anti-recruiting print (subtitled: Exposed to the Horrors of War, Pestilence and Famine for a Farthing a Day) was published by William Humphrey in October 1775, when relentless enlistment drives were being undertaken throughout the country. A thin emaciated recruit is being implored by his near-naked children and pregnant wife not to go to war for the pittance being offered. His wages are unfavourably compared (left) with those of a coachman at three shillings a day, a driver at two shillings, even a chimney sweep's boy at a shilling. On the right the gaunt figure of Famine beckons to him beneath the motto COURAGE BOYS! If you gentlemen soldiers should die & be damn'd/ Your wives and yr Infants may live and be cramm'd, while two Yankee soldiers sustain a murderous cannon and musket-fire on the hapless soldier. The watchword on their hats proclaim they are fighting for their freedom (DEATH OR LIBERTY); what is he fighting for?*

BOTTOM RIGHT
The Parricide. A Sketch of Modern Patriotism. *Anon: This rare attack on the leading opponents to the war was published in April 1776, when their parliamentary assaults on the Ministry had reached a crescendo. America (left) with tomahawk and head-dress attacks her sister Britain with the encouragement and active assistance of the Opposition. The Duke of Grafton pinions one arm, Alderman Hayley the other while Lord Camden in his judge's regalia restrains the outraged British Lion. Other identifiable accessories to this act of 'parricide' are John Wilkes with his squint (pointing, behind the figure of America), Charles James Fox (predictably, as a fox) and Lord Chatham, extreme right, hobbling on his crutches.*

The Parricide.
A Sketch of Modern Patriotism.

BIRTH OF AN ARMY

Throughout the muggy summer the American volunteers encamped around Boston, a tourniquet of some eight or nine miles cutting the city off from all communication by land. No one emerged, except those rebelliously inclined citizens whom Gage thought prudent to send packing. Despite the arrival of the four regiments intended for New York (and hurriedly intercepted by the general) he did not feel strong enough to take any offensive by land. By sea, though, the odds were still on the British and the occasional coastal raid had the double advantage of inconveniencing the enemy and of supplementing a diet that sooner or later was bound to take its toll in dysentery. Bristol, Rhode Island, required only a skirmish to hand over its ransom of forty sheep; Falmouth preferred to watch three quarters of its houses blown up first.

Meanwhile the events at Boston had transformed the Congress at Philadelphia from an assembly for passive resistance into an energetic war-council. Slow to adopt the one army it did have outside Boston, it diligently voted money for gunpowder for a Continental army which as yet existed only on paper, established a postal service, dispatched advice on defence to all corners, authorized the recruiting of riflemen, and looked round for a commander-in-chief. Several names were canvassed. There was old Artemas Ward, already on active service but ailing. There was Charles Lee, experienced and sophisticated but an Englishman in his bones. And there was John Hancock himself, President of Congress but inexperienced in warfare—and a New Englander (and this was to be all America's struggle). How badly he thirsted for the job we will never know, though John Adams records that when, on June 14, he rose to propose the gentleman from Virginia who had sat listening day after day to all the arguments resplendent in his old militia uniform (George Washington), Hancock expressed 'mortification and resentment as forcibly as his face could exhibit them'. Nevertheless Washington's election was unanimous, his reply everything Congress could have hoped for: 'Though I am truly

sensible of the high honour done me in this appointment, yet I feel great distress from consciousness that my abilities and military experience may not be equal to the extensive and important trust. . . . I beg leave to assure the Congress that as no pecuniary consideration could have tempted me to have accepted this arduous employment at the expense of my dome..ic ease and happiness, I do not wis.. to make any profit from it'.

Early in July the new Commander-in-Chief with his retinue arrived to take command of the Boston army, belatedly adopted by Congress. What he saw did not impress him: 'I daresay the men would fight very well (if properly officered) although they are an exceedingly dirty and nasty people' he confided to his brother. There were also fewer of them than he had been led to expect (for many thought nothing of returning to the comfort of their homes when things got slack) and most of them deficient in engineering equipment, powder, artillery, clothing and discipline. So far as the last was concerned, time was on Washington's side. Summer passed, with the British dormant in their impregnable position, and turned into Fall. Week succeeded week with more fighting going on inside the camp than outside, as the diary of Aaron Wright shows: 'Sept 10. Great commotion on Prospect Hill among the riflemen, occasioned by the unreasonable confinement of a sergeant. . . . Oct 7. Peace with our enemy, but disturbance enough with rum, for our men got money yesterday. . . . Oct. 15. Our clergyman preached with his hat on.'

Slowly and patiently Washington fashioned his army, taming the recalcitrant with the lash, cashiering the more unscrupulous officers, mending inter-colonial jealousies, even uncovering duplicity in high places (Benjamin Church, Director General of Hospitals, was discovered in the act of sending a coded message to the enemy). 'I flatter myself' he was soon able to write, 'that in a little time, we shall work up these raw materials into good stuff'. As winter came and their period of enlistment expired, many returned home; but thousands stayed to re-enlist in the Continental army. These were the men who were to march the length and breadth of the

colonies with Washington for the next six years.

Behold the Yankies in there Ditch's
Whose Conscience gives such griping twitch's
They'r ready to Be S—t their Brechs. Yankie Doodle
&c

Next see the Hypocritic parson
Who thay all wish to turn an A—s on
Altho' the Devil keeps the farce on. Yankie &c

The Yankie Doodles Intrenchments Near Boston 1776
Publish'd as the Act Directs

See Putnam that Commands in Chief Sir
Who looks & Labours like a thief sir
To get them daily Bread & Beef sir. Yankie &c

Their Congress now is quite disjoint'd
Since Gibbits ois far them appointed
For fighting gainst ye Lords Annointed. Yankie doodle

EVACUATION OF BOSTON

So melancholy a place did Boston become following the débâcle on Bunker Hill that Gage positively forbade the ringing of church bells for funerals. Not even General Burgoyne's efforts at amateur theatricals did much to relieve the torpor of the long summer days or, as winter approached, the bleak nights. Men deserted, plundered or simply amused themselves tormenting the hapless Whigs incarcerated in the town. From time to time the guns would splutter ineffectually at the rebels but, as one eye-witness put it, 'it seemed to be rather in jest than in earnest . . . during the whole blockade little else was done but keeping both armies out of the way of idleness, or rather the whole scene was an idle business'.

On September 26 a letter from Dartmouth arrived summoning Gage back to England, ostensibly to discuss the coming year's campaign. No one, least of all Gage himself, expected him to return. Nearly a year had passed since his dismissal had been first mooted in London. In the meantime he had been instructed to be circumspect and aggressive, coercive yet conciliatory. Whatever he had done he was self-evidently not the man to have affected the course of events in 1775 one whit. On October 10 he sailed back to England for good leaving Howe to hold on by his fingernails till winter passed.

Things were worse, in fact, than Howe imagined. Absorbed in his logistics Washington had refrained from an assault on the city until his men and ammunition were up to it. When on January 24 the new Colonel Commandant of Artillery, Henry Knox, trudged into camp with 43 cannon and 16 mortars which he and his men had dragged three hundred miles across ice and rivers from the captured fort at Ticonderoga, Washington determined that the time for action had come. Like Howe he had been contemplating the commanding position of Dorchester Heights to the south of the city. By the beginning of March he was ready to occupy it. Someone suggested that March 5 would be an auspicious day being the anniversary of the Boston 'massacre'.

And so on the night of the fourth, some of the precious cannon, seven or eight hundred bundles of hay and a strong garrison under General Thomas were silently transported up the hill. All night the men worked furiously entrenching themselves and erecting forts; in the morning they settled in and awaited the inevitable attack. It never came. Waking to find his situation turned perilous overnight, Howe was overheard to exclaim 'Good God! These fellows have done more work in one night than I could have made my army do in three months'. The weather was turning inclement for an all-out attack; he also had his orders from England—unknown to the rebels—to abandon Boston. Getting an unofficial communication through to Washington promising not to fire the city if allowed an unimpeded retreat, he packed his sick, his soldiers and loyalist supporters, their wives, children and servants, bag and baggage into every inch of ship he had available and sailed to Nova Scotia.

Noddle Island or How are we decieved. *Darly: Noddle's Island, just to the north-east of Boston harbour, had not featured in the blockade except to suffer a few incursions by British troops in search of cattle. But the pun on noddle (in use at the time, meaning the back of the head) and How (continually resorted to by cartoonists in reference to Howe) was too much for the artist. Matthew Darly, a London engraver and publisher, specialized in caricatures of the monstrous prevailing fashions in hair-styles (see page 72). This is a relatively rare example in that it contains a political allusion, very probably to the surprise occupation of Dorchester Heights (right) and Howe's army hastily taking to the boats (bottom).*

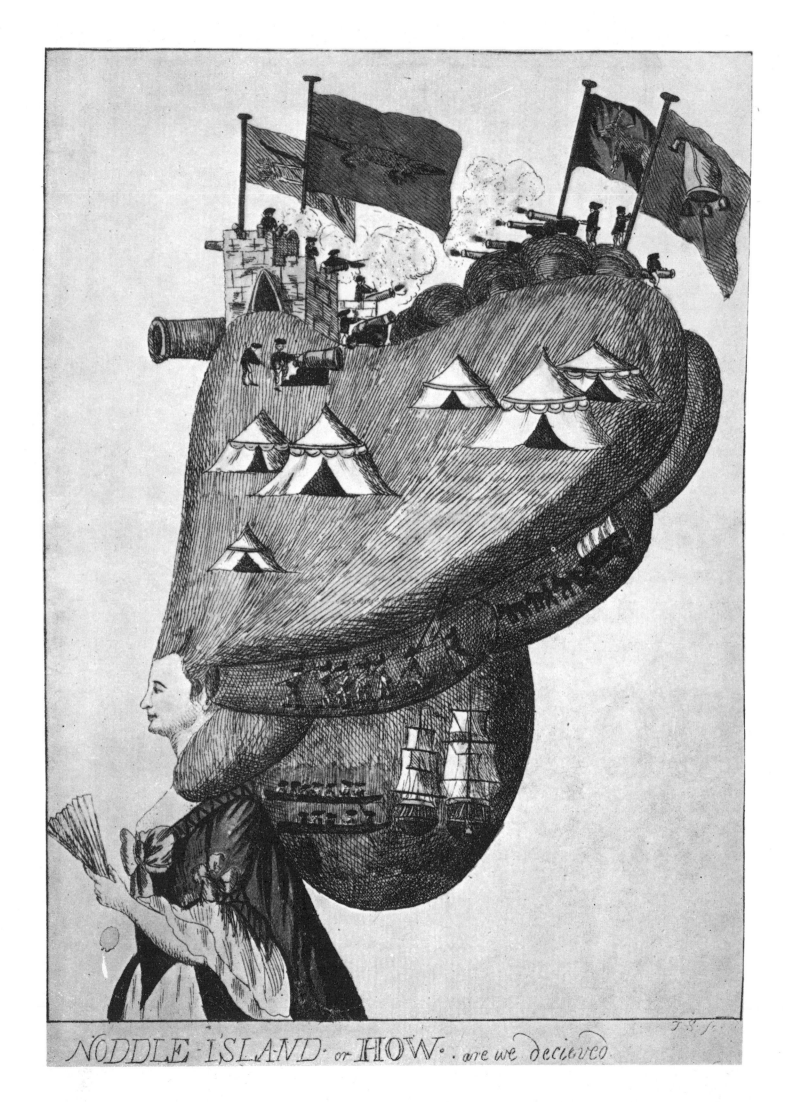

NODDLE ISLAND or HOW. are we decieved

THE BATTLE OF CHARLESTON

Since the summer of 1775, when the royal governors of Virginia, North and South Carolina and Georgia had impetuously declared their confidence in raising huge troops of loyalists, the Middle and Southern colonies had been regarded in Britain as easy prey. But the stately expedition which was going to reduce them —seven regiments, two artillery companies, eleven warships and thirty transports under Admiral Sir Peter Parker—failed to set sail from Cork until the middle of February 1776. It was to rendezvous with a detachment from Boston under General Clinton who, only too eager to leave behind the tensions of that beleaguered city for a more congenial climate, had embarked a month earlier.

Yet even before this new army was battling with the winter seas, events in Virginia were dismally proving the governor's expectations too sanguine by far. Lord Dunmore, after scavenging together a force of loyalists, marines and negro slaves, was convincingly beaten at Great Bridge (south of Norfolk) on New Year's Day. Norfolk itself became an inferno, its patriot houses blown up by Dunmore's artillery, its Tory houses ignited by the rebels. In North Carolina, where numbers of recent Scottish immigrants (including the romantic Flora MacDonald) were expected to rise as readily for King George as they had against his grandfather in 1745, Governor Martin had been equally precipitate. At the end of February 1,700 loyalists set out to meet a nonexistent fleet at Wilmington; instead they met a thousand patriots at Moore's Creek Bridge (missing a few vital planks). According to a local newspaper 'the battle lasted three minutes. . . . This, we think, will effectively put a stop to Toryism in North Carolina.' And so, together with the subsequent surrender of 850 loyalists, it did for the time being.

By the time Parker met up with Clinton early in May, there was nothing they could do to help the North Carolina loyalists, but they did hear that the patriots were fortifying Sullivan's Island, which guarded the entrance to Charleston harbour—and set off to win back South Carolina. The appearance of the British armada outside Charleston did indeed cause great alarm among the rebels, but the arrival within three weeks of General Charles Lee (newly-appointed to command the Americans in the South) with his rough manners and ridicule of the redcoats, boosted their morale— 'equal to the reinforcement of a thousand men' claimed the local commander gratefully.

The combined British land-sea assault on Sullivan's Island, though it took three weeks in the preparation, when it came proved a model of mismanagement. Clinton stationed his troops on adjacent Long Island on the mistaken assumption that at low tide he could walk his men across to Sullivan's Island through eighteen inches of water (it proved to be seven feet). Parker manoeuvred his ships into a position where they could bombard the rebel fort, only to find the enemy's fire more accurate, the wind and tide against him making retreat impossible and three of his vessels ran aground. By nightfall the British fleet had taken such a battering, the admiral wisely saw fit to retire out of reach. Only the traditional shortage of powder prevented the rebels from completely disabling Parker's flagship, the Bristol. For three weeks the fleet hovered around Charleston harbour, its carpenters working overtime, then sprinted off in search of Clinton who had long sailed in the direction of New York.

ABOVE

The Female Combatants. *Anon: This somewhat generalized print appears to be a comment on one of the early patriot successes in the war (the dateline has been removed)—Bunker Hill or, possibly, Charleston. America (as an Indian) has just landed an admirable straight right to her mother's face, who is clearly in a terrible temper with her 'slut' of a daughter.*

BELOW

Charles Lee, Esqr. *Anon: At the defence of Charleston Lee was at the height of his popularity. From contemporary accounts, this caricature seems to have caught him in a typical posture, dapper, dour and brisk and always attended by his dogs. After his capture by the British, however, he was of increasingly little value to the Continental army—possibly because of his mercurial temperament. After the battle of Monmouth Courthouse Washington found it necessary to court martial him—in spite of his great regard for this erratic Englishman. Lee was to spend his short retirement writing bitter letters of recrimination against the Commander-in-Chief and his conduct of the war.*

RIGHT

Miss Carolina Sulivan. *Darly: Another in this engraver's series of satires on the extravagant hair-styles of the period (see page 81). Dated September 1 1776 it takes its theme from the news of the British failure in South Carolina which had just arrived in Britain. The muzzle of the cannon is dedicated to Peter Pop Gun (which could, charitably, be a pun on the name of the commanding admiral, Peter Parker).*

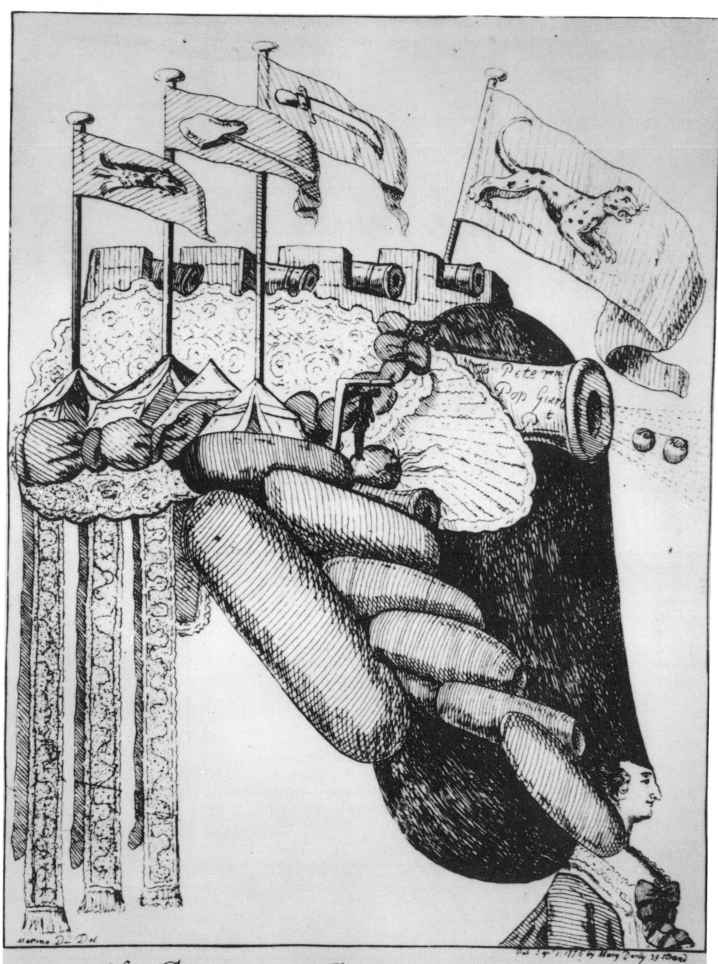

Miss CAROLINA SULIVAN
one of the obstinate daughters of America, 1776

A PAIR OF POLITICIANS waiting for the EXTRAORDINARY GAZETTE.

FROM SUCCESS TO DEFEAT

The fall of New York to the arrival of the French

1776-1779

1776	August 27	*Battle of Long Island*
	September 15	*Capture of New York*
	October 28	*White Plains*
	November 16	*Fort Washington taken, and Fort Lee (20th)*
	December 26	*Hessians defeated at Trenton*
1777	January 3	*Princeton*
	April	***Lafayette in America***
	August 16	*Bennington*
	September 11	*Brandywine*
	September 19	*Bemis Heights*
	September 20	*Paoli massacre*
	September 26	*Howe occupies Philadelphia*
	October 4	*Germantown*
	October 17	*Burgoyne surrenders at Saratoga*
	November 15	*Articles of Confederation adopted by Congress*
	November 20	*British control of Delaware*
	December	*Washington moves to Valley Forge*
1778	February 6	*Franco–American treaties signed: Britain declares war on France*
	February 17	*North's Conciliatory proposals*
	April 5	*Peace Commissioners appointed*
	April 7	*Chatham's last speech: dies (May 11)*
	June 18	*Philadelphia evacuated*
	June 28	*Monmouth*
	July 3–4	*Wyoming massacre*
	July 5	*Fall of Kaskaskia*
	July 8	*D'Estaing's fleet arrives at the Delaware*
	August 29	*Siege of Newport abandoned*
	September 4	*Commercial treaty between Holland and America*
	November 11	*Cherry Valley massacre*
	December 29	*Capture of Savannah*
1779	February 25	*Fall of Vincennes*

In 1776, with many a misgiving and dissident voice, Congress moved towards the final rupture with Britain, independence. By that summer revolutionary governments had replaced British administration everywhere, the publication of Paine's *Common Sense* had cogently and forcibly argued the benefits to be reaped from independence and demolished the sentimentality of unreasoning allegiance to 'a crowned ruffian'. Many patriots believed that their aims would only ever be achieved outside the framework of British imperialism; many concluded they were already beyond the pale; pronounced rebels by the King, about to be set upon by Indians and Hessians they no longer had recourse to their rights as Englishmen—they must affirm their natural rights as men. As the war progressed, every skirmish, every infantry charge, every hand-to-hand engagement with British soldiers made it increasingly difficult to look upon them as brothers. And yet there was hesitation to snap the links with Britain finally and irrevocably. When Richard Henry Lee of Virginia brought forward his resolution that 'these United States are, and of right ought to be, free and independent states, that they are absolved from all allegiance to the British Crown . . .' six delegations dissented from it, and a decision was postponed for three weeks. By July 2, however, twelve colonies were prepared to endorse the resolution and two days later they formally adopted Thomas Jefferson's draft of the Declaration of Independence.

That momentous document, enshrining its appeal to natural rights and theory of political association, and enumerating the injuries inflicted on America by George III, needs no re-statement here. What is relevant to this survey is that not one single echo of it appeared in any contemporary cartoon (so far as is known). The news of it was received in London in a dispatch from Howe which arrived early in August, but it appears to have been accepted with equanimity by the Ministry and in deafening silence by the cartoonists. Perhaps the prevailing feeling was that the outcome of the war would decide who was independent and who wasn't, that this particular declaration was not to be distinguished from any of the other declarations of one sort or another which had emanated from there in the past.

This period of the war is marked by a relentless decline in the fortunes of the British armies in America. It begins with the defeat of Washington's forces on Long Island and their subsequent evacuation of New York, but by the summer of 1779 after two hard and expensive campaigns that city (and Savannah) was still the only major foothold the British could claim on the continent (they still held Newport, but evacuated that too in the fall). In the meantime Britain's fearful mercenaries, the Hessians, had been defeated at Trenton; an entire army under General Burgoyne, attempting an invasion from Canada, had surrendered; and France had entered the war on the American side. True, the vast sums of money extracted from the British taxpayer and the prodigious energy expended by her troops had been rewarded by small compensations: for ten dizzy months the redcoats had occupied Philadelphia and spent a gay, comfortable winter there while Washington's Continentals shivered to death at Valley Forge; in formal pitched battle the disciplined British regular had proved himself superior to the ill-trained, ill-equipped Continental. But this was not a war fought by European rules; every mile marched deeper into hostile territory endangered the already critical communication and supply lines. In spite of the cheery predictions from Ministers in London, the anticipated uprising of loyalists just failed to materialize.

In London, disappointment over the failure to crush the rebels swiftly and decisively was attended by fierce recriminations between ministers and officers. The spate of parliamentary inquiries and court martials during these years was meat and drink to the cartoonists, as was the virtual admission of defeat implied in North's peace proposals of 1778. Several times the Ministry faltered, then rallied and with each rally the war policy remained as entrenched as ever. Slowly, it came to be recognized that, at the root of everything lay the King's intransigence. By 1779 he, too, had made a come-back in their satires.

CANADA

MONTGOMERY 1775

Quebec

Chaudiere River

St. Lawrence River

Montreal

St. John's

BURGOYNE 1777

ARNOL

Lake Champlain

VERMONT

NEW HAMPSHIRE

Crown Point

Concord

ST. LEGER 1777

Ticonderoga

Connecticut River

Merrimac River

NEW

Lake Ontario

Oswego

Fort Stanwix

Saratoga

Bennington

Concord
Lexington
Cambridge

YORK

Oriskany

Mohawk River

MASSACHUS

Niagara

Albany

CONNEC-
TICUT

Hartford

Hudson River

Newhaven

Delaware River

West Point

PENNSYLVANIA

Stony Point

New York
Brooklyn

LONG
ISLAND

Wyoming
Valley

Easton

WASHINGTON 1776

HOWE 1776

Susquehanna River

Princeton
Trenton

Monmouth Court
House

Allegheny River

Valley Forge

Philadelphia

NEW JERSEY

Pittsburg

Lancaster

HOWE 1778

Head of Elk

Wilmington

HOWE 1777

HOWE 1777

Baltimore

[88]

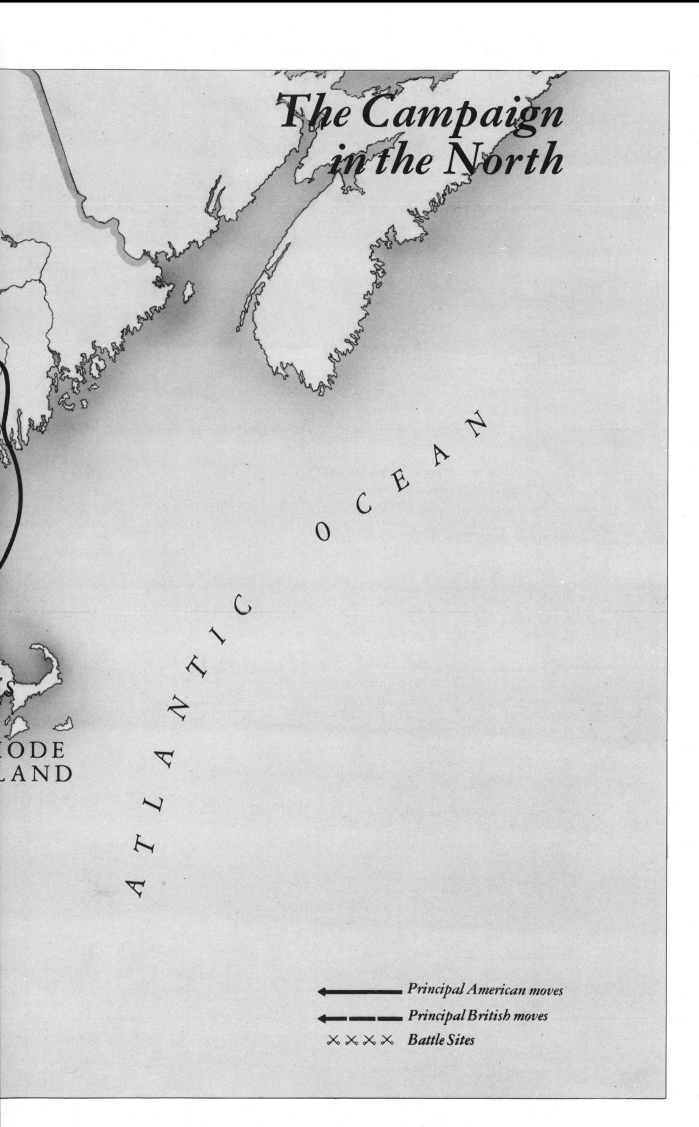

The Campaign
in the North

ATLANTIC OCEAN

RHODE ISLAND

ATLANTIC

⟵⟶ Principal American moves

⟵– – – Principal British moves

×××× Battle Sites

NEW YORK: LORD HOWE AND MR. WASHINGTON

Even as the patriots of New York were celebrating the news of the Declaration of Independence by melting down King George's handsome statue on Broad Way for musket balls, there was converging on them from all directions a veritable juggernaut of an expedition. From Nova Scotia in the north came General Howe's bored but as yet unbeaten Boston army. From the south came Clinton and Parker, shaking off the memory of their futile Charleston adventure. Across the Atlantic from Germany came nine thousand Hessians, and from Britain assorted battalions of Highlanders and others. It was the largest concentration of forces yet to appear in American waters, a sobering sight for the troops manning the Hudson batteries who, to Washington's annoyance, could only sit and gape. 'A weak curiosity at such a time' he very properly warned them in General Orders, 'makes a man look mean and contemptible'.

With good reason had New York been selected in London as the principal objective for the summer's operations. Not only was it an excellent springboard from which to invade New England, join up with Carleton's victorious Canadian army and re-conquer the northern colonies. It also possessed a formidable and die-hard core of loyalism. Far from cowering in their homes to avoid arbitrary arrest or other indignities (which was the lot of many loyalists elsewhere), it was even reported that the Tories of New York had contrived a plot to carry off General Washington himself. The plot was detected, and in it the hand of the Governor (like most of his fellow governors, safe aboard one of His Majesty's cruisers) and the Mayor (who was accordingly thrown into jail). One soldier was executed for his part in this dubious enterprise and Washington took the opportunity to warn his army 'to avoid lewd women who, by the confession of this poor criminal, first led him into practices which ended in an untimely and ignominious death'. But such was the blind loyalty which the Ministers in London daily expected to assert itself and smother the rebellion.

So ran the theory. In command of this putative *coup de grace* were the brothers Howe, Sir William in charge of the army, Lord Richard the navy. Lord Howe in particular was known to be uneasy about his country's policy towards the colonists and his own involvement in the war. As a sop to his conscience he (with his brother) had been designated a Peace Commissioner, an ambassador in the now familiar charade of offering the Americans an olive branch in an iron fist. In practice the terms offered the rebels nothing, and Howe's early efforts to acquaint Washington with them proved as fruitless as they were tactless. On July 14 he sent a letter addressed to 'George Washington Esq., etc., etc.'; it was promptly returned to sender with the message that no one of that designation was known in the patriot camp.

When by the middle of August further (and more courteous) negotiations had foundered, the Howes embarked unhappily on their military alternatives. By the end of the month they were in possession of Long Island, over a thousand prisoners and two patriot generals (Sullivan and the so-called Earl of Stirling) by smartly outflanking Putnam's somewhat straggling left wing. Only by an improvized and brilliant night evacuation across the **East River did Washington save the** bulk of his Long Island garrison. On the advice of his staff he prepared to evacuate New York also and in doing so only managed to escape the disastrous effects of yet another of Howe's flanking movements through that general's inexplicable reluctance to deliver the knock-out when his opponent was on the ropes. By mid-October Washington had relinquished the whole of Manhattan to the British, except for 3,000 men in Fort Washington on the banks of the Hudson. Still in dilatory mood Howe followed the patriot army onto the mainland, and found them turned to face him at White Plains. Delay this time not simply saved the Americans, it had provided them with much-needed food, drink, moral and tactical advantage. The days after an inconclusive battle found Washington entrenched on higher **and stronger ground and Howe** returning to the Hudson where, now that British boats had the run of the river, Fort Washington was temptingly vulnerable.

THE JERSEY CAMPAIGN

Looking back after the war Washington would most surely have counted the months of November and December 1776 as the nadir of his fortunes. New York was abandoned, and with it Forts Lee and Washington and their precious stores and equipment. From White Plains his army, barely 3,000 'much broken and dispirited' men, had been hounded through New Jersey by a surprisingly vigorous force under Cornwallis. To Newark, New Brunswick, on to Princeton and Trenton his exhausted men dragged their shoeless feet through the freezing cold, spurred on only by the relentless reports of the British never more than a day's march behind. At last, the Delaware. As Cornwallis entered Trenton, Washington's last few boats were pushing off for the safety of the Pennsylvania shore.

It was December 8. At the end of the month his army would once again begin to melt away as its period of enlistment expired. Lee, with 2,700 men, was on his way from the Hudson 'for the salvation of America' as he was extravagantly inclined to put it, but with infuriating slowness. Indeed so slow was he on the morning of the 13th that he was caught in dressing-gown and slippers by a British patrol, in an inn some three miles from his main army. While their general retired from the fray to partake of British hospitality in New York, his men ploughed on to the Delaware. Appeals for more men garnering only a handful of Pennsylvania militia, Washington boldly determined to throw his tortured troops back onto the offensive. He knew (as Howe knew) that the long line of British garrisons across New Jersey was painfully exposed at its southern end. Trenton itself was manned by 1,500 Hessians, whose particular brand of plundering was viciously oppressing the inhabitants. Success now might hold his army together for another campaign.

Christmas Day in Trenton was celebrated with traditional German conviviality, the beer and the singing interrupted only briefly by a false alarm to the north, and not at all by the thought that their commander in his arrogance had omitted to construct any form of earthwork.

At eight in the morning he was still asleep after a tiring night at cards; within minutes he had been informed of the surprise American attack, had mounted his horse and fallen mortally wounded. For the hired mercenaries of Hesse this little township was not one they had any great desire to be sacrificed for, nor was the impromptu street-fighting the kind they had been trained for on the parade grounds of Europe. Their cannon was bottled up, their flintlocks sodden in the pouring rain; they were confused and out-manoeuvred. Whole companies surrendered; barely a third escaped to the plains. The patriots suffered but four casualties, one of whom, Lieutenant Monroe, survived to propound his doctrine from the White House fifty years later.

Washington now hankered after New Brunswick, and by New Year's Day had assembled 5,000 troops at Trenton to make the march, but the next day the dogged Cornwallis was sighted hurrying through the mud. Snipers kept the British from entering Trenton before nightfall, but there was no retreat for the Americans this time over the ice-packed Delaware. Nor, to judge from the activity and fires in the American camp, was there any such idea in their heads. The real activity, however, was elsewhere as the muffled cannons and silent battalions were shepherded away on a back road to Bordenstown. Not for the first time in the campaign had Washington extricated his army from between the water and overwhelming odds. On the road to Princeton—almost as if a reward for his ingenuity— Washington encountered three regiments of redcoats hurrying to Trenton. The British had the advantage of breakfast, the Americans of numbers and, as it turned out, of their General's own bravery in rallying his exhausted men in the teeth of the muskets. The battle of Princeton lasted for one savage hour until all final resistance around the College chapel was extinguished (where one unacademic cannon-ball was said to have removed the head from a handsome portrait of George the Second).

With this victory Washington wisely retired into secure winter quarters at Morristown. His army had held together; his own reputation was assured. The Continentals had proved themselves none of Tom Paine's 'summer soldiers and sunshine patriots'. Men, money and clothes began to arrive at the American camp. A letter from Robert Morris to Washington must have been as welcome for the sentiments it contained as the fifty thousand dollars it enclosed. 'The year Seventeen seventy-six is over' wrote Morris, 'and I am heartily glad of it, and hope that you, nor America, will be plagued with such another'.

HEAD QUARTER'S.

A HESSIAN GRENADEIR

FRENCH INTEREST

On the face of it, it was an unlikely union: the aspiring republic and the absolute monarchy. But both America and France had their own convincing reasons for forgetting that within living memory they had been implacable enemies on American soil. Congress quite simply needed allies and experience, men, money and munitions on whatever terms they were offered. Hardly was the ink dry on the Declaration of Independence than Congress had dispatched an assortment of quasi-diplomats off to the courts of Europe from St. Petersburg to Madrid. Now perhaps their efforts would no longer be viewed across the Atlantic as a romantic adventure, but as the life-and-death struggle of a new nation. It was not to be expected of course that dynasties would rise up with one accord and joyfully embrace republicanism (nor did they) but in Paris, if nowhere else, there were sympathetic and well-placed ears.

It was thirteen years now since the war had ended in which Pitt and his armies had stripped the French of their colonies, crippled their economy and annihilated their trade. But the scars were deep and there were ministers at Versailles unwilling to let them heal; first Choiseul, for whom no opportunity of bringing on a conflict had been too remote; and now there was Vergennes who had been indulging in all manner of cloak-and-dagger conspiracies, since the first shot had been fired, to supply secret aid to the patriots. He even infiltrated one of his secret agents into London, a remarkable adventurer by the name of Beaumarchais whose pen (amongst other things he wrote The Marriage of Figaro) was as sharp as his duelling sword. Under cover of a fictitious shipping company, Roderigo Hortalez and Co., French guns and mortars were already finding their way to American ports with the royal fleur de lys stamp unaccountably missing.

Few politicians in Britain were under any illusions about French duplicity. As far back as May 1774 Edward Foley had bet Charles Fox fifty guineas at Brooke's Club 'that England would be at war with France before this day two years, supposing Louis XV dead'. Well, Louis XV was dead but as yet the ineffectual Louis XVI continued to suffer the British Ambassador's repeated protests against French gun-running pacifically. In the meantime, Vergennes had been busy sounding out **France's Bourbon ally, Spain,** seeing they too had suffered miserably at Britain's hands. Yes, they were willing to fight—in principle and at a price. Indeed they were already contributing large sums to the Americans both via Beaumarchais' phoney Spanish company and directly. But it was evident Charles III was going to choose his own time to join the proceedings.

Such was the state of diplomacy when the American commissioners, Lee, Deane and Franklin arrived in Paris. They were a disparate trio: Silas Deane was subsequently proved to have sold information to the British, Arthur Lee contrived to offend his would-be ally, and only Franklin was accepted with enthusiasm both in political and in intellectual circles. America could have had no better ambassador to tap the **growing reservoir of goodwill towards its cause in Paris.**

of a new breed of aristocrat in France. A soldier, exceedingly rich, fashionable and a staunch republican. Like a number of his compatriots he was stirred by news of the Declaration of Independence to finance his own expedition to fight in the war. His enterprise was entirely unofficial ('The French court appears to be very angry' wrote Gibbon in London, but that is to be doubted). In the winter of 1776 he was hob-nobbing with Lord George Germain at soirées in London, by **spring he was sailing for Philadelphia.** *Congress, suspicious of foreign mercenaries who invariably demanded preferment over native Americans, prepared to give the young nobleman a chilly reception. But his credentials and his integrity established, Lafayette became a Major General and ultimately a folk-hero of the Revolution.*

TOP RIGHT

The Family Compact. *Anon: Since the War of the Spanish Succession (when Austria unsuccessfully disputed the legacy of the throne of Spain to Louis XIV) France and Spain had been bound together by their Bourbon family ties. Since 1733 this had taken the concrete form of an alliance against Britain (the First Family Compact). It had been renewed in 1743 on the eve of France declaring war on Britain and lapsed in 1749 after the Peace of Aix-la-Chapelle. The Third Family Compact had been concluded in 1761, again during hostilities with Britain. It was still technically in force and although its primary intention was to safeguard Bourbon possessions, Spain traditionally regarded it as a means of wresting Gibraltar from Britain's clutches. So it was widely recognized in London that if France declared war, Spain would not be far behind. This print, in fact, was published in 1779 after Spain had indeed joined in the fray. Here, Charles III and Louis XV (right) have joined with the devil in a threesome reel over a carpet of (symbolic) American colonies.*

BOTTOM RIGHT

Marquis Lafayette. *Gillray(?): At 19 Lafayette was a typical example*

PASSING THE BRANDYWINE

As the British were sweeping through the Jerseys in the fall of 1776, the Continental Congress in Philadelphia was waxing indignant at a 'false and malicious rumour by the enemies of America' that it was preparing for instant flight. Still indignant, it resolved the very next day to retire to Baltimore, where it remained until Washington's successes at Trenton and Princeton assured the safety of Philadelphia, however temporary. Charles Lee might damn them for 'a whole stable of cattle', but their concern for the centre of government was very real. Washington, revitalizing his army in hibernation at Morristown in early spring, pondered over his intelligence from New York and shared their anxiety. What would Howe do when the campaign season re-opened? Meet up with Carleton and isolate New England? Or head south into the Middle Colonies and Philadelphia?

Howe, for his part, was undecided. At different times, indeed, he opted for both courses of action and informed Lord George Germain in London to that effect. On November 30 he had recommended sending a substantial force up the Hudson and another against Boston. Three weeks later he was devising an entirely new operation: a march against Philadelphia, leaving a token army on the Hudson to act 'defensively' and depending on 'the state of things at the time' as he ambiguously put it. Therein the general's fickleness was germinating the seeds of disaster. For, unknown to him, Burgoyne was busy in London canvassing for command of the Northern army over Carleton's head and his much-admired 'Thoughts for Conducting the War from the Side of Canada' fortuitously coincided with Howe's first proposal. In Lord George, Burgoyne had an eager patron; by mid-March he had obtained the King's approval of Burgoyne's proposals and appointment (the other contender, Clinton, being bought off with a knighthood). On March 27 Burgoyne sailed for Quebec a happy man—happier than if he had known that his plan lay in ruins even before he left London.

For the Secretary for America had also consented to Howe's plan for marching in entirely the opposite direction, and had neglected to inform Burgoyne of that fact. Worse still, he subsequently omitted to acquaint Howe of Burgoyne's expectation of making a junction of the two armies at Albany. It was a masterpiece of mismanagement which left the two British armies in North America operating for the rest of the year at complete cross-purposes. There is a shred of evidence for believing that Germain assumed that Howe could both take Philadelphia *and* get back to Albany in time to meet the northern army. If so, he was ascribing to the general a superhuman speed, while in practice Howe was surpassing even his own previous circumspection. For months the fleet lay idle in New York harbour (he had decided to sail to Philadelphia now). On July 23 the ponderous armada containing 19,000 men set sail, arriving at the Delaware six days later. To Washington's astonishment it sailed straight past and on to Chesapeake Bay, where on August 25 it discharged its cargo of sickened soldiers and dead horses.

The behaviour of the British had been puzzling Washington throughout the summer. He had divined their objective successively as the Hudson, then Philadelphia, then even Charleston—forcing him to march and counter-march his men up and down New Jersey to keep ahead of the game. Earlier in the year he had judiciously declined to be tempted into open battle at Middlebrook; at last he could make a stand and chose to bar the road to the capital on the northern bank of Brandywine Creek. The morning of September 11 found the British marching to the attack and Howe at his most workmanlike; a typically rapid flanking march by Cornwallis caught the Americans by surprise, and only some staunch rearguard stuff from Nathanael Greene's division and the timely intervention of nightfall prevented their withdrawal turning into a rout. In the process Washington lost two men for every redcoat.

Only the river Schuylkill lay between Howe and Philadelphia. On the night of the 20th, a final pocket of resistance under Anthony Wayne at the village of Paoli was extinguished with such steely efficiency by British bayonets as to earn the engagement the title of 'massacre' thereafter. Five days later Howe was in possession of the city of brotherly love, once again empty of its Congress which the week before had decamped with some urgency to the comparative safety of York. But Washington, for one, had not yet given the city up for lost. In the foggy dawn light of October 4 he mounted a surprise assault on the main British position at Germantown outside Philadelphia. Everything went wrong: the fog, some obstinate resistance from a farm outpost in the American's line of advance, the collision of two attacking companies (who fired on each other and fled) all conspired to enable Howe to form his lines and beat off the attackers. Philadelphia was now his for a more or less comfortable winter.

TOP RIGHT

Flight of the Congress. *Anon: Three days after Howe's triumph at Brandywine, Congress voted to re-convene at Lancaster (from where it moved on to York). Its papers had already been sent to Bristol for safekeeping. A Tory account of its departure from Philadelphia recalls it as being 'with the utmost precipitation and in the greatest confusion', an account with which this anonymous artist does not see fit to quarrel. In his Congressional menagerie he identifies John Hancock (President) as an ass, Henry Laurens, Samuel and John Adams and Richard Henry Lee, but is clearly stuck for any more names since he has included Israel Putnam, the old warrior from Massachusetts and, as an armadillo, George Washington (a rare reference to the Commander-in-Chief in prints). In the guise of an owl Benjamin Franklin (top right) is flying off on his diplomatic mission to Paris to induce the French to enter the war. On a branch of the tree (centre top) a squirrel is scattering scraps of Continental paper currency, which being flooded on to the market in ever-increasing quantities was leading to desperate inflation (and by 1780 had become virtually valueless). Earlier in the year Congress had been forced to ask individual states to stop printing their own—with absolutely no response. This print is additionally interesting in that it develops the snake motif which was to gain considerable currency after Yorktown. It*

is also one of the relatively few satires extant which is favourable to the Ministry.

RIGHT
The Conference between the Brothers HOW to get Rich. *Anon: Throughout September and October 1777 no news from the Howes was received at all in London. Germain was constantly complaining 'that the General should be so fond of concealing his operations'. His apparent dilatoriness in prosecuting the war was becoming a byword in England, and he had certainly taken an unconscionable time in reaching Philadelphia by a roundabout route. Some opponents put it down, unfairly, to the Howes' supposed American sympathies. Others would have it that Sir William was for ever being detained by his mistress, Mrs. Joshua Loring, the wife of his commissary of prisoners, and took immense delight in retailing the popular ditty which was currently going the rounds: Awake, arouse, Sir Billy/ There's forage on the plain/ Ah, leave your little filly/ And open the campaign. Yet others believed the Howes were extending the war for their own enrichment. Ac-*

cording to Horace Walpole 'the nation from impatience of news grew much dissatisfied and the Howes were infinitely abused and accused of thinking of nothing but their vast profits'. If this artist had not already made it abundantly clear that such was his theory, he has included rows of cabbages outside the door (left)—'cabbaging' being a current slang expression for 'pilfering'.

TO CONTROL THE DELAWARE

Life in Philadelphia promised to be unusually pleasant for the British officers and young ladies of the town for the duration of winter. What with plays, balls, concerts and assemblies 'I have been but three evenings alone since we moved to town' scribbled one enthusiastic young Tory lady. The Quaker City, with its handsome public buildings and wide boulevards was the perfect place for winter quarters—except for one thing: without control of the Delaware, the lifeline for the supply ships from New York, the army and the inhabitants would slowly starve. Salt was already selling for sixteen shillings a bushel and flour could not be had for any kind of money, golden guineas or continental dollars. It was a job for Lord Howe's fleet, which on receiving the good tidings of Brandywine had begun returning its useless journey from Chesapeake Bay.

The American blockade of the Delaware was an elaborate arrangement: beneath the water, sunken obstacles of every description including an ugly iron-studded trellis-work; on the surface a flotilla of frigates and floating batteries; and on the banks, gun entrenchments at Billingsport and Fort Mercer, and Fort Mifflin on an island in the middle of the river (known locally, and with good reason, as Mud Island). Even before His Lordship's fleet arrived at the Delaware (on the very same morning that Washington was assaulting Germantown), the army had scored its first naval victories—more by luck than judgement. The crew of the frigate Delaware, in attempting to bombard the river-front of the city, had succeeded only in running the boat aground. It was promptly boarded by the Royal Marines who put out the fires and refloated her. Within a few days Billingsport, and the entire complements of several ships, had surrendered, and much of the obstruction cleared. Forts Mifflin and Mercer, however, were made of sterner stuff, manned by Virginian and Rhode Island regulars.

The first attack came on October 22, on the Jersey shore against Fort Mercer. It was the Hessians, intent on renaming it Fort Donop. At their head Von Donop himself, who had begged this opportunity to restore the honour of Hesse so shamefully lost at Trenton. He was not to be the officer to regain it; forty minutes later when the Hessians flung off their cumbrous knapsacks to flee the deadly fire of the patriots, Von Donop was left behind mortally wounded, amid stacks of his slain compatriots, a rich haul for their Landgrave at thirty crowns a head in compensation. Lord Howe's ships fared little better in the engagement: one ship of the line and a sixteen-gun cruiser caught fire and were destroyed by their own exploding magazines.

From then on the offensive progressed with greater caution. For three weeks engineers laboured in the swamp which divided Fort Mifflin from the Pennsylvania shore building causeways and gun platforms. At dawn on November 10 the bombardment commenced which systematically reduced the buildings on Mud Island to rubble. In the ensuing six days between 250 and 400 casualties were reported (depending on the source of the report), but the gallant garrison was reinforced each night by volunteers prepared to risk the hell on earth. So much importance did Washington attach to the siege that he is said to have offered a hundred pounds to every man who would join the garrison and see it through. On the 15th two of Howe's ships succeeded in getting near enough to lob hand-grenades into the defences, and to rake every corner of the island with grapeshot. That night the remnants of the garrison vacated the ruins which had cost so much American blood.

With Mud Island gone, Fort Mercer was worthless and was abandoned before Cornwallis' ten battalions reached it. The American flotilla, too, decided it had had enough. The crews of seventeen ships put ashore at New Jersey, and fired their vessels. Philadelphia was not in for a hungry winter, after all, even if the supper-parties were destined to be held under a cloud: early in November Howe had announced to his army the reason for the jubilant salvoes fired from American guns all along the Delaware on October 18. Burgoyne had surrendered at Saratoga with his entire army.

RIGHT

The takeing of Miss Mud I'land. *Anon: This print is apparently based on Howe's dispatch of October 25 describing the action at Fort Mercer on the 22nd (which reached London on December 2). It was not therefore entirely accurate, even for an anti-ministerial satire. Fort Mercer is that marked at Red Bank (centre right). It does, however, show the chevaux de frize, the iron-tipped obstructions employed by the Americans (bottom and top right). The Isis (bottom centre) was one of the warships destroyed in the action on that day. Below, the mastheads of the Eagle, Howe's flagship are just visible.*

THE TAKEING OF MISS MUD ILAND.

THE NORTHERN CAMPAIGN: THE MARCH ON ALBANY

Blissfully unaware of the new battle-orders for 1777 winging between the War Office and Philadelphia even as he was on the high seas, Burgoyne arrived in Quebec to take up his command of the northern army early in May. From Carleton he obtained more co-operation than, as a usurper, he had a right to expect and by the middle of June had assembled a motley but well-armed force of redcoats and Germans, Tories, Canadians and Indians. Those in Britain who were acquainted with the indiscriminate nature of Indian warfare were deeply shocked by their enlistment as allies. Gentlemen Johnny had no such scruples, imagining that by his flowery philippics he could at once rouse them to fury with the patriots *and* civilize their implacable scalping-knives. 'Have you read Burgoyne's rhodomontade (Walpole summed up the feeling at home) in which he almost promises to cross America in a hop, step and a jump? He has sent over, too, a copy of his talk with the Indians, which they say is still more supernatural.'

Burgoyne's first confrontation on the road south to Albany, at Fort Ticonderoga, certainly did much to vindicate his early optimism. The 3,500 patriots there under St. Clair were ill-prepared for sustained resistance, the able-bodied far outnumbered by the sick and dying, and had even neglected to fortify the dominant Sugar Loaf Hill. Burgoyne succeeded in dragging his cannon to the top, to discover no necessity to even load them; under cover of the night of July 5 the garrison slipped away from the menacing muzzles. But the British were up early in the morning of the 6th, and by three in the afternoon had overtaken one set of fugitives in their boats at Skenesboro. The next morning General Fraser caught up and dealt severely with St. Clair's rear-guard at Hubbardtown. Soon Fort Anne to the South and Fort Edward on the Hudson had been abandoned to the advancing redcoats.

If it was a moment of pure elation for Burgoyne, it was a most trying few weeks for his opposite number, Philip Schuyler. Not only was he fighting the British, he was contending with a pathetic lack of resources and desertions on an agonizing scale, as well as insinuations in Congress that he was in the pay of King George and the insistent importuning of Horatio Gates to take over his command. But Schuyler's tactics, unappreciated in higher circles, were beginning to bite. The further Burgoyne progressed the more isolated he became, the more flimsy his lines of communication appeared. The terrain, however much it might look like Gloucestershire on maps in Whitehall, was well-nigh impassable, mountainous, swampy, densely forested. With Schuyler's men blocking roads, flooding open ground, razing crops on their route, the British were obliged to devote every ounce of energy to shifting the army—and thirty carts full of their general's personal belongings—a few miles a day.

By the early days of August Burgoyne's war-machine had ground on as far as Fort Miller on the Hudson. The time gained by Schuyler had been put to good use by General Lincoln, sent north by Washington to rally the New England militia in defence of their territory—threatened for the first time since that fateful march on Lexington. There also joined Lincoln at Manchester the mercurial figure of John Stark, who had been granted an independent commission by the New Hampshire legislature and resolutely refused to join the Continental army. Burgoyne had not even guessed at the strength of this new opposition when on August 11 he dispatched Colonel Baum's Hessians to confiscate some rebel supplies at the village of Bennington, Vermont. Heavily outnumbered, Baum sat and waited for help or the enemy, whichever came first, to reach him. He sat and in the belief that they were Tories come to the rescue (for he spoke not one word of English) watched the Americans outflank him at their leisure. The Germans lumbered about in their spurs valiantly but to no avail; they were completely surrounded. Within two hours Baum had fallen, his army dispersed to the winds, even as a formidable relief force under Colonel Breymann approached to within the sound of cannon-fire.

But those two hours, which if Breymann had marched even 'two miles an hour any given twelve hours' (complained Burgoyne afterwards) could have saved Baum, now served only to compound the disaster.

The Closet. *Anon: These two small panels make up part of a much larger cartoon published in January 1778, after London had had time to digest the news of Saratoga (the largest frame on this cinemascopic print can be seen on page 107). The first shows the flight of Burgoyne's Scottish troops, and the fall of one of his generals, Simon Fraser (not the one referred to on page 70). It is clear from the captions that the Hessians were also included in the rout. In the second panel Burgoyne himself leads his manacled troops away to captivity. He is dressed in the costume and buskins of a theatrical star (back home he enjoyed a small reputation as a playwright) and carried copies of his plays.*

Le general Burgoyne a Saratoga. *Anon: This French print was produced in 1782 as a companion to Le general Cornwallis a Yorck (see page 156); intended to underline the passive nature of Burgoyne's surrender (though the fact that the French were present only at the siege of Yorktown may have something to do with this myth). The implication is, of course, that it is easier to trap a turkey than a fox. The choice of animal for Burgoyne may or may not have been suggested by the turkey-calls used by Morgan's riflemen as signals to one another.*

le général burgoyne à Saratoga, le 17e 8bre 1777
a été pris prisonnier de guerre avec toute son armée

THE NORTHERN CAMPAIGN: SARATOGA

Nothing but bad news seemed to arrive at Burgoyne's headquarters that August. Even before the Bennington fiasco, Burgoyne had belatedly heard from Howe that he was bound for Philadelphia and, except in the unlikely event of Washington turning northwards, would not be putting in an appearance at Albany. Then came the thunderbolt out of the West: St. Leger's diversionary force which had set off on July 27 to sweep the Mohawk Valley clean of patriots had foundered at Fort Stanwix. The garrison had held out stubbornly and against all expectation—knowing perhaps that safe conduct meant nothing to the 1,000 Iroquois marching with St. Leger. One relief force under Nicholas Herkimer had been turned back, but another under Benedict Arnold was on its way, a small one it was true but sending before it exaggerated accounts of its vast size. Unhappily for St. Leger his Indian allies fell for this ruse of Arnold's and deserted British rum for the safety of their forests. St. Leger was left with no alternative but to remove himself and attempt (in vain) to meet Burgoyne by a safer route.

September came, with the army still forty-five impossible miles from Albany and abandoned by virtually all its Canadian and Indian allies. But Burgoyne's orders to break through to Albany had been quite unequivocal, and in spite of setbacks he was determined to do it. He edged forward and cast the die on the 13th by crossing the Hudson to the west bank; there was to be no retreat now, as he dismantled his bridge of boats behind him. The symbolism was greater, perhaps, than he intended. Arrayed against him, and ensconced on the solid protection of Bemis Heights, were more than 7,000 Continentals, now under the guiding hand of Gates (whose machinations at Congress had finally removed Schuyler just two days after victory at Bennington). On the 19th Burgoyne led his army in three columns against the American positions, bravely but blindly—for he knew neither the numbers nor the disposition of his enemy. 'It was', he claimed afterwards, 'a smart and very honourable action . . . which

must demonstrate our victory beyond the power of even an American newswriter to explain away.' He omitted to add it was also a pyrrhic victory; the British were in possession of the field but it was a worthless field, where only the wounded groaned all night, unaided in the freezing fog.

The army could advance not one inch farther. Burgoyne's only hope now lay with Clinton in New York, who must by now surely have started on his way up the Hudson to relieve him. Two days after the battle Burgoyne learned that he had not, because no reinforcements had arrived from England. With mounting urgency Burgoyne dispatched a string of couriers to Clinton begging immediate help. Several were caught and summarily executed; two got through and persuaded Clinton to move in force despite the emaciated nature of the new troops he had now received from London. Another message reached Clinton en route, asking for orders; but Henry Clinton could already foresee the tragic outcome of this misadventure and refused to be dragged into the inevitable recriminations by offering either orders or advice. More practically he took Forts Mongomery and Clinton on October 6 with economical efficiency and sent on General Vaughan with 2,000 towards Albany on the 13th. Two days later Vaughan's transports came to a halt in the shallows at approximately the same distance to the south of Albany as Burgoyne's beleaguered army was to the north.

He would have been too late, in any event. Rations had been drastically reduced on October 3. A desperate foray against Gates's left flank on the 7th had lost Burgoyne another 600 infantrymen and any slim hope he might have cherished of making it to Albany. The next night, after three weeks of entrenched stalemate with every passing hour on Gates's side, Burgoyne withdrew to Saratoga as slowly and painfully as he had advanced. The enemy methodically tightened the net around Burgoyne, sealing off any conceivable passage to Ticonderoga, till not even a fire could be lit without the certainty of drawing sniper-fire like a magnet. On October 14 Burgoyne informed Gates he was prepared to sign a 'convention', the terms of which (emanating

as they did from his own fertile imagination) were exceedingly generous to the British. They would lay down their arms in return for a free passage to England on their oath never to serve again in North America. Gates hesitated—as well he might have—but not knowing the precise whereabouts of Clinton's columns, he agreed—even to permitting the British to march out of their camp with colours flying. But the cordial toasts and politeness (Gates replied to Burgoyne's toast to Washington with a health to the King) did not disguise the fact that it was a complete surrender, that the Americans were now masters of five thousand eight hundred prisoners, including it was said six MPs. Congress, when it later was apprised of all the facts, viewed the convention somewhat differently and successfully employed every legal quibble to prevent the 'Convention troops' (as they came to be known) from leaving their shores and returning to Britain where they would most assuredly have freed an equal number of fighting men from garrison duties there.

TOP RIGHT

The Yankee's triumph, or B------E beat. *Anon: Horatio Gates receives Burgoyne's sword in surrender while his men cheerfully feed the famished redcoats, who in the final days before capitulation had been reduced to catching rain-water in their hats and mixing their half-ration of flour into an inedible paste. In fact the Americans were rather more generous than this print implies; they provided fresh meat rather than homony and 'dirty pudding'. The spoils of victory included 42 pieces of artillery, 5,000 muskets and 70,000 rounds of ammunition; the military chest, however, was somewhat depleted for Burgoyne had taken the precaution of paying every one of his soldiers what was due to him before the surrender.*

BOTTOM RIGHT

The Political Raree-show. *Anon: This print, published later in the year in July, pins the guilt even more firmly on Burgoyne. Once again it is just one small scene from a much larger dramatic satire (therefore considerably enlarged). Burgoyne snoozes in his tent, while his hapless army surrenders most abjectly to the Americans and his correspondence to General*

THE YANKE'S TRIUMPH, or B——E BEAT

Howe lies undelivered on the ground. It is, of course, a gross calumny on Burgoyne but the Opposition was at this time still concerned with championing Howe against Germain and was only prepared to defend Burgoyne so long as he did not implicate Howe in his defence.

VALLEY FORGE: HAMMERING INTO SHAPE

By one of history's strange ironies the hill on which Washington's army was to spend the most miserable, most famine-ridden winter of the war went by the name of Mount Joy. Under happier circumstances it might well have earned it's title; it's wooded slopes flanked by the curving banks of the Schuylkill River promised an almost impregnable position to healthy soldiers with the wherewithal to fortify them; its situation, around the little village of Valley Forge, was well within cavalry-reach of any British foraging parties venturing out of Philadelphia—had there been any horses strong enough to bear the weight of a man. Here the army arrived on December 18 and set about constructing its fortress out of wood, the only vegetation the surrounding countryside provided in generous measure. By Christmas Day one of the army surgeons, Dr. Albigence Walbo from Connecticut, was complaining 'we are still in tents when we ought to be in huts. The poor sick suffer much in tents in this weather.' For it was a fortunate man that freezing winter who possessed a blanket; doubly fortunate if he could lay claim to a shirt as well. Some lacked even the means of decency.

For food, the troops existed on fire-cake, lumps of dough baked on an open fire. 'A general cry through the camp this evening among the soldiers', wrote Waldo, ' "No meat! No meat!" The distant vales echoed back the melancholy sound "No meat! No meat!" ' That was in December; by the middle of February the situation was quite as hopeless, a part of the army having been a week without any kind of flesh, according to Washington. The toll was terrible enough utterly to distress as hardened a campaigner as General Wayne who confessed that he would 'most cheerfully agree to enter into action once every week in place of visiting each hut in my encampment, where objects strike my eye and ear whose wretched condition beggars all description. The whole army is sick and crawling with vermin.' But for the sick to take refuge in one of the several hospitals was little more than a death-warrant. Out of forty men

sent into hospital from one regiment, three emerged alive. For every man who died of wounds, ten to twenty perished from dysentery or jail fever.

Yet for want of transport there were stockpiles of clothes and shoes rotting within reach. There was food and money to be had farther afield but for the mismanagement of the Quartermaster's department which General Mifflin had permitted to slide into a state of supine negligence; but for the ineptitude of successive Commissaries and the apathy of a Congress more inclined to lend its ear to stories of the Commander-in-Chief's inefficiency than the sufferings of their troops. There is no direct evidence of a concerted conspiracy to oust Washington in the course of that dreadful winter, but it was without doubt a season of smears and exaggerated claims on behalf of Gates, the victor of Saratoga. Some leading politicians actively canvassed for Gates to take over command, men like James Lovell, Benjamin Rush and General Thomas Conway, a Franco-Irish malcontent whose merit as an officer, Washington had said, 'exists more in his own imagination than in reality'. Nor can it be said that Gates emerged from the affair with his own loyalty and honour intact.

Washington himself proved dignified in the face of abuse and equal to his bitterest detractors. Even Conway, whose name tradition has linked inextricably with the so-called Cabal, eventually recanted on what he well believed to be his deathbed: 'Justice and truth prompt me to declare my last sentiments. You are in my eyes the great and good man. May you long enjoy the love, veneration and esteem of these states whose liberties you have asserted by your virtues' (he wrote, having been shot in the face in a duel over that very subject). Slowly, with the restoration of confidence in Washington came restitution of the army's fortunes. In spite of the fact that 'history had never heard of a Quartermaster' Nathanael Greene took over from the inadequate Mifflin and revolutionized the flow of supplies. In the place of Conway as Inspector General, there stepped up a genial German baron, lately arrived in camp after twenty-two years' service with the King of Prussia (so he claimed). Von Steu-

ben's credentials were perhaps not everything he would have had Washington believe, but he knew his army training and armed with a barrage of foreign oaths and an interpreter constantly by his side he jovially instilled into the Continentals the rudimentary principles of the parade-ground, of retreating and advancing in order, and of bearing their arms with discipline. For his efforts it was a more soldierly army which emerged with intense relief from the horrors of Valley Forge the following June.

RIGHT
A view in America in 1778. *Anon: This viciously anti-American production crudely satirizes the sufferings of the Continentals during the winter of 1777–78. A member of Congress (left) snugly warm in his fur-lined overcoat is indifferent to the fate of his tattered army. Two well-wrapped officers appear to be positively glorying in their men's hardships—a totally unjustified slur on the majority of Washington's senior officers. Congress and the various colonial assemblies may have been dilatory in providing food and clothing, but the officers suffered no less than the men that winter at Valley Forge. In the right foreground lies a negro apparently wounded by a cannon-ball; an ill-informed comment on the Americans' treatment of slaves (in fact, the Continental Congress had voted on October 20 1774 for the total discontinuance of the slave trade). The style and sympathies of this print are similar to The Yankee-Doodle Intrenchment (page 79).*

A   VIEW   IN   AMERICA   IN *1778*

GENERALS IN THE FIRING-LINE

Official confirmation of Burgoyne's surrender reached London in letters from Carleton on December 3. The country was stunned; the Opposition beside themselves with vituperation. The stock market plummeted—but no faster, nor to greater depths, than the Ministry's credit. In the months that followed the battle of Saratoga was re-fought with batteries of accusation, recrimination and self-justification. The hapless generals stranded in America made frantic efforts to return to England to defend their sorry reputations; the American Secretary tried all he knew to postpone their embarrassing arrival. Who was responsible for this disaster? Where were the guilty men? Even when news of the fate of Burgoyne's army was still a matter of informed speculation Fox had made up his mind: 'an army of 10,000 men destroyed through ignorance, the obstinate wilful ignorance and incapacity of the Noble Lord called loudly for vengeance . . .' he thundered. Only the intervention of Christmas came to Germain's rescue —not because it brought with it a measure of goodwill, but because it signalled the parliamentary recess. Lord North flatly refused to make any relevant papers available to the Opposition, adjourned the House as fast as he dared and kept it adjourned for the next six weeks.

The generals, meanwhile, were quite frustrated in their attempts to leave America. Burgoyne, as a prisoner of war, needed Congress's permission. Howe's resignation was stalled officially in the name of the King, while Clinton's was turned down pointblank (as it was to be on subsequent occasions). In a weak and uncharacteristic moment Germain himself toyed with the thought of resignation, then pulled himself together, and prepared to resist the onslaught which was brewing for the next session. It came in the middle of March with a full-scale inquiry into the causes of Burgoyne's surrender. With the support of the country gentlemen the government scraped home with one of its smallest majorities of the war, under forty (one of which was, unprecedently, Germain's). A scapegoat remained to be found.

He arrived in England on May 13. After repeated entreaties to Congress, Burgoyne had been permitted to return to his native country. He went with Washington's sympathies in one of the most cordial letters a defeated commander could ever have received ('And wishing you a safe and agreeable passage, with a perfect restoration of your health, I have the honour, etc. . . .'). He discovered, also, that he had the best wishes of the Opposition provided he did not attempt to implicate Howe in the disaster. But that was the sum total of his good fortune. He was refused an audience with the King. Germain would not agree to a court martial nor a parliamentary inquiry; instead he was heard in camera by a special board. The board did not get past its first question to Burgoyne for, on hearing that the general was still on parole, it refused to continue in case it prejudiced the fate of the troops held prisoner in America. But Burgoyne did eventually get a public hearing—as an MP. The Opposition moved for a committee to inquire into his conduct and the ensuing debate (although the motion was predictably defeated) enabled Burgoyne at last to air the grievances he had bottled up against the American Secretary. The scene in the House was reminiscent of Billingsgate, so Walpole reported, with 'Burgoyne bullying . . . and Lord G. scolding like two oysterwomen'.

There remained yet another hurdle for Lord George: the return of Howe on July 2. It would be difficult to off-load the blame on to him, for he was a friend of the King. Lord North wanted his brother in the Cabinet, and the Opposition was determined to support him willy-nilly. A hearing was not organized until April the following year but, to the dismay of the Ministry, witnesses were permitted. On behalf of Howe many distinguished soldiers gave testimony including Carleton and Cornwallis, while Germain could only call upon (according to one far from unbiased witness) 'the evidence of a set of thieves, contractors and commissaries'. True or not, the hearing looked like turning out as a triumphant vindication of Howe. It looked, at one point, almost certain to disintegrate the Ministry. But once again Germain was saved not by his own virtues but by the turn of events—in this case the declaration of war by Spain which absorbed public attention to the exclusion of the inquiry. Germain lived to fight yet another calamitous campaign. It was only many years later that the story of Germain's unsigned, unposted dispatch to Howe (ordering him to co-operate with Burgoyne) found in a Whitehall pigeon-hole was revealed. By which time no one cared much whether it was true or not (and many people doubted it) and it was too late anyway.

QUALIFYING for a CAMPAIN.

A PEACE INTERLUDE

'Be certain also,' Beaumarchais had written to Vergennes on the first day of 1778, 'that the English Ministers restrain the universal resentment only by assuring all their friends that they are working sincerely for peace with America.' And there was indeed a germ of truth in the jibe. Hard-liners like the American Secretary might have committed themselves to a relentless war, with no quarter asked or given. But Lord North had never ceased to delude himself that the acceptable peace formula was just around the corner. Officially, there had been a peace commission in America since the summer of 1776 in the persons of the Howe brothers; but their status was utterly discredited, their repeated proclamations of pardon grown tedius, even comical by repetition. Now, with taxes rising and the stocks plummeting after news of Burgoyne's disaster, there were pressing economic as well as political reasons for more whole-hearted negotiation.

On February 17 Lord North unveiled his peace terms to a glum and silent House. He was prepared, he said, to erase from the statute books every one of the Acts which had alienated the colonies. There was to be no more meddling in the Constitution of any of the colonies, no more taxes for the imperial revenue, no shipping of political prisoners to England; American opinion on the appointment of governors and magistrates was to be respected. He would even consider granting them representation in Parliament, he added kindly. With these concessions he hoped to pre-empt the imminent Franco-American alliance, admitting in almost the same breath that 'it was possible, nay too probable' he was too late. He was, of course, two years too late. Nothing short of Independence, as Fox was insisting, now would end the war. The unpalatable truth of this was brought home when on March 13 the French Ambassador officially announced his country's recognition of the United States. Yet with ever less conviction North pressed on with his commission.

Much thought was given to choosing members of the commission who would be acceptable to both the King and the Opposition. William Eden, one of the Ministry's handymen, found favour. George Johnstone, who had formerly governed East Florida and once done his damnedest to kill Lord George Germain in a duel in Hyde Park, seemed an appropriate choice. As head of the Commission Frederick Earl of Carlisle, a reformed rake, seemed very young at thirty for such responsible diplomacy. But, as Walpole philosophically concluded, he was a very fit Commissioner for making a treaty that would never be made. These gentlemen were to treat 'with any body of men, by whatever name known or distinguished, who may be supposed to represent the different provinces' and further, bearing in mind Lord Howe's earlier *faux pas*, they were 'to address them by any style or title which may describe them'.

They also discovered on embarking on April 22 that they were directed to sail to New York. Mystified, they prevailed on the captain to take them to Philadelphia as they had intended. Not until they entered Delaware Bay early in June, and came upon the British warships loaded for New York, did the truth dawn on them: Philadelphia was being evacuated. Whatever slim chance their negotiations had stood of bearing fruit had vanished overnight. In fact it had evaporated on March 21 (one whole month before they had left Portsmouth) when secret orders had been shipped to Clinton, outlining an entirely new and defensive strategy for the British forces in North America. With France's entry into the war, the offensive against Washington must be laid aside for the moment in favour of conserving manpower and strengthening British possessions in the West Indies—whither the French would undoubtedly be focusing their greedy eyes before long.

Torn between disappointment that their mission had become a farce and irritation at Germain for double-crossing them ('Never one syllable in Allusion to it,' complained Eden), the Commissioners tried to make the best of a bad job. They applied to Washington for a pass for their secretary, a Doctor Ferguson (who gloried in the title of Professor of Pneumatics at Edinburgh University) to no effect. Eventually, under a flag of truce, they succeeded in forwarding their proposals to Congress. But before they could get a reply, Clinton had marched his army out of Philadelphia and the Commission deemed it no part of their duty to remain isolated and unprotected on enemy territory.

TOP RIGHT

A Picturesque View of the State of the Nation for February 1778. Anon: This famous plate was the cartoonist's first reaction to the Conciliatory Propositions. It was widely copied in Britain, on pottery as well as by other cartoonists, in France, America and Holland. Such universal favour no doubt sprang from the fact that it demonstrated that North's humiliating peace proposals were the result of torpid administration and inadequate leadership. Because it emanated from Britain, it seemed to lend weight to the claim that Britain was beaten. The English cow (as a symbol of the country's commerce) is being milked by Holland, while France and Spain gratefully carry off their share of the milk. America saws off her sharp horns—to the fury of an honest Englishman who beats his breasts in anger. The British lion slumbers oblivious to the dog urinating on it. Across the water, Lord Howe's flagship is laid up and the commanders slumber away their days. (Indeed life in Philadelphia had not been at all unpleasant. To honour General Howe's departure in May a lavish 'mischianza' was held—a feast-pageant-ball with no expense spared. One shop alone counted £12,000 spent on silks and fine clothes.)

BOTTOM RIGHT

The Commissioners interview with Congress. *Darly: Published a full two months before the Peace Commission even arrived in America, this print is pure fantasy—for the much-desired interview never took place. It was inspired, in fact, by a remark made by the Duke of Richmond during the debate on the Conciliatory Bill on March 9: he claimed, it seems, that Congress had been much offended by one of the governors who had taken exception to them wearing woollen caps in Council (though in this he may have been confusing the Massachusetts Provincial Congress which had instituted this degenerate habit in the cold winter of 1774). Accompanied by the kilted and ubiquitous Lord*

A Picturesque View of the State of the Nation for February 1778.

The Commissioners interview with CONGRESS.

Bute (who, needless to say, had not the remotest connection with the commission) the Commissioners approach with what may be charitably described as appeasing gestures; Lord Carlisle with snuffbox, followed by the bureaucratic William Eden and the thick-set Governor Johnstone.

A PEACE INTERLUDE
(continued)

THIS PAGE
The English and American Discovery. *Anon: This good-natured production appeared in November 1778, when all peace initiatives had foundered irrevocably. An English gentleman (John Bull?) and his brother Jonathan nostalgically share a bottle and a plug of tobacco, having reconciled their differences and admitted they were 'both in the wrong'. On the wall a picture of clasped hands underlines the comfortable scene. The sentiments in this print were those very close to the heart of Lord Chatham, who was forever referring to the colonists as 'our countrymen' and had declaimed before the war began that he trusted 'it will be found impossible for freemen in England to wish to see three millions of English-men slaves in America'. But Lord Chatham was dead, killed in May by the disease that had been consuming him for many years. On April 7 he had dragged himself to the House for the last time to denounce the American war, and had collapsed in the chamber. Even then there were those who saw no other hope for peace than to hand over the government to Chatham, but the King had adamantly refused to address himself to what he called 'Lord Chatham and his crew'. Now it was too late anyway.*

design to which a speculative caption has been added by a French publisher. It bears a great resemblance to the numerous satires on the militia camps which mushroomed in Britain in 1778. These camps (such as the one at Coxheath) became popular for a day's outing by fashionable society (the lady and gentleman being given a guided tour in this print would seem to be prime specimens of that breed).*

ABOVE RIGHT
A Tete a Tete between the Premier and Jn. Hancock esqr. *Anon: This stylized and moralistic effort purports to show that the conciliatory proposals had foundered because there was nothing whatever in common left between the British and Americans. It is absurd—the implication is—for the dapper be-Gartered Lord North to communicate with the earthy, home-spun Hancock and his mountain tiger. The accompanying verse further implies that it is North's policy which has reduced the colonists to this primitive level of living, but they would persist in it rather than return now to the fold.*

BOTTOM RIGHT
La visite du Camp Americain par les Comissaires Anglais. *Anon: Whatever else this print portrays, it is meaningless as the English Commissioners visiting the American Camp. Most likely it is a pirated English*

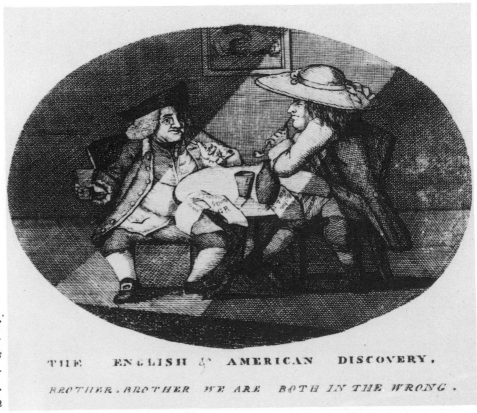

THE ENGLISH & AMERICAN DISCOVERY.

BROTHER. BROTHER WE ARE BOTH IN THE WRONG.

HANCOCK, and North, Supposd to meet.
And thus, *the first,* his thoughts repeat.
Let some, like Spaniels, own my plan.
In me, behold a different MAN.

A TETE, á TETE
between
The PREMIER & Jn Hancock, esqr.

J. Hancock, Gov. of
Massachusetts
Oct. 1780.

Who eer hed call thy House his Home.
Wou'd with the mountain Tyger, roam.
Live on the Roots, pluck'd from the Earth.
From whence Himself, like Thee had Birth.

La visite du Camp Américain par les Comissaires Anglais.

The Anglican Commissioners visiting the American Camp.

FRENCH INTERVENTION

In Paris the news of Saratoga was greeted with undiluted joy. When Howe's capture of Philadelphia had become known, Vergennes had hesitated to pursue his chosen course, unconsoled by Franklin's conviction that it was in reality Philadelphia that had taken the British. But now within two weeks confidence in the patriot armies was dramatically restored; no longer would Louis pander to his scruples about stabbing a fellow-monarch in the back (the less so with wily Frederick of Prussia so strenuously plotting to embroil him in America and pre-empt any interference in his machinations against Bavaria). The arrival in December of a British agent, Paul Wentworth, to wean away the Commissioners from their vacillating friends with succulent offers of a peace treaty, brought matters to a critical pitch. Within twenty-four hours Vergennes had accommodated the Commissioners handsomely.

More than that, he was offering them the total fulfilment of their ambitions: formal recognition of the United States of America, renunciation forever of any claim to Canada and lands to the west of the Mississippi, an alliance both offensive and defensive. In return Congress had only to guarantee not to make a separate peace with Britain. On February 6 the treaties were signed; on March 12 Franklin—by now the idol of Paris, his features adorning the walls of countless French homes and the lids of the most aristocratic snuff-boxes in the capital—was ceremonially received by the King. His only recorded reaction to this momentous moment in American history was that he would have liked to give Versailles a jolly good scrubbing.

Although it was to be four months before the British and French fleets were to engage in earnest, Louis' navy was already in fine shape. His shipwrights and carpenters had built no less than ten new ships of the line in the previous year. A formidable squadron lay at Toulon under D'Estaing, bound where? At Brest some twenty-five frigates and thirty men-of-war under D'Orvilliers threatened to dominate the Channel, even to mount an invasion. The prospect plunged Lord Sandwich

and the Admiralty into an agony of indecision: divide or concentrate? He could muster only thirty-three ships of the line in home waters and in battle-trim. To add to his discomfiture his commander of the Channel Fleet was one of the most entrenched critics of the American war and an Opposition MP, Admiral Keppel, whose preoccupation of the moment appeared to be prophesying disaster rather than searching out the enemy.

By the end of April reports arrived that D'Estaing was under sail and very likely on his way to America. On June 5, to Keppel's disgust, a detachment under Admiral Byron was sent in pursuit. Keppel himself was by this time patrolling the Channel with twenty ships and had very soon picked up a couple of stray French frigates—a convenient action which the French used as an excuse for a formal declaration of war on July 10. Seventeen days later Keppel and D'Orvilliers finally met, on equal terms, seventy miles west of Ushant. It was an inconclusive action, and on the following day the British woke to see the last three French ships disappearing over the horizon. Claiming he had won a splendid victory Keppel failed to pursue them. The next month when the French newspapers arrived in London he was shaken to read that D'Orvilliers too claimed a victory.

TOP RIGHT

Monsieur sneaking Gallantly into Brest's skulking-hole. Anon: The British version of the Battle of Ushant. According to Keppel the French 'put their lights out about half-past eleven o'clock, and the morning of the 28th showed they were gone, the circumstance of which and some rockets that were seen in the night, makes it probable that they began to run before midnight'. Unfortunately for him, it took three weeks to get the fleet back on patrol again, while the French were back in the Channel within two weeks—which lent a certain lustre to their claim to have won a victory.

BOTTOM RIGHT

An Extraordinary Gazette, or the Disappointed Politicians. Anon: News of any important event, victory or defeat, was promptly published in an extraordinary edition of the London Gazette, where a general's dispatch

would be printed in full—provided it satisfied the Government censors. The dispatch in question here is Clinton's on the engagement at Monmouth Courthouse, claiming it as a victory for Britain (the patriots also claimed a victory—see page 114). This print satirizes the reaction to the news amongst the Opposition. One gentleman, who has obviously been dwelling on past glories and mulling over Marlborough's dispatch from Blenheim (the date of which should read 1704 not 1710), has to grip the table to recover himself. Decorating the wall behind are two maps, one delineating the glorious extent of the American Empire under Pitt's administration, the other devoured by serpents emphasizing its pitiful state in 1778. A playbill advertises a performance of 'All in the Wrong' with Mr. King—both play and player quite genuine it happens, but too good a double entendre not to include in the satire. The drawing of 'A Mountain in Labour' is a pertinent comment on the enormous resources mobilized by Britain in America to produce such meagre results.

Monsieur sneaking Gallantly into Brest's sculking Hole after receiving a preliminary Salutation of British Jack Tar the 27 of July 1778

Publ. as the Act directs by W. Richardson No. 68 High Holborn.

AN *EXTRAORDINARY*. Gazette. or the *DISAPOINTED* POLITICIANS.

RETREAT TO NEW YORK

Congress's reply to the peace commissioners did not reach them until they were many miles from Philadelphia. It contained no surprises, merely informed them of its decision of April 22 not to treat until such time as Britain either recognized America's independence or removed her army and navy completely. Perceiving the futility of their position, they begged leave to return 'since to persist any longer in our pacifick advances ... would be to expose his Majesty and the State of Great Britain to insults'. Nevertheless they lingered on in New York for some months, published an appeal to the Americans in general and individual states in particular, the only spirited response they got being from Lafayette, who took offence at their references to French conduct and challenged Carlisle to a duel. The earl prudently declined. Governor Johnstone meanwhile was meeting with such little success at his clandestine attempts to bribe senior American leaders that his fellow-commissioners were obliged to disown him.

By the first week in July Clinton's army was safely in New York. But it had been a scorching and dangerous odyssey. He had chosen to march rather than sail, since his transports were barely sufficient to accommodate his sick, his baggage and all the distressed loyalists of Philadelphia who preferred exile to the vengeance of their patriotic countrymen. It would be expedient, moreover, to keep between his objective and Washington's forces. The Commander-in-Chief observing Clinton's straggling caravan cover only 40 miles in a week resolved to make the redcoats turn and fight at the first opportunity. A number of his officers argued against the plan, none so vociferously as Charles Lee (who appeared to have developed an unhealthy respect for the British infantry during his enforced sojourn among them). At first he even declined to lead an advance party; but by morning had, for reasons known only to himself, changed his mind.

Lee's division sighted the British on June 28—the hottest day within living memory—at the hamlet around Monmouth Courthouse. Finding himself opposed not by a small rearguard but by the flower of Cornwallis' regiments, Lee manoeuvred to take up defensive positions. Some witnesses insisted he retreated. To Washington advancing close behind it looked like a rout. There was a brief, sharp exchange between the two generals—one officer claimed that for the one and only time in his hearing Washington swore: 'Sir, on that ever-memorable day, he swore like an angel from Heaven'. In the ensuing battle the heat took its toll as savagely as the muskets; an official account of the battle states that more than sixty British soldiers 'fell dead as they advanced, without a wound'. Yet others ran amok from the sun—not entirely surprising in their thick woollen uniforms. But perhaps the major casualty of the battle was Lee himself who claimed he had been slighted on the field of battle by Washington ('instigated by some of those dirty earwigs who will forever insinuate themselves near persons in high office') and demanded a court of inquiry. He was promptly granted it, found guilty of disobedience, misbehaviour and disrespect, and suspended from the service for a year. Disgruntled and embittered he took himself off for good to continue his own petty vendetta against his commander for the remaining five years of his life.

TOP RIGHT

The Olive Rejected, or the Yankees Revenge. *Anon: A French view of Congress's rejection of the terms of the Conciliatory Bill, based clearly on the resolution of April 17 before those terms had been formally presented to it. There appears to have been some confusion in the artist's mind as to the author of the Bill; Le Lord Burthe could be a mix-up between Burke and Lord North (or is it Lord Bute popping up once more?). Whoever it is, is attempting to regain the safety of Britain on a donkey because—according to the caption—'his fleet is dispersed or defeated'. The French (rightly) interpreted the peace overtures as an effort to split Congress and overthrow the French treaty.*

BOTTOM RIGHT

Dedié aux Generaux de l'Armée de la Grande Bretagne par un zelateur de la Liberté. *Corbut: A somewhat premature and chauvinistic print, which could surely have done little good to the cause of Franco-American relations. The British army is shown in panic-stricken retreat from Philadelphia pursued by the avenging angel of France! It was far too early for the French to claim any glory yet from their new alliance: D'Estaing's squadrons arrived at Philadelphia to find it already evacuated and there were no French troops at all on land except for the freelancers like Lafayette who had enrolled in the Continental army. Nevertheless the inscription asks us to note the frivolous Americans rejoicing in the 'Golden Age' round a liberty pole adorned with a liberty bonnet; and to admire the fleur de lys, the flaming sword and the war-like Médusa of the French angel.*

NEWPORT: THE ALLIES IN ACTION

On April 15 the Comte D'Estaing's squadron, twelve ships of the line and five frigates, sailed proudly out of Toulon to make an end of the affair in America. If he had moved, perhaps, with more speed and less dignity he might have rendered his new allies a notable service by catching Lord Howe before he had completed his evacuation of Philadelphia. But arriving at Delaware Bay he learnt he was too late and turned about to pursue his quarry to New York. There Howe and Clinton were busy preparing a spirited and efficient reception for him. Nevertheless the combined weight of the French fleet and Washington's army (now over 16,000 strong) at White Plains would surely crush even the redoubtable defences of the British headquarters. The admiral's calculations overlooked only one fact: that his mighty warships drew too much water to cross the sand-bar which lay across the entrance to the harbour. In paroxysms of frustration he offered gigantic rewards to any pilot who could get them through, all in vain. There was no alternative but to settle for a lesser prize for the time being—Newport, Rhode Island.

The garrison at Newport, under the veteran of Bunker Hill Sir Robert Pigot, waited for the inevitable as the French ships of the line sailed almost insolently past the British batteries and 10,000 infantry and militia under John Sullivan occupied the north end of their island. The *coup de grace* was jointly arranged for August 10. On the 9th Howe's fleet appeared on the horizon battling in the teeth of opposing winds. He had been joined by the front-runners of Byron's fleet which had sailed from Britain in early June in pursuit of D'Estaing but had been scattered up and down the Atlantic by a heavy gale (the ill-fortune of 'Foul-weather Jack' Byron in his treatment by the elements was to become a legend in the Royal Navy). Howe's arrival persuaded D'Estaing to re-embark the troops he had put ashore in support of Sullivan and give battle on the open seas. Once again he was to be frustrated, as a hurricane descended to wreak havoc on both the fleets.

Lord Howe returned to New York to repair his battered boats as swiftly as he could.

To the delight of the waiting Americans, whose camp also had been flattened in the storm, D'Estaing returned to Rhode Island. He had only come though, he said, to tell them he was off to Boston for a rest and a refit. And to Boston he sailed, deaf to the entreaties of his allies. 'The devil has got into the fleet,' moaned Greene, and despair had enveloped the militia—half of whom were gone home within the week to attend to the harvest. Now outnumbered and threatened by the imminent return of Howe, Sullivan organized a hasty and harried withdrawal. It had been an inauspicious overture to Franco-American operations. Sullivan fumed and hoped 'the event will prove America is able to produce with her own arms that which her allies refused to assist her in obtaining'. A Frenchman found the sight of American militia 'a laughable spectacle . . . I guessed that these warriors were more anxious to eat up our supplies than to make a close acquaintance with the enemy'. Which were the very sentiments many patriots were entertaining about the French sailors at that moment cheerfully baking their own bread in front of a flour-starved crowd in Boston. Out of the riot which ensued (in which a French lieutenant was killed) an unbridgeable rift might have developed but for the speed with which the Massachusetts Assembly tactfully appropriated money enough for a statue in the anonymous lieutenant's honour.

TOP RIGHT

The Curious Zebra, alive from America. *Anon: Marks a rare appearance in satires of Washington (right). He grips the tail of the zebra (America) like a rudder to steer the animal away from both the French King who boasts that it 'will look very pretty in my menagerie' and from Lord North (left) who is determined to hold on to the reins 'until the beast is subdued'. Behind the zebra Grenville is attempting to saddle it with the Stamp Act (a somewhat antediluvian reference in view of the fact that the Government's policy in 1778 was notable for its proposals to repeal all colonial taxes). Since the peace commissioners (left) had returned empty-handed, perhaps the author assumes that repressive policies will now re-assert themselves. The reference to Washington as 'Fabious the Second' (after Favius Cunctator, the Roman general renowned for his defensive strategy) would, one feels, have been more appropriate for the following year's campaign than for this.*

BOTTOM RIGHT

Untitled: *This emblematic print was published in the* London Magazine *for August 1778, when the race between the French and British fleets across the Atlantic was still under way. Neptune is here scoffing at the new alliance between the patriot and the Gallic cock and consoling Britannia. On the open seas he was being less generous—scattering Admiral Byron's fleet all over the ocean (see above).*

THE ADMIRALTY KEEL-HAULED

Apart from Lord North himself, the longest serving member of the Cabinet was Lord Sandwich, First Lord of the Admiralty. No other minister (with the possible exception of Lord George Germain) epitomized the folly or the genius—depending on your political standpoint—of the government's policy. He had come to office in January 1771 (his third tour of duty at the Admiralty) and had stuck as close as a limpet to his premier through every stormy political passage since then. His personal misfortune was to be one of the most unpopular men in the country. He might have been forgiven—even celebrated—by the good old English tar for keeping a notorious mistress, Martha Ray, even after seeing the wrong side of sixty. But for attacking Wilkes for writing a dirty poem there was no forgiveness. Still less for committing himself with such enthusiasm to the anti-American cause. History perhaps has done him a favour in associating his name primarily with a form of food rather than the Royal Navy.

In the course of the war the Admiralty had sustained many a broadside in Parliament for the vagaries of its naval estimates. But in 1779 it received a battering for which it was not truly at fault. The quarrel arose out of the disputed engagement at Ushant on July 25 1778 (see page 112) in which Admiral Keppel had neglected to pursue and destroy a French fleet he claimed to have beaten. The disappointment of the indecisive battle (for since the days of Hawke and Boscawen anything short of total victory against the French *was* a disappointment) might have worn off in time had there not appeared an anonymous article in the *Morning Advertiser* accusing Keppel's Vice-Admiral, Sir Hugh Palliser, of being responsible for the indeterminate outcome. The whole episode emitted the unsavoury tang of party politics, for Keppel was an Opposition MP, Palliser a member of the Board of Admiralty and a staunch government supporter. But Palliser's personal honour was affronted and he found himself with no alternative but to demand courts martial for himself and his commanding officer.

Palliser's case was that he had been ordered 'to chase to windward' by Keppel's Chief of Staff; in doing so his division had become dispersed and had been unable to support the rest of the fleet during the battle. His own boat had run the gauntlet of savage French fire and been so disabled that when Keppel signalled for the line to be reformed he had not been able to take up his station. It carried little weight, however, at Keppel's court martial—for if Palliser thought he had the strong arguments, Keppel knew he had stronger friends, not least of whom were Rockingham and Richmond. Keppel was acquitted with honour and his acquittal was the signal for a series of outrages by the mob against ministry supporters. Palliser's house, as well as Lord North's and parts of the Admiralty suffered damage quite as bad as anything the French fleet had undergone on the 25th.

Palliser himself, though obliged to resign before his own trial came up, was also honourably acquitted. Keppel refused to serve any longer —to the relief of Lord Sandwich— and Fox took the opportunity to attack the ministry once more for setting up a sinecure for Palliser after the event. The long-term results of the affair were not dissimilar to those which followed upon Germain's public inquisition after Saratoga, a widening of the breach between the administrators in Whitehall and the commanders on the sea.

TOP RIGHT
Dedié aux Milords de l'Amirauté Anglaise par un Membre du Congrès Americain. *Corbut: This satire has to be taken as a threat of things to come rather than a parody on things as they were at the date of publication (1778). A British admiral in the guise of a bird of prey (1) has been tied to a tree. An American (2) snips his claws, a Spaniard (3) grasps a wing while it is clipped by one Frenchman (4) and another (5) takes over the tobacco trade—forcing an Englishman (6) to smash his pipes in frustration. The 'fat' Dutchmen meanwhile (7 & 8) join in the sport and carry on their illicit trade. From the moment the French signed the American treaty it was clear that the British fleets would be inadequate to protect shipping, guard the Channel and prosecute the war—though this was only to come home to the public in the next two years. The Admiralty was to be ceaselessly criticized for its lack of ships, men and foresight.*

BOTTOM RIGHT
They reigned for a while . . . *Anon: This satire, published soon after the result of Keppel's court martial, emphasizes that the Opposition's campaign was not just against Palliser but the Admiralty as a whole. Keppel's supporters row in triumph past a double gibbet from which hang Palliser (Sr. H. Knt.) and Lord Sandwich (Twitcher). Palliser wears a scarf round his neck inscribed 'Formidable', the name of his flagship, and '5 Lies' presumably referring to the five charges brought against Keppel; his Log Book hangs like a weight from his feet, a reminder that Palliser's log book was found to have been altered on some crucial pages. A similar weight is attached to Sandwich's ankles (£400,000, which if it was intended as an indictment of the number of ships lost so far in the war was a somewhat conservative estimate). The First Lord is labelled 'Essay on Woman'—harking back to the origins of his unpopularity in 1763, when during the debate on Wilkes's famous issue no. 45 of* The North Briton *Sandwich produced a copy of an indecent poem ascribed (dubiously) to Wilkes and thereby helped to discredit him. This had ever since been held against Sandwich, who had kept quite as undesirable company as Wilkes, and earned him the nickname of Jemmy Twitcher (the character who betrayed Macheath in Gay's* The Beggar's Opera). *Upper left on the print, the devil points out the fate of his supporters to an unusually ethereal Lord North.*

They reign'd a while but 'twas not long | As they had turn'd from Side to side
Before from world to world they swung | And as the Villains liv'd they dy'd.

Hudibras

THE WAR ON THE FRONTIER

From the earliest days of the war the Americans had been fighting on another front an enemy far more unpredictable and savage than any redcoat. From the Allegheny River in the north to the Alabama in the south the Indian tribes who roamed the backwoods presented an ever-present menace to the border settlements which had sprung up deeper and deeper into the west since 1763. In the south the Cherokee had invaded parts of Georgia and South Carolina in the summer of 1776 and occupied the attentions of no less than four patriot armies. From 1777 the Shawnee plundered wholesale in the region of the Ohio Valley, while the Iroquois terrorized the pioneer homesteads of New York and Pennsylvania. Indiscriminate and uncontrollable, these were Britain's allies. Not, it must be said, from any deep-rooted opinions on the constitutional issue between Parliament and Congress, but seduced for the most part by liberal issue of British rum and other handouts. Nor had it been a difficult task for the British agents to persuade them that in the land-hungry settlers lay their ruin, and in the great Benefactor from across the ocean their salvation. By no means all the tribes, however, rose up for King George. Stockbridge Indians had joined the rebel siege of Boston (which, for what it was worth, had provided the Ministry with its justification for recruiting red men) and, most notably, the Oneida tribe subsequently opted for the patriots through the blandishments of a New England missionary.

By the middle of 1778 the frontier savagery had reached unprecedented heights. In June Colonel John Butler at the head of a mixed expedition of Tories and Iroquois swept into the beautiful Wyoming Valley in northern Pennsylvania, all but exterminated some 300 defiant frontiersmen and devastated their land. In August an Iroquois chief by the name of Joseph Brant (he had had an English education and James Boswell had been tickled to exhibit him to fashionable society in the old days) razed the village of German Flats on the Mohawk. Three months later he was on the warpath once more, down the Cherry Valley where amongst their exploits his men,

according to a survivor, 'killed, scalp't and most barbarously murdered thirty-two women and children . . . and committed the most inhuman barbarities on most of the dead'. Petitions flooded into Congress from the frontier folk, begging protection.

The most satisfactory means of stemming the tide of butchery—by annihilating the British supply-bases for the Indians—was beyond the resources of the Continental army. Pensacola (which kept the Cherokee in tomahawks in the south) eventually fell to the Spanish in 1781. Niagara in the north and Detroit, where Henry 'hair-buyer' Hamilton presided over the grisly trade, appeared out of reach. In the summer 1778 the Virginia Assembly did attempt to attain that end by commissioning an experienced Indian fighter, George Rogers Clark, to march on Detroit. Clark's swashbuckling approach paid early dividends; the predominantly French towns of Kaskaskia, Cahokia and Vincennes in Illinois country fell willingly, almost with relief, into his hands. Clark did not reach Detroit, but Henry Hamilton reached him which was quite as satisfying. Marching 600 miles in seventy-one days Hamilton's small troop reached Vincennes on December 17 and secured the surrender of the garrison (three men and the commandant). But an even more impressive forced march through floods, Clark was on the spot in seventeen days. With a show of sheer bravado (and by tomahawking five Indians in the face of the enemy) he obtained Hamilton's capitulation and marched him back to Virginia, and his fate.

Not until 1779 did Congress respond materially to the pioneers' pleas. At its request Washington dispatched 600 formidable Continentals against the western offenders among the Six Nations, at the same time placing 4,000 men under John Sullivan with the explicit instructions not merely to overrun their country but to destroy it. This Sullivan's Expedition accomplished with as ardent single-mindedness as any Indian scalping-party. Apart from a brief and ineffectual resistance by Brant's Iroquois and Walter Butler's Tories at Newtown on August 29, they were permitted to go rampant and unimpeded about

the Indian lands. Advertised by the swirling of fife and the beat of drums they advanced on village after village, invariably deserted, and eradicated them from the face of the earth.

The succession of punitive raids and inevitable reprisals did not diminish in consequence of the activities of 1778 and 1779; it became more violent than ever. The flow of British arms was not staunched nor the activities of the agents curtailed, until news of the Peace filtered into the backwoods. The patriots and pioneers suffered greatly, but they tenaciously held on to their land.

TOP RIGHT

The Allies—Par nobile Fratrium. Anon: According to the imprint, 'Indignatio' produced this print, indignation against Britain's continued use of Indian allies over whose brutalities she had no control. George III is depicted sharing a cannibal feast of the bones of colonists with his 'allies'. The dismembered body of a child lies nearby; it is enough to make the dog in the foreground sick. An Anglican cleric (probably Achbishop Markham, see page 122), however, finds the scene much to his liking, and his lackey hurries to deliver his gift-box of 'scalping-knives, crucifixes and tomahawks' explaining 'D . . n my dear eyes, but we are hellish good Christians'. The Bible stands up-turned at the foot of the cross and the King's proud standard proclaiming him to be Defender of the Faith has mouldered away into shreds.

BOTTOM RIGHT

Yankee-Doodle, or the American Satan. Wright: Published by 'Ebenezer Scalpp 'em on the banks of the Ohio' some time in 1778, this engraving of a decidedly un-Satanic young patriot appears to have as its motive the discrediting of Tory claims that Indian atrocities were matched (at least) by the ruthlessness of the border colonists. Or it may be a belated reference to the activities of the Grand Ohio Company which had been formed before the war to develop former Indian lands, and in which even Cabinet Ministers had had a stake.

YANKEE - DOODLE, or the
American SATAN.

THE WRATH OF THE CHURCH

Rightly or wrongly, it was an almost universal belief among the Evangelical clergy of the colonies that the triumph of American arms would ensure religious liberty. Prayers from the pulpit for the victory of freedom over tyranny became as commonplace as the more orthodox variety for rain on the crops; it was not unknown for the preacher himself to march into battle at the head of his parishioners. At the same time there was a widely-held conviction among Anglican clergy in England that a more propitious moment for establishing that elusive episcopacy in America than the crushing of the rebellion would never come their way. Some of the most vociferous supporters of Lord North's war were to be found among the senior prelates of the Church. And foremost of them was Archbishop Markham (see below) who was translated to the see of York in 1777.

Events in 1776 and the years that immediately followed added fuel to the Anglicans' war fervour. The Declaration of Independence effectively sounded the death-knell on the prospects for an episcopacy, for by law no deacon, priest or bishop could be ordained or consecrated who could not take the oath of allegiance to the King. Then, in state after state, the authority of the Church of England crumbled. In Maryland, under that colony's Bill of Rights in 1776, the Anglicans were forced to bow in the face of religious freedom. By the new constitutions of Georgia in 1777, of North Carolina and South Carolina in 1778 their Church was disestablished for ever. One of the first Acts of the infant Virginia legislature was to suspend the salaries of the Established clergy, though the internal controversy raged on for several more years. It was all the more humiliating, therefore, for the hierarchy in England to have to watch the Congregationalists of New England battle to hold on to their privileges as tenaciously as they battled to keep the armies of Clinton and Burgoyne at bay.

OPPOSITE TOP

The Church Militant. *Gillray: An army of prelates marches on to prosecute the war against the Americans,* the Archbishop of York on a charger at their head. There is no positive identification but probably among the ecclesiastical corps are Cornwallis (Archbishop of Canterbury) and Butler (Bishop of Oxford) whose dogmatic views on the rebellion were well known. As they go they chant their litany: Give us good Beef in store/ When that's gone, send us more/ And the key of the cellar door/ That we may drink/ From labour and industry, Good Lord deliver us. The implication is that in wishing to extend the episcopacy to the colonies, the Bishops really desired an extension of their own power and wealth.

OPPOSITE BOTTOM LEFT

Spectatum admissi, risum teneatis, amici. *Anon: Once again the soldier-cleric takes the field, using as his shield the Thirty-nine Articles of the Church of England. He is surrounded by the accoutrements of war, in particular a cannon inscribed 'alliance between Church and State'. It was widely rumoured that many senior churchmen applauded the war because they relied on ministers for their preferment, and therefore the administration made full use of their oratory and literacy to propagandize. Walpole wrote in his* Journals (December 16 1776): 'The Fast Sermon let loose all the zeal of the clergy, and contributed to raise the infatuation of England against America. Indeed it was no wonder, for the Court had now at their devotion the three great bodies of the clergy, army and law. Lord Mansfield encouraged writings full of all the old exploded nonsense of passive obedience and non-resistance. . . . On the Fast, too, a sermon against all the principles of the Revolution was preached and licensed at Oxford by Dr. Miles Cooper, late President of the College at New York. This was severely attacked in the public papers in a letter to the Bishop of London, who was called on to know if Cooper had received any share of the subscription for the suffering American clergy. . . .'

OPPOSITE BOTTOM RIGHT

General Sanguinaire Mark-ham. *Anon: Half-cleric and half-soldier, the new archbishop of York prepares to do battle. Of all Anglicans the most entrenched supporter of the American war, he had fulminated against the colonists from his pulpit, most notably at St. Mary-le-Bow's before the Society* for the Propagation of the Gospel (which before the war had great aspirations to spreading Anglicanism in America). This particular sermon (see the blade of his sword) had roused the Opposition in the House of Lords to the utmost fury at 'his pernicious doctrines'. 'A pert, arrogant man' Walpole had summed him up, and referred to him as 'that warlike metropolitan archbishop Turpin'.

THE CHURCH MILITANT.

THE WAR AT SEA

The British blockade of American ports, which Lord North's Prohibitory Act had put under way, struck deep at the colonists' trade, forcing many of them to perfect those smuggling skills that had been practised since the dawn of the Navigation Acts. Against Lord Howe's men-of-war the embryonic American navy under Esek Hopkins could not hope to accomplish much in formal battle; nevertheless by the end of the war it was able to chalk up nearly 200 successful assaults on enemy shipping. But even more lethal to the British merchantmen, which ferried across the Atlantic bloated with provisions or money for the troops, was the heterogeneous fleet of American privateers who by the end of 1778 had, it was estimated, relieved the Exchequer of a good two million pounds' worth of goods. It became a very expensive business indeed in London to insure any cargo bound for colonial waters; the odds against it reaching its destination were currently given as three to one, if it was unarmed.

The most remarkable and daring of the privateers was John Paul Jones whose apprehension was required (if the *Annual Register* is to be believed) in distant parts of the Empire for a number of capital offences already. His name became a byword in the very harbours and coastal towns of Ireland and England, where he indulged in the same kind of reprisals which were being exacted on the fishing-villages of New England by British raiders. In the summer of 1778 he invaded the fortress at Whitehaven, spiked the guns and set fire to the shipping in the harbour. Ranging the Irish Channel, he played havoc with the commercial traffic, and took on and captured one of His Majesty's sloops whose name, *Drake*, must have appealed enormously to this other sailor of fortune. But Paul Jones's most memorable engagement came on September 23 1779 when he got to grips with the British frigate *Serapis* in the North Sea. In the murderous fighting his own ship was crippled, but the *Serapis* was captured and sailed triumphantly off to France. The physical damage inflicted by the American's depredations was bad enough; the effect on morale was worse. For the first time it was brought home to the ordinary Englishman just how utterly vulnerable the demands of the colonial war had left his own shores.

TOP RIGHT

The Liberty of the Subject. *Gillray: The voracious demands of the British fleet for man-power were met almost exclusively by the barbarous practice of impressment, described to the House of Commons by Admiral Vernon as follows: 'When our ships are to be fitted, an impress is sent into the streets, to bring those who shall fall in the way, by force into the vessels; from that time they are, in effect, condemned to death, since they are never allowed to set foot again on shore, but turned over from ship to ship, and when they have finished one expedition hurried into another without any regard for the hardships they have undergone'. During the American war press-gangs were a regular feature of daily life in London and elsewhere. In this scene a tailor (scissors and tape in his pocket) is being carried off for service in the war by a gang of sailors under the command of an officer (right). The only attempt to stop them appears to be made by the womenfolk (left). The better-dressed citizens of London (NB St. Paul's in background) who were usually spared by the press-gangs look on passively. (1779.)*

BOTTOM RIGHT

John Paul Jones Shooting a Sailor. *After John Collett: John Paul (he is said to have aided Jones to escape detection for his crimes) was the first lieutenant to be commissioned in the Continental Navy. After a remarkable series of successes in and around American waters he was given command of a dilapidated French frigate, which he renamed the* Bonhomme Richard *(as a compliment to Franklin), and sailed around the coasts of Britain in 1778–9. For his exploits in these campaigns Louis XVI awarded him a gold-hilted sword and Congress a formal vote of thanks, and after the war a gold medal (he was the only naval officer to obtain such a decoration). Jones ended his career as a Rear-Admiral for Empress Catherine of Russia in her war against the Turks. This print illustrates an incident (probably apocryphal) during his celebrated engagement with the* Serapis. *By his own admission 'the scene was dreadful beyond the reach of language' during that three-hour battle. Both ships were lashed together, firing point-blank at one another.*

COUNT DE GRASSE

Taking a peep in the west Indies

Sold by W.Humphry. N.º 227 Strand.

CHAPTER

5

THE END OF AN EMPIRE

From the ministerial crisis
to Yorktown

1779-1781

1779	June 16	*Spain declares war on Britain: opens siege of Gibraltar*
	July 16	*Stony Point*
	August	*Sullivan's expedition*
	August 19	*Paulus Hook*
	August	*Combined Franco-Spanish invasion attempt*
	October 20	*Siege of Savannah*
	September 23	*John Paul Jones in* Serapis
	October	*British abandon Rhode Island*
1780	January 16	*Rodney defeats Spanish at Cape St. Vincent*
	February 8	*Yorkshire petition for Parliamentary reform*
	March 10	*Russia's declaration of Armed Neutrality*
	April 17	*Martinique*
	April 19	*Dunning's resolution*
	May 12	*Fall of Charleston*
	May	*Burke's Bill for economic reform*
	June 2–8	*Gordon riots*
	July 10	*French under Rochambeau arrive at Newport*
	August 16	*Camden*
	September 23	*Capture of Major Andre*
	October 7	*King's Mountain*
	December	*Britain declares war on Holland*
1781	January 17	*Cowpens*
	March 15	*Guilford Courthouse*
	June 19	*End of siege of Ninety-Six*
	September	*De Grasse defeats British fleet in Chesapeake Bay*
	September 8	*Eutaw Springs*
	September 28	*Siege of Yorktown begins*
	October 19	*Surrender of Cornwallis*

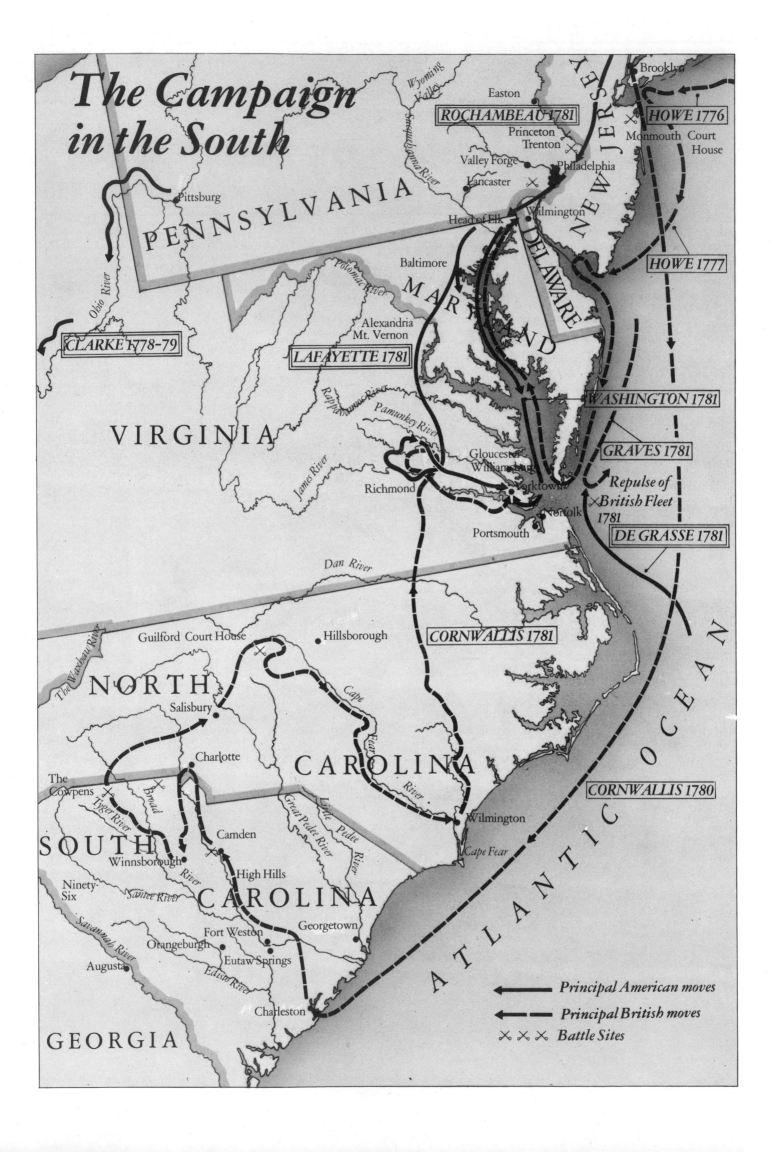

The Campaign in the South

ROCHAMBEAU 1781
HOWE 1776
HOWE 1777
CLARKE 1778-79
LAFAYETTE 1781
WASHINGTON 1781
GRAVES 1781
GRAVES 1781
DE GRASSE 1781
CORNWALLIS 1781
CORNWALLIS 1780

PENNSYLVANIA
NEW JERSEY
DELAWARE
MARYLAND
VIRGINIA
NORTH CAROLINA
SOUTH CAROLINA
GEORGIA
ATLANTIC OCEAN

Pittsburg
Easton
Princeton
Trenton
Valley Forge
Lancaster
Philadelphia
Brooklyn
Monmouth Court House
Head of Elk
Wilmington
Baltimore
Alexandria
Mt. Vernon
Gloucester
Williamsburg
Yorktown
Richmond
Norfolk
Portsmouth
Repulse of British Fleet 1781
Guilford Court House
Hillsborough
Salisbury
Charlotte
The Cowpens
Camden
Winnsborough
Ninety-Six
High Hills
Wilmington
Cape Fear
Georgetown
Fort Weston
Orangeburgh
Eutaw Springs
Augusta
Charleston

Wyoming Valley
Ohio River
Susquehanna River
Potomac River
Rappahannock River
Pamunkey River
James River
Dan River
The Waxhaw River
Cape Fear River
Broad River
Tyger River
Little Pedee River
Great Pedee River
Santee River
Savannah River
Edisto River

Principal American moves
Principal British moves
Battle Sites

In the concluding three campaigns of the war Britain was forced to adopt a completely new strategy on the American mainland. The entry first of France into the war, then Spain (1779) and Holland (1780) threatened not just her Atlantic trade but her supremacy at sea. She had to look to the defence of Gibraltar, Minorca, her West Indian possessions, even at one dark hour in 1779 her own shores. No more men could be spared for America, yet the war could not be allowed to be lost there by default. There seemed to be one hope: that the residue of loyalism in the Southern colonies could be resuscitated by a British initiative there. At first it looked as if this policy might work. Savannah was successfully defended against combined French and American forces, and Charleston captured. Cornwallis began an offensive through South and North Carolina into Virginia, which to observers in Britain who had no conception of the difficulties and distances to be overcome looked as if it might be decisive.

The meddling interference of the European powers plunged Britain into an all-out war effort, but so much activity on so many fronts against so many enemies proved to be an alarming drain on the country's resources. Men started to question not just why all this money was being spent, but how it was being spent. They looked at the host of pensioners and placemen in Parliament and the executive who were keeping alive the ministry and the King's policies, and clamoured for economies and the abolition of sinecures. As always the prints dutifully reflect the preoccupations of the Opposition in Parliament, increasingly the King appears in unflattering roles, as a despot, as the watchman asleep while his ministers conspire and connive all round him. In 1781 their attention was rudely diverted back to America by the shattering news of Cornwallis's surrender. His advance had run out of steam in Virginia, where he had been caught between the pincers of the French fleet and the massing American Continentals and militia. It was all over, except that the King of course persisted in his belief that the colonists could be reduced by force.

A most notable addition to the ranks of the cartoonists at this time was James Gillray. He will always be best remembered for his scathing attacks on Charles Fox (not to mention Boney) during the Napoleonic wars, but it was on the American war that he cut his engraving teeth. His prints of this period are less single-minded in their virulence, show scant attention to facial character, are still inhibited by the limitations of the engraver's technique. Nevertheless those which can be attributed to him show a greater freedom of composition and confidence of line than most of his contemporaries possessed (since, at this stage of his career, he followed the customary practice of not signing his work, most attributions before about 1782 must remain doubtful). Another distinctive artist whose work is featured in this section was Henry Bunbury (see *The Coffee-house Patriots*, page 153). He was counted the leading amateur of this period, though little of his work was of a political nature. His designs were etched by leading engravers, notably Darly; primitive designs, certainly, but never lacking in appeal.

How the End Came. *The news of Cornwallis' surrender at Yorktown as reported in a special edition of the* Boston Gazette.

Cornwallis TAKEN !

BOSTON, (Friday) October 26, 1781.

This Morning an Exprefs arrived from Providence to HIS EXCELLENCY the GOVERNOR, with the following IMPORTANT INTELLIGENCE, viz.—

———

PROVIDENCE, Oct. 25, 1781. Three o'Clock, P. M.

This Moment an Exprefs arrived at his Honor the Deputy-Governor's, from Col. Chriftopher Olney, Commandant on Rhode-Ifland, announcing the important Intelligence of the Surrender of Lord CORNWALLIS and his Army; an Account of which was Printed this Morning at Newport, and is as follows, viz.—

NEWPORT, October 25, 1781.

YESTERDAY Afternoon arrived in this Harbour Capt. Lovett, of the Schooner Adventure, from York River, in Chefapeak Bay, (which he left the 20th inftant,) and brought us the glorious News of the Surrender of Lord Cornwallis and his Army Prifoners of War to the allied Army, under the Command of our illuftrious General; and the French Fleet, under the Command of His Excellency the Count de Graffe.

A Ceffation of Arms took Place on Thurfday the 18th Inftant in Confequence of Propofals from Lord CORNWALLIS for a Capitulation.—His Lordfhip propofed a Ceffation of Twenty-four Hours, but Two only were granted by His Excellency General WASHINGTON. The Articles were compleated the fame Day, and the next Day the allied Army took Poffeffion of York Town.

By this glorious Conqueft, NINE·THOUSAND of the Enemy, including Seamen, fell into our Hands, with an immenfe Quantity of Warlike Stores; a Forty-Gun-Ship, a Frigate, an armed Veffel, and about One Hundred Sail of Tranfports.

— — — — — — — —

Printed by B. Edes and Sons, in State Street.

THE SECOND HALF

Brooding cheerfully, as was his custom, on the misfortunes of the Ministry as the war took on a new and more desperate complexion Horace Walpole summed up the state of the country at the beginning of 1779: 'The navy disgusted . . . a rebellion ready to break out in Ireland, many of them well-wishers to the Americans and all so ruined that they insisted on relief from Parliament or were ready to throw off subjection; Holland pressed by France to refuse us assistance . . . uncertainty of the fate of the West Indian islands; and the dread at least that Spain might take part with France; Lord North at the same time perplexed to raise money . . . such a position and such a prospect might have shaken the stoutest king and the ablest administration'.

The ministry was shaken indeed, at times almost to the point of disintegration. Throughout 1779 there was a constant stream of defection from its ranks: Lord Bathurst had already resigned as Lord Chancellor the previous June, largely in protest at Germain's conduct of the war; Lord Barrington quit as Minister of War complaining of an administration which had 'no system, no steadiness and little concert'. Lord Suffolk, Secretary of State, inconveniently died and deprived the Cabinet of one of the firmest props of its American policy. Lord Gower, President of the Privy Council, and Secretary of State Lord Weymouth both sickened of the war and resigned before the year was out. In June even Lord North applied to leave office, an application the King studiously ignored: 'No man has a right to talk of leaving me at this hour,' he wrote peevishly.

Presenting his budget that year North frankly confessed to the House that he was short by at least a million pounds. The cost of the armed forces had nearly doubled from £11 million to £20 million a year, and so had the interest due on the National Debt; interest rates were soaring and every new loan meant fresh taxes. But if the Exchequer was having difficulty in making ends meet, merchants and manufacturers all over the country were rapidly sinking into bankruptcy. In Yorkshire the wool trade was virtually at a standstill, with thousands out of work and the price of land fallen twenty-five per cent. West Indian merchants in London were going broke with colossal debts, tobacco traders in Glasgow were selling up. In Liverpool where Burke had complained earlier in the war 'they are literally almost ruined by this American war, but love it as they suffer from it' they were soon changing their tune. For want of a convoy, merchant ships idled in port amassing crippling expenses; for a West Indian or Eastern convoy to arrive home unscathed and unplundered was becoming a matter for public rejoicing in the City (from 1779 Britain was losing, on average, some 600 ships a year).

TOP RIGHT

Mr. Trade & Family or the State of ye Nation. *Anon: Thomas Tradeless with his wife and barefoot, ragged children appeals to General Washington (not, note, the King or Parliament) for alleviation from their distress. The only references to the King in fact are as a toy being pulled by the smallest child and addressed as Sultan by the owls on the withered tree (at about this time drawings of George III as an omnipotent potentate in a turban were coming into vogue—see page 142). Out of the man's pocket hangs a credit note (or possibly a government security) now 'worthless', though in the background the landed gentry still seem able to pursue their leisurely activities. On the horizon Norfolk (bombarded by Lord Dunmore in January 1776) and Aesopus (burnt by General Vaughan in October 1777) are holocausts—a reminder that these sufferings extended to the ordinary* people of America, too. *All the houses in the street on the left are 'to let' (it is estimated that in the City of London alone there were over 1,100 buildings vacant at this period).*

BOTTOM RIGHT

A Birthday Ode. *Anon: Throughout the miseries of this period of the war, there were those who stuck faithfully to the King and his policies. Here they perform an ode to the King on his birthday (June 4 1779) entitled The Distresses of the Nation: North on the viol, Germain on the hautboy, Sandwich on the kettle-drums. The vocal parts are supplied by the Lord Mayor of London (Samuel Plumbe, most unpopular for his ministerial sympathies) and the Bishop of London.*

BELOW

The Present State of Great Britain. *Anon: A forlorn John Bull is being protected from the depredations of America, Holland and France by, of all people, a Scotsman. This favourable representation of Scotland is exceptional in all the war satires, possibly because recruiting was going well there by comparison with the rest of the country.*

STALEMATE IN THE NORTH

For the armies in the North the campaign season opened late in 1779, and in desultory fashion. The winter had been kind to Washington based on Middlebrook; more plentiful provision and French shipments of clothes alleviated the lot of the soldier in the ranks, even if individual states (now required to support their own lines) tended to favour the militia at home in preference to their Continentals at New Jersey; for the officers there was even the semblance of a social life with its 'pretty little frisks'. Shut up in New York, however, Clinton passed the winter months engaged in an arduous and increasingly short-tempered correspondence with his American Secretary. In October he had attempted to resign what he called 'his mortifying command'. He had been shackled by instructions, he complained. His army was debilitated, his own powers curtailed. At the whim of Whitehall he had been obliged to siphon off some 10,000 men of his command to the South, to Florida and the West Indies. And by his own esoteric method of accounting Lord George Germain continued to insist that Clinton's army numbered nearly 50,000 (by including the sick, missing and captured, as well as those serving 3,000 miles away from New York).

Clinton knew he had only a fraction of that number at his disposal for operations in the north during 1779. Yet Germain's instructions in January included the maintaining of a garrison at New York of 12,000, raids on the New England and Chesapeake Bay coasts, and the luring of Washington into a pitched battle. It was true there were 5,000 hypothetical reinforcements on their way and the West Indian troops would be returned 'as soon as the season for offensive operations in that climate was over'. But by May Clinton had lost all patience with his overlord. 'For God's sake, my Lord,' he wrote, 'if you wish me to do anything, leave me to myself and let me adapt my efforts to the hourly change of circumstances!' Nevertheless, at the end of May he did attempt to goad the patriot Commander on to the offensive by pushing up the Hudson as far as forts at Stony Point and Verplanck's

Point, without making any strenuous demands on his precious manpower. The assault on Stony Point cost him just one wounded soldier.

But Washington was not to be drawn. Diversions to the Chesapeake, at King's Ferry, even rampages around the Connecticut coast failed to budge Washington from his secure perch higher up the Hudson—until July 15, when Clinton had retired to New York to resume his fruitless vigil for those reinforcements from England. That night Anthony Wayne launched a sudden, typically audacious onslaught on the precipitous fortress at Stony Point. At Paoli his men had been cut down by the silent British bayonets: it was a lesson Wayne had learned well. Scrambling over the British defences in the moonlight, his little army captured more than 500 and carried off $150,000 worth of equipment without a shot fired. It was a brilliant counterthrust, contributing inestimably to the army morale (if little to its strategic position: the fort was judiciously abandoned within two days). A month later 'Light-horse Harry' Lee, not to be outdone by Wayne's infantry, overran another British outpost at Paulus Hook, captured most of its inhabitants and retreated back to the safety of his lines. Lee's lightning stroke, conducted under the very noses of the British on Manhattan Island, effectively concluded operations in the north for the year. Clinton re-built his forts but Washington had safeguarded his position on the Hudson at West Point and, more important, he had contained the enemy, living up to his honourable nickname of Fabius.

He had achieved more, perhaps, than was at first realized, for Clinton decided in the fall to evacuate Rhode Island to concentrate his men still further. His reinforcements had finally arrived in August, to his disgust barely half of what he had been promised and those so racked with the fever that they had soon passed it on to over 6,000 of his fit and healthy men. He began to suspect, rightly, that the energies and enthusiasm of the American Secretary were directed elsewhere, the English Channel, Gibraltar, the West Indies—anywhere but New York. 'Not a word from Europe this month, not a farthing of money, no

information, no army. Good God!' he exploded. No one would even accept the resignation he once more tendered in despair.

TOP RIGHT
The Horse America, throwing his Master. *Anon: In the summer of 1779 (this print appeared in August) it seemed as if Britain was conceding the war through sheer inertia. Almost no positive move had been made since the assault on Savannah the previous December. Washington's tactics of attrition seemed to be paying off— after all, how could an army bottled up in New York and Newport, waging a defensive war, hope to bring the rebels to their senses. Time only multiplied the number of our enemies. Ultimate defeat for Britain is the message of this print: the King with his crop of sabres and tomahawks is bucked from his saddle. More alarming still, a Frenchman runs up (to take over from the unseated rider?).*

BOTTOM RIGHT
Prattle the Political Apothecary. *Darly: At home there were any number of armchair strategists happy to give the generals in America the benefit of their vast military knowledge at such a time. The coffee-houses of London were, no doubt, full of Prattles and Lud Fiddlefaddles prepared to parade their total ignorance of American geography to anyone who would give them the time of day. This print (published August 1779) celebrates a particularly virulent epidemic of ear-bending which followed the official inquiry into Lord Howe's conduct.*

THE SIEGE OF SAVANNAH

Not for two years, since Henry Clinton had withdrawn from his fruitless escapade at Sullivan's Island, had the southern colonies been unduly disturbed by the alarms of war. But as 1778 drew to its close it erupted in the plantations with undiminished fury. By the spring of the next year, as one patriot general wryly noted, there were no less than five armies marching about Georgia and South Carolina to different purposes at the same time. Not until Cornwallis' surrender three long campaign seasons later was there to be any respite.

As far back as the spring of 1778 the thoughts of the Ministry had begun to turn from the north—where the British armies seemed to have manoeuvred themselves into a state of passivity, if not total surrender—to the south with its tempting prospects of opening a back door on Washington's army. Lord George Germain had never ceased to cherish his fond illusions about the upsurge of loyalist sympathies which would greet the arrival of a substantial British force in those colonies. Ordering Clinton to detach an expedition from New York against Savannah in Georgia he added 'it is not to be doubted that large numbers of the inhabitants would flock to the King's standard and that His Majesty's Government would be restored in that province (North Carolina) also'. So it was that in December two British forces were to be found converging on the valuable tobacco port of Savannah, from the north 3,500 men under Colonel Archibald Campbell and from the south General Prevost with a detachment from the Florida garrison at St. Augustine. Finding the only patriot army in the vicinity (a meagre 850 men) under Robert Howe arrayed against him outside Savannah, Campbell resorted to the tactical stand-by which had served so well in the past against the Americans, a flanking movement through the swamps against the enemy's right. Once again it succeeded; by nightfall on December 29 the town was his. 'I may venture to say, Sir,' he reported, 'that I have ripped one star from the rebel flag of America.' And indeed after Augusta and Sunbury had fallen

within the month it did look as if Georgia had been restored to the Empire convincingly enough for the former Royal Governor, Sir James Wright, to return to his duties from London.

It would have gladdened Germain's heart to see how the Georgia Tories were suddenly emboldened to take up arms. But patriot resistance stiffened too under Colonel Pickens, and soon had the double satisfaction of routing a loyalist army on its way to Augusta *and* hanging its leaders. General Lincoln, who had proved his worth in rallying the New England militia against Burgoyne, was sent south to repeat the performance. Twice he attempted to push back into Georgia. At Briar Creek on March 3 he lost four hundred men in the attempt. At the end of April he moved again against Augusta, only to discover his quarry turned hunter and that Prevost was making for Charleston, bold as brass. In fact Prevost was only pretending—until it dawned on him that his way to Charleston was wide open. He drove on, and might have made it if his troops had been a little less systematic in their looting of the grand plantation mansions along the way. When the British arrived at Charleston on May 12, Lincoln was close behind them. Called on to surrender, Governor Rutledge stalled, offering the fatuous (but effective) counter-proposal that his city be granted neutrality. His procrastination saved Charleston—for the time being.

But Savannah was still in enemy hands and remained so throughout the long, hot summer. Then at the beginning of September, in response to Congress's urgent summons D'Estaing arrived with his fleet, hotfoot from his triumphs in the West Indies (where he had seized the islands of St. Vincent and Grenada). He could only spare two weeks, he said, since the hurricane season was approaching. But with the 4,000 men he had on board, Lincoln's militia and Count Pulaski's newly-arrived Legion, that would be sufficient. Unhappily, the rains were on schedule, not allowing the siege to get under way until October had begun. On the 4th the bombardment opened, continued day and night till 'there was hardly a house which had not been shot through'. But the British held out longer than D'Es-

taing's patience. He ordered an assault for before dawn on the 9th. It was a fiasco. D'Estaing arrived late, charged bravely but recklessly at the entrenchments without reference to his allies and concentrated the murderous fire on his hapless men. Not since Bunker Hill had a single engagement taken such a toll: 637 Frenchmen and 457 Americans killed or wounded, against 55 redcoats lost.

That was enough for D'Estaing. No persuasion on earth could keep him at Savannah, and Lincoln had no option but to raise the siege. For the French admiral it was the end of a short but sorry association with his new allies. He had already, as one of his countrymen later wrote, disillusioned them on three critical occasions: on the Delaware for lack of speed, at Sandy Hook for lack of water and at Rhode Island for lack of fine weather. He now finally deserted them, for lack of patience.

There me had him.

Pub by E Hedge Royal Exchange

DESTAING

ENTER SPAIN: THE NEW ARMADA

On April 12 1779 His Most Catholic Majesty King Charles the Third of Spain—who for four years had remained officially aloof from (if unofficially alert to) the progress of the American war—graciously consented to append his name to 'an amicable and reciprocal engagement' with his Bourbon brothers from France. In so many words, he was now prepared to make war on Britain. If it meant allying himself temporarily with those objectionable revolutionaries across the Atlantic, that was a price he was prepared to pay. The rewards would be substantial: the return of Minorca, and the addition of the whole of Florida including Mobile and Pensacola to the Spanish Empire. But the most glittering prize of all, which Vergennes now dangled before his eyes, was the re-conquest of Gibraltar. All that was diplomatically required was some sort of casus belli. Since none technically existed, Floridablanca the Spanish Minister concocted what must be rated one of the most transparent in the history of European diplomacy. He offered to mediate between France and Britain (neglecting to mention that his country was now secretly allied to one of the parties) then threatened to declare war if Britain rejected his two-faced offer.

Britain, of course, refused, and on June 16 Spain declared war, a mere technicality by that time since the allied fleets (a total of sixty-six ships of the line and fourteen frigates) were already in the process of massing off Corunna for the invasion, no less, of Britain. On the coasts of Normandy and Brittany since May an army of 50,000—it included Lafayette whose 'blood was boiling in his veins' at the prospect—waited only for a decisive victory by the combined fleet to begin swarming all over the Isle of Wight. Between this juggernaut and the Bristol Channel lay only the Channel Fleet under Sir Charles Hardy with less than half the number of vessels. But on land, from the Ministry in London to the contingent of Cornish tin-miners who marched into Plymouth, picks at the ready, that old 'Armada' spirit had asserted itself. 'It was the vigour of mind shown by Queen Elizabeth,' wrote the King appropriately, 'and her subjects, added to the assistance of Divine Providence, that saved this island when attacked by the Spaniards.' It was a happy allusion, and his country responded.

Meanwhile the new Armada had got off to a bad start. The Spanish contingent under Don Luis de Cordoba (whose punctuality came a poor second to his conspicuous piety) arrived six weeks late; the two fleets discovered they could make neither head nor tail of each other's signals and frittered away valuable weeks devising new ones. Worst of all, scurvy had begun to decimate D'Orvilliers' crews until, by the time he came in sight of Plymouth on August 16, he doubted his ability to put up any kind of fight. He continued to doubt for two days as he contemplated the town's heavy artillery pointing at him. Then the weather made his decision for him; it gathered itself into a gale and spreadeagled his ships all over the Atlantic. A fortnight late he attempted to give battle to Hardy, half-heartedly at best. Under the ravages of disease the incapacity of his Frenchmen to man the boats was equalled (he now realized) only by the natural incompetence of his Spanish allies to do so. On September 3 he returned to Brest, to the disappointment of the British Ministry, and soon after the Spaniards sailed off to Cadiz. The net profit of the whole expensive enterprise was the lone ship *Ardent*, whose misfortune had been to sail straight into a fleet hardly anyone else had been able to set eyes on.

TOP RIGHT

The British Tar at Omoa. *Gillray: With the entry of Spain officially into the war, the West Indian squadron turned its attention to some of the rich Spanish possessions in the Caribbean. On October 16 1779 Omoa in the Bay of Honduras was successfully stormed, and the prizes captured in Omoa harbour were estimated to be worth 3,000,000 dollars. The incident depicted here was said to have been based on a genuine report of how one sailor surprised a Spanish officer just out of bed.*

BOTTOM RIGHT

Britannia Protected from the Terrors of an Invasion. *Anon: By January 1780 (when this print appeared) it was clear that the Allies had abandoned all efforts to invade Britain, and there was every justification to display gloating satires on how easy it had all been, after all. The French were, in fact, to attempt an invasion of the Channel Islands the following January—but it was to be of little consequence.*

BELOW

John Bull Triumphant. *Gillray: Another paean of praise for Britain's triumph at Omoa—in spite of the efforts of ministers and pseudo-ministers to inhibit the rampant bull. Right to left, Bute, North and Mansfield tug at the animal's tail, giving as their battle-cries the names of their respective stately homes.*

The British Tar at Omoa.

A loud crying Woman & a Scold shall be sought out to drive away the Enemies.

SECRET SERVICES AND CONSTITUTIONAL CRISES

North's ministry, in the long course of the war, had stumbled from one parliamentary crisis to another. But on all issues which directly affected its American policy or its administration of the war itself it had emerged bloodied and abused, but more or less intact in the face of defeat and disaster, inquiries and resignations. In 1780 it was granted a respite on this front, for not even the bitterest of its opponents could claim that the good news from America was outweighed by the bad. Instead it was assailed from new quarters and before the year had advanced many weeks found itself caught between a flanking movement from another of its rebellious territories, Ireland, and a frontal assault by the Opposition on the question of economical reform. Nor was either of these burning issues quite so remote from the American war as it might have appeared.

Ireland had been hit considerably harder by the economic depression of the war years than Britain since Parliament, as with the colonies, placed severe restraints on both its imports and its exports. It had always required the presence of a substantial garrison—in 1775 there had been 12,000 troops stationed there—but the voracious demands of the war had reduced this to a dangerously low level. In its place there had arisen an *ad hoc* militia which called itself the Volunteer Movement, for the defence of the country. Its allegiance to the Crown was not, for the time being, in question but its very existence was not viewed in Westminster with undiluted pleasure by any means, at a time when the demands from popular Irish bodies for constitutional freedom were growing more insistent with every month. To Lord North it was ominously familiar; was it to be the American experience all over again? For the Irish leaders had not been slow to learn from the colonists' example nor, as Henry Grattan candidly expressed it, 'to attack Great Britain in her weakness and obtain freedom to their constitution'. The Ministry, under pressure, showed it too had learned something from experience and in December 1779 freed Ireland's trade from its restrictions. But it had no answer to the constitutional issue which was brought to a head the following April by Grattan's demands for Home Rule.

Nor did it have much defence against the concerted barrage of complaints which fell on its head from all parts of Britain in the first session of 1780. A petition from the freeholders of Yorkshire was presented to Parliament on February 8, and was followed by others from twenty-five counties and eight towns. The country was broke (so the petitions ran) yet public money was being squandered in staggering amounts, largely in the payment of state sinecures and pensions and in reimbursement for 'secret services'. The Crown, moreover, had acquired an unconstitutional influence which was threatening the fundamental liberties of the country. It was an attack on the very basis of North's ministry, on the government placemen who dutifully sacrificed their principles at every division of the House in order to stay on the Ministry's payroll. The further implication was also unavoidable: that the Ministry was only being propped up at the country's expense in order to effect the King's obstinate will on the American war. There were even those who went so far as to say that the war was being deliberately prolonged by fortune-hunters. What answer had the Ministry when even one of its own supporters, Admiral Rodney, inveighed against 'the long train of leeches who seek the blood of the State', the quartermasters, barrack-masters and commissaries who were coining princely fortunes 'and laugh in their sleeves at the Generals who permit it'?

The Opposition were not backward in exploiting the public resentment. In the Lords Shelburne introduced a proposal for a Commission of Public Accounts; in the Commons Burke introduced his Establishment Bill, aimed at removing redundant offices and stamping out 'secret corruption almost to the possibility of its existence' (a truly high-minded ethic to parade in an eighteenth-century parliament). Then on April 7 John Dunning well and truly grasped the nettle by bringing forward his resolution 'deploring the increased influence of the Crown' and demanding that it be diminished. Typically the King was less distressed by the fact that the majority of the House agreed with Dunning than that Lord North should interpret the success of the motion as a vote of no confidence in his government. The Prime Minister plunged into one of his black fits of depression, while the King attempted to shore up his ebbing spirits and refused to let him resign. The Opposition, meanwhile, looked forward with keen anticipation to an imminent change of ministry.

The Bull Roasted: or the Political Cooks Serving their Customers. *Anon: A variation on the same theme. Lord North serves up choice pieces of his country to the enemy. Germain turns the spit, Sandwich ladles the gravy, Bute (as usual) supervises. The memorial broth requested by Holland (squatting on the floor) is a reference to the succession of memorials presented to the United Provinces by the English Ambassador in protest at their continued trading with France.*

The Bull Over-Drove: or the Drivers in Danger. *Anon: It was the common people of England the Opposition claimed to speak for when they launched their attack on parliamentary corruption. Here the artist has taken them at their word and introduced a crowd of huzzaing Britons to watch the Ministry mauled by an infatuated bull (Britain). The beast's hind legs attend to North and Germain while it tramples all over Sandwich (who calls out the name of his late mistress, Martha Ray, murdered on the steps of Covent Garden in April 1779 by an unrequited suitor). Spain (right) and France, observing the unleashed fury of the bull, liberated from the control of sinecurists, steal out of their American alliance in sheer nervousness.*

The BULL ROASTED: or the POLITICAL COOKS Serving their CUSTOMERS.

Behold the poor Bull! once Britania's chief boast.
Is kill'd by State Cooks, and laid down for a Roast:
While his Master, who should all his Honours maintain.
Turns the Spit tho' he should such an Office disdain.

Monsieur licks his gills at a bit of the Brown.
And the other two wish for to gobble him down.
But may ill digestion attend on the treat.
And the Cooks every one soon be roasted & Eat.

Publish'd as the Act directs Feb.ʸ 12, 1780. by I. Harris. Sweetings Alley. Cornhill. London.

The BULL OVER-DROVE: or the DRIVERS in DANGER.

The State Drovers to madness, had drove the poor Bull.
Their Goads and their Tethers no longer can rule.
He Snorts Kicks and Tramples among the curst rout.
Who fall by his Fury or Stagger about.

O! may all such Drovers thus meet with their Fate.
Who Hamper: and Gall so, the Bull of the State.
May his Terror: thus fill them with fear, and dismay.
While the People all Chearfully Cry out. Huzza!

London Publish'd as the Act directs Feb.ʸ 21, 1780. by I. Harris, Sweetings Alley Cornhill.

SECRET SERVICES AND CONSTITUTIONAL CRISES
(continued)

BELOW

The State Tinkers. *Gillray: In anticipation of Dunning's famous motion to curb the influence of the Crown, this print (published February 1780) portrays the King turbanned in the fashion of a despotic sultan, applauding as his ministers tinker with a leaky 'national kettle' (the Constitution). Sandwich and Germain hammer at the outside while Lord North chisels away at the inside and Bute shares in the general approbation in the background.*

TOP RIGHT

Argus. *Anon: In this production, however, published three months later in May, the sleeping King is unaware of the threat to his Crown. In the tale of the legendary sleeper he is about to have it snatched away by a Jacobite plot; the Scottish Lords Bute and Mansfield, and an unidentified Jacobite conspire to carry it off to the pretender (if not to place it on Bute's own head). A bedraggled Briton and a disconsolate Britannia are in despair; the British lion is padlocked. An Irishman takes his harp and goes his own way, America (behind the King) makes the point he has no crown to fight for and lose, a mercenary Dutchman is taking the opportunity to spoon some honey from the royal hives.*

BOTTOM RIGHT

The appointment of ye brave Adml. Rodney & Jemmy Twitcher in ye Dumps. *Anon: Of all the ministers it was Sandwich at the Admiralty who was most consistently accused of filling senior posts with his own friends and supporters. It was not an entirely justified complaint—he had employed prominent Opposition supporters, like Keppel and Howe, as his senior commanders. On the other hand, his critics pointed out, there was his shabby treatment of Admiral Rodney to answer for. It was well known that Sandwich had spited Rodney in the past, and that the Admiral for his part could not stand the sight of the First Lord. Heavy debts had obliged him to go and live in that bankrupt's haven, Paris; but ever since the outbreak of war he had persistently written to the Admiralty begging for employment. Only after five years and* a procession of admirals of varying competence did Sandwich consent to recall him (strangely, his debts were paid off by a Frenchman). He was over sixty by now and in ill-health, yet his first commission was an outstandingly dangerous one: the relief of Gibraltar, under blockade by the Spanish since the middle of June. Rodney sailed in December. The following March the news arrived back in England that not only had he succeeded in relieving the beleaguered garrison, he had captured a Spanish convoy and trounced the Spanish fleet off Cape St. Vincent on January 16. The country was ecstatic, but by that time their hero was on his way to take up his command in the West Indies. This print (published May 25) belatedly crows over Sandwich's supposed discomfiture at his enemy's success—indeed it plunges further into defamation, by suggesting that the First Lord (right) opposed Rodney's appointment and favoured Sir Hugh Palliser for the job. Rodney (left) is seen kissing hands and promising his sovereign he will never 'fear a Lee Shore' (one of Keppel's alibis after Ushant).

ARGUS.

Ireland   L? Mansfield. L? Bute.   George 3. America   Holland   Pub? May 15? 1780. by W. Renoal.

THE FRENCH ASHORE

On May 10 Lafayette rode into winter quarters at Morristown after more than a year's leave in France, bringing the most welcome news Washington had heard all winter and spring: a French army, some 6,000 strong, was on its way. In view of their unhappy experiences with D'Estaing's squadrons American hearts might have been forgiven for sinking at that moment. But Washington had cause for elation; his own army was in parlous condition. It had suffered more—if that were possible—that winter at Morristown than at Valley Forge. It had never been colder, the Hudson freezing from bank to bank so hard that cavalry could ride across it. Men had been reduced to gnawing wood or roasting the shoes they so badly needed. There was even the first rumblings of mutiny in the Continental ranks; to be sure, no violence and few reprisals followed, but it was an ominous sign. Many of the soldiers' three-year enlistments were expiring (as late as mid-July Washington could count on little more than 3,000 active men) and many States were laggard in fulfilling their new quotas. As one officer passionately reproached his own tardy legislature: 'Send your men to the field, believe you are Americans, not suffer yourselves to be duped into the thought that the French will relieve you and fight your battles. . . . When they arrive they will not put up with such treatment as your army have done. They will not serve week after week without meat, without clothing and clad in filthy rags.'

In July Count de Rochambeau disembarked with his army at Newport, which Clinton had evacuated the previous autumn. That evacuation Sir George Rodney called 'the most fatal measure that could possibly have been taken. It gave up the best and the only harbour of consequence in America during this unhappy war.' Now that the French had landed Clinton, too, was having second thoughts and hastily girded up an army from Long Island to attack the newcomers. But quite as peremptorily he called the project off, possibly fearing to leave New York vulnerable to Washington, possibly daunted by the numbers of militia and minute-men flocking to Rhode Island—or more possibly still, sceptical of the reliance he could put on the latest admiral of the fleet, Marriot Arbuthnot, seventy years old, ill and generally agreed (except by Lord Sandwich) to be utterly incompetent. The crusty admiral was not pleased by Clinton's vacillation: 'Sir Henry Clinton's amusing me with his troops in transports and aides-de-camp dancing backwards and forwards with reports of intelligence kept me in constant hope . . . till time slipped from under my feet and obliged me at last to retire'. Sooner or later, it was clear, one of the commanders would have to go (in the event, it was Arbuthnot).

Rodney arriving off Sandy Hook in September with ten warships from the West Indies was livid to find the attack abandoned. The French were permitted to remain in Newport unmolested. But until the promised squadron from France under de Grasse arrived, and restored the balance of power at sea, neither were they of any practical value to Washington. It must have seemed like yet another nail in the coffin of Franco-American co-operation when, on August 25, news arrived that de Grasse was himself under blockade in Brest and had no idea when he might be expected.

Count de Rochambeau. French General of the Land Forces in America Reviewing the French Troops. *Anon: Through Rochambeau the French and American forces were ultimately successful in co-ordinating their efforts (at Yorktown). This was due in large measure to the cordial relations between Washington himself and the French commander. Their arrival at Newport, however, was not at all so propitious. The reception party was late and the Count arrived to find 'no one in the streets; only a few sad and frightened faces in the windows' and was forced to stay the night at a local inn. Only the next day, when matters were sorted out, did Newport greet its welcome guests with bells and illuminations. This print bears the hand of the same artist who rejoiced in satirizing D'Estaing at Savannah (see page 137).*

The French Spy. *Colley: An English officer, with his Frenchified hair-do and decorated breeches, has been 'caught' by a bevy of English lasses and is forced to kneel for mercy. It took several more years of war with France for the influence of Paris fashion to lose its attraction for clothes conscious males.*

COUNT DE ROCHAMBEAU
25 Nov. 1780

French General of the Land Forces in America Reviewing the French Troops

The FRENCH SPY,
taken Prisoner by English Girls.

TREASON AT WEST POINT: ARNOLD AND ANDRÉ

While the armies of three nations lay dormant in the northern department through almost the entire campaign season of 1780, one man had been very hard at work indeed attempting to turn the tide of war in his own way. Since the spring General Benedict Arnold had been the commander of West Point, the patriot stronghold on the Hudson—a sedentary post for the energetic hero of Ticonderoga and Saratoga, but it was by way of being a favour from the one man who held Arnold's talents and integrity in high esteem, George Washington. For Arnold was no friend of Congress, which owed him vast expenses and appeared to value his undoubted achievements so meanly as to consistently pass him over for promotion in favour of lesser men. Nor, for that matter, was Congress a friend of his for it had upheld four of the eight charges of misconduct brought against him by the Council of Pennsylvania while Arnold had been governor of Philadelphia. A court martial had found him guilty of two of those charges, but let him off with a reprimand. Back on semi-active service (for he had a severe leg wound) he pleaded for..and obtained..what he had set his sights on, command of West Point.

He had his reasons for such a request. For more than a year he had been in secret correspondence with the English commander, with a view to defecting from the patriot cause which had failed to recognize his true qualities. His asking price, of course, was high. His debts were enormous, his socializing wife a constant drain on his diminishing resources, his family commitments alarming. Not unnaturally, Clinton wanted something more substantial for his money than a single general —say, the surrender of a corps of 5,000 to 6,000. West Point fitted the bill perfectly.

These negotiations spread over many months were conducted with all the trapping of high espionage: ciphered messages, invisible inks, a trusty courier, and as negotiator on the British side a discreet major by the name of John André, who had flirted with Arnold's future wife in those heady Philadelphia days of 1778. As Adjutant General of the forces, André was close enough to Clinton to be entrusted to a secret meeting with Arnold to arrange final details, on September 21. It would be a hazardous undertaking, since the meeting was to be behind American lines; but André with his enthusiasm for theatricals was game for the adventure. Everything seemed to go wrong for the unfortunate Major André; the protracted interview forced him to remain in the enemy's positions beyond daybreak, he was obliged to carry secret papers from Arnold (which his orders had expressly forbidden him to do), and the boat by which he was to make good his escape was bombarded and forced to retire without him aboard. As he made his way back through no-man's-land (where neither side was safe from predatory guerillas) he had the bad luck to fall in with a group of militia, who took a liking to his fine boots. Inside the boots were the secret papers.

That day Washington happened to be inspecting the fortifications at West Point. If he was shocked by the air of neglect about the place and puzzled by the non-appearance of Arnold, all was made disturbingly clear when that afternoon André's papers were disclosed to him. On the 26th the whole army heard in General Orders what had happened: 'Treason of the blackest dye was yesterday discovered. General Arnold, lost to every sentiment of honour, of public and private obligation, was about to deliver up that important post into the hands of the enemy.' Arnold was at that moment safe with his tarnished honour in British lines, where he ultimately received his £6,000 reward from King George, a commission in the army and the opportunity to ravage the homeland he had once so ardently defended. But André's fate was sealed. In Washington's book, he was a spy. Clinton pleaded for his favourite aide, but refused to exchange him for Arnold. André was hanged publicly on October 1.

Shaken by this treachery, the patriot army was destined to suffer further blows to its unity—if not its very existence—that winter. The habitual lack of clothing, food and shelter in winter quarters was heightened in January 1781 by the utter collapse of the Continental currency. 1,700 Pennsylvania troops mutinied and marched on Philadelphia to air their grievances in Congress. Clinton lost no time in offering to pay the mutineers in solid English guineas, if only they would march to New York. Instead, his intermediary was hanged and the mutineers accepted Congress's offer. There was to be more disaffection in the patriot ranks, especially among the New Jersey contingents, but the Continental army emerged into spring and the warmer weather more or less intact, if not entirely unscathed.

TOP RIGHT

Representation of Figures. *Anon: This engraving, published in the Pennsylvania Gazette in November 1780, shows how in his absence Benedict Arnold's two-faced effigy met with its traditional fate. Preceded by a lantern illuminating his crime and a figure of the Devil looming behind him, he was paraded through the streets of Philadelphia before being consigned to the flames. The caption describes how the event was attended 'with a numerous concourse of people, who after expressing their abhorrence of the Treason and the Traitor . . . left both the effigy and the original to sink into ashes and oblivion.' The original Arnold, after an initially courteous reception by the Court on his arrival in London in 1782, did indeed sink into oblivion (to be disturbed ten years later when the Earl of Laudedale unwittingly insulted Arnold in a speech and was called to satisfaction one Sunday morning).*

BOTTOM RIGHT

The Unfortunate Major André. *Anon: André, confronted by three militia men (not two as this print suggests), had mistaken their uniforms and identified himself as a British officer. Realizing his error he then produced a pass from General Arnold. He then attempted to barter for his release (here, he is seen offering his captors his watch—who are, it would seem, horrified and outraged at such venal approaches). It was probably as well for the Americans that they were deaf to his blandishments: they became heroes overnight and were awarded silver medals by Congress and generous pensions for life.*

THE UNITED PROVINCES: A QUESTION OF NEUTRALITY

At the end of 1780 Britain was obliged to add to her already imposing list of enemies yet another, one whose maritime interests had coincided with her own for more than a century. The United Provinces had been bound to Britain by friendly treaties since 1674, and by defensive alliance since 1716. The quarrel between the two countries stemmed from the different interpretations (and priority) they gave to these various treaties. Holland claimed the right to trade in enemy ports under the agreement of 1674; Britain resented Holland's failure to provide military assistance against her enemies, as had been arranged in 1716. Worse still, Holland's unrepentant trafficking with the French was making nonsense of one of Britain's strongest weapons—her naval blockade. When, at the end of 1779, the Dutch assigned convoys to her merchant shipping the state of uneasy intolerance flared abruptly into armed confrontation.

The Dutch were warned: curtail the trade with France, or no longer be regarded as allies but as neutrals (whose shipping Britain had long been searching with all the assurance of a nation to whom mastery of the seas was almost a birthright). No satisfactory reply having been received by April 17 the Royal Navy forthwith proceeded to subject the ships of the United Provinces to the same indignities as everyone else. But to declare Holland neutral, as the Ministry soon discovered, involved a delicate diplomatic problem. The root cause of this problem lay far away in the person of the Empress Catherine of Russia, who had devised a scheme for a League of Armed Neutrality to protect her own shipping from arbitrary arrest and search (not by Britain, ironically, but by Spain who had been impudent enough to seize two of her ships at the beginning of the year). Unless carrying contraband (to be defined by agreement) neutral ships, she declared, were to be given freedom of enemy ports. Sweden and Denmark had already joined (by the end of the war all the naval countries of Europe were to have followed their example) and if the United Provinces were also to join this would effectively put an end to the blockade or else, if Britain persisted in harassing Dutch trade, bring the fearful wrath of Moscow down on her head.

Clearly, since the Dutch had every intention of joining the League, there was no alternative but for the Ministry to declare war on them *before* they could conclude the terms of their entry. There were grounds enough to prove Holland's more than cordial relationship with the colonists. For one thing, she had offered harbour facilities to John Paul Jones. And, by a stroke of good fortune, the capture of Henry Laurens on the Atlantic had brought to light that negotiations of a sort were under way with Congress. On November 10 the British ambassador in Amsterdam demanded that the Dutch disown their American negotiations. On December 11 he demanded again, and received no satisfaction. On December 20 Britain declared war, in the nick of time. For the Empress Catherine, who had no taste for unnecessary fighting, was enabled to turn a deaf ear to Dutch entreaties that it was due to, and in violation of, their accession to the League.

The Dutch as enemies proved to be far less troublesome to Britain than the Dutch as allies; their tiny navy was helpless to prevent the arrest of dozens of their merchant ships in the years that followed. Through the unorthodox diplomacy of John Adams, however, the States-General was able to materially assist their new allies to the tune of five million guilders and with a commercial treaty (albeit one which they were powerless to put into effect).

TOP RIGHT

Jack England Fighting the Four Confederates. *Anon: This cartoon reflects what could, arguably, be described as the high point for the Ministry during the latter years of the war. Certainly Walpole was complaining at the turn of the year that the Government were more popular than the Opposition. In America the capture of Charleston and victory at Camden in 1780 seemed to indicate that perhaps the back of American resistance was broken, after all. Spanish islands were in peril all over the Caribbean; a French landing on Jersey had been beaten back by the determination of the island's small garrison. An additional war with the Dutch was highly popular, and little feared in any quarter.*

BOTTOM RIGHT

The Dutch in the Dumps. *Anon: No sympathy whatever was wasted on the Dutch by the cartoonists; they had been as unrelenting enemies to the French King as any Briton once upon a time. Now they could reap the harvest of their perfidy. On the declaration of war, a London newspaper claimed, the 'Change was more of a bustle than it had been in thirty years, but the Admiralty were brashly confident of recovering costs by the increase in prize-money.'*

1. Yanky Doodle   2 Monsieur Louis Baboon.   3 Don Diego   4 Mynheer Frog.   20 Jan. 1781

JACK ENGLAND Fighting the FOUR CONFEDERATES.

To Arms you Brave Britons to Arms the
Road to Renown Lyes before you.

Printed for Jn.° Smith N.°35 Cheapside, Rob.° Sayer & Jn.° Bennett N.° 53 Fleet Street, Jan.° 20: 1781

THE GENERAL ELECTION

The spring of 1780 blossomed and with it the Opposition's genuine expectations of ousting the Government. The success of Dunning's motion and the Ministry's disarray in the face of popular agitation for economies were but the first satisfying gulps at the fountain of power. But the Opposition had underestimated the Ministry's resilience; given a short and unexpected breathing-space by the Speaker's illness, the Government made full use of the recess to whip in its diffident support from all ends of the kingdom. The Opposition's majority dwindled and disappeared—with the help of circumstances which not even the most prescient among them could have foreseen. On June 15 the news of Clinton's capture of Charleston reached the capital, apparently justifying the strategy of the entire Southern campaign. In a bout of elation, Ministers even talked as if the end of the war was in sight.

Another event had occurred that month which was to hasten the reaction in favour of the Ministry. On June 2 a procession headed by the bigoted Lord George Gordon marched to Parliament to petition on behalf of the Protestant Association for repeal of the Catholic Relief Act of 1778. It got out of hand and for a full week the mob roamed through London pillaging anything which caught its fancy or offended its eye. Prisons and distilleries, Catholic chapels and ministerial mansions were indiscriminately looted in those seven days of anarchy. Politicians observed the collapse of law and order and pondered deeply on the undesirable results of undermining the established government. Even Lord Rockingham agreed to attend the Privy Council while it decided how to quash the violence.

Lord North emerged from his demoralized state and turned his thoughts to how he could best fortify his regime. Rockingham's co-operation over the riots encouraged him to believe the time was ripe for a coalition, and with the King's reluctant approval began the delicate negotiations. Rockingham's faction was indeed moving away from its uneasy alliance with Shelburne's, but it did not relish the idea of falling into the arms of Lord North on the rebound. Rockingham

was categorical on the question of American Independence; he also demanded that Fox and Richmond be appointed Secretaries of State. A coalition was therefore out of the question. But the King had another idea: 'As soon as we have hobbled through the next session' there must be a general election. Early in July North consulted his colleagues and, finding them enthusiastic, threw himself headlong into plans for a premature dissolution. Parliament had the best part of a year still to run and initial calculations seemed to show that the Ministry might lose a few marginal seats. On the other hand, the Opposition would be caught on the hop and the Ministry's stock was higher than anyone had dared hope at the beginning of the year.

Parliament was duly dissolved on September 1 to the 'exceeding vexation' of Rockingham, and the lobbying and electioneering got under way. The relatively high number of constituencies contested in the 1780 election (as opposed to being sold or donated to supporters) reflected the rapid growth of the parliamentary opposition as a political force; five years of war had divided the House into two clear-cut 'parties' and provided an over-riding national issue for the hustings. The unprecedented expenditure from the King's 'election fund' (well in excess of £60,000) equally reflected the Ministry's strenuous efforts to invalidate all the Opposition's high-minded talk of political corruption. Whether or not Lord North considered he got his £60,000 worth, the returns for the new session showed the Ministry had failed in its primary objective —to strengthen its hand in the Commons. On paper, in fact, it was possible its majority had been reduced to a dangerous level. That such was not the case emerged from the early divisions of February 1781 which the government carried with its old familiar majorities. Even its conduct of the war seemed to have regained a measure of approval when Fox's motion for an inquiry was soundly defeated.

The Virtuous and Inspired State of Whigism in Bristol. *Anon: In the port of Bristol, with its flourishing and lucrative trans-Atlantic trade, the American question played a greater part in local politics than almost anywhere else in the country. In the 1774 election two uncompromising opponents of the war had been returned: Edmund Burke, himself a colonial agent, and Henry Cruger, born and educated in America and therefore one of the small handful of MPs who had any first-hand knowledge of the colonies. The local factions in Bristol were focused on two political clubs, the Standfast Society (which in general followed the ministerial line) and the Union Club (the Whigs' headquarters). During the course of the last Parliament, however, Burke and Cruger had fallen out, with the result that the Union Club entered the lists in 1780 in disarray. Burke eventually quit the contest and Cruger found himself without the support of a number of influential officials. The Tories capitalized on their opponents' wranglings and regained both seats. But that was not the end of it. Sir Henry Lippincott, one of the new members died almost immediately and a by-election was held in February 1781. This print portrays Cruger's renewed attempts to win back his seat against the new candidate, George Daubeny. Proclaiming American Independence Cruger is drawn in state by two supporters who trample the scales of justice and the crown into the dust. His carriage is attended by a devil and a patriot astride a garlanded bull; citizens of Bristol watch the parade affirming their support or opposition to 'Croker'. In the foreground a party official and a parson have reduced the political debate to the level of personal abuse.*

Liberty Enlightened. *Anon: By February 20 both candidates were neck and neck; then Daubeny began edging ahead. Here the collapsing Cruger is being supported by his father-in-law Samuel Peach, a noted slave-trader. A fiddler is trying to rouse his spirits with a ditty about the days of Oliver Cromwell, while (left) a group of Americans mourn the loss of one of their staunchest allies at Westminster. The pile of rope addressed 'to Congress' in the foreground is intended to imply that Cruger had been exporting stores to the Americans. Daubeny's flag flying from the church tower recalls that Cruger, in the previous election, was supposed to have flown the American flag on public buildings.*

PROFIT AND LOSS IN THE WEST INDIES

To the merchants of the City the most disturbing aspect of French participation in the war was not the renewed impetus given to the patriot armies, but the threat to their incalculable West Indian trade, the ever-present menace to their priceless convoys of sugar, rum and cotton. Nearly two years of skirmishing in the Caribbean had confirmed their worst fears; since the summer of 1778 three British possessions, Dominica, St. Vincent and Grenada, had fallen to the French, with only Barrington's capture of St. Lucia to chalk up on the credit side. Once the French had forfeited their chance of striking at Britain's heart by direct invasion, it was clear to any English sailor (even the Admiralty) she would now attempt to strike at her stomach by conquest in the West Indies. Which they did without delay, posting off a strong squadron under Comte de Guichen thither at the beginning of February. He reached Martinique only days before Rodney with his squadron put in at St. Lucia.

With Rodney, the victor of Cape St. Vincent, went his country's highest expectations (and £2,000 p.a. for life). The admiral immediately set about proving himself worthy of both his popularity and his pension by bearing down on the French fleet as it stole out of Martinique on April 17 with every intention of attacking Barbados. It seemed certain the French centre would crumble under this concerted attack, had not fellow admirals (Parker and Rowley) misinterpreted the signals from the flagship and dispersed their ships in fruitless pursuit. They had snatched an inconclusive result from the jaws of certain victory. Hopping mad, Rodney penned furious letters to Lord Sandwich about such 'barefaced disobedience to orders and signals' but, much to the First Lord's relief, did not press for a court martial. The remainder of the season was squandered in a leisurely game of hide-and-seek between the two fleets, at the conclusion of which the balance sheet recorded no ships sunk or captured, no islands lost or gained by either side.

Even the rapture which greeted the news of Rodney's capture of the Dutch island of St. Eustatius on February 3 was prematurely snuffed out when the convoy bringing home the first instalment of the booty (estimated at a million pounds) was seized by the French in virtually English waters. The island itself was of some importance to Britain, for under the flag of Dutch neutrality it had served as a major supply-base for the Americans. But any temporary advantage its capture may have provided was cancelled out in April by Rodney's failure to reach Tobago in time to prevent its capitulation to de Grasse. This was a disaster of the highest order; for while the commanders in the West Indies might denounce the enthusiasm of its inhabitants ('being highly indebted to the merchants at home') to succumb to the enemy, in Britain nearly 20,000 cotton-workers of Lancashire suffered greatly as the principal source of their raw material dried up. Public opinion grew even more resentful when it was learned that de Grasse's arrival in the West Indies might have been prevented in the first place but for an inept piece of manoeuvring by Rodney off Martinique. That admiral's first tour of duty in the Caribbean had done little to enhance his reputation; he soon retired to England to recover his spirits and his health, leaving Hood to cope with de Grasse as best he could. He chose to sail in a ship of the line, one which events demonstrated the fleet in America could ill-afford to lose.

TOP RIGHT

The Late Auction at St. Eustatia. *Anon: In spite of Rodney's acclaim for his successes, as a ministerial supporter he qualified for the unstinted abuse of the Opposition, especially in connection with his treatment of the inhabitants of St. Eustatius. These had included Englishmen whose property he had seized and put up for auction, along with that of other nationalities. Rodney's defence is contained in a letter (March 1781) to Germain: 'Except for supplies from the island and from British subjects there, who meanly condescended to become Dutch burghers (and as such they shall be treated) the American Revolution had long been at an end'. In May Burke had demanded an inquiry into the affair, and Rodney himself was for a long time to come plagued with lengthy lawsuits arising out of his seizure of English goods. In this hostile print he is depicted as an auctioneer (top right), the army-commander General Vaughan as his clerk. A truly cosmopolitan assembly (French, Dutch, Spanish) is bidding for the confiscated goods; cap in hand an Englishman pleads to be allowed to buy back his property and export it. Another Briton (centre) is suggesting that if Rodney had not lingered so long on the island the French reinforcements would not have slipped past him at Martinique.*

BOTTOM RIGHT

The Coffee-House Patriots: or News from St. Eustatia. *Bunbury: The report of Rodney's capture of the Dutch island is being greeted with anything but rapture by the merchants in this print (published belatedly in October 1781). It was widely rumoured that some merchants were using St. Eustatius themselves as an entrepôt for trading with the enemy.*

CHARLESTON TO GUILFORD COURTHOUSE

In spite of the striking successes at Savannah in the fall of 1779, it was with no great enthusiasm that Clinton was persuaded to escalate the war in the south the following year, in deference to the American Secretary's nagging dispatches. Added to Lord George's silvery prose there were the equally insistent entreaties of his second-in-command. Lord Cornwallis had returned to New York the previous summer (armed with a dormant commission to succeed Clinton whenever word came from London) and was finding the lassitude of life at headquarters not to his taste. So at the end of 1779 Clinton gave in and set sail southwards with more than 7,000 troops. He arrived at the mouth of the Savannah river a whole month later having lost all his horses at sea and one transport full of Hessians (which later turned up in England). By February 11 the army was within striking distance of Charleston, which Lincoln's patriots were stubbornly preparing to defend to the bitter end.

Doubtless remembering his earlier débâcle against this city (see page 82) Clinton approached the siege with exemplary method. Over two months he inexorably cut off all escape routes from the city by land or sea, except that to the north protected by General Huger's cavalry. Before dawn on April 14 even this life-line was abruptly severed by the bayonets of Banastre Tarleton's British Legion, a loyalist unit which was to become notorious for exacting more than its pound of flesh. On the night of May 9 the British opened up an artillery barrage, which however much it looked to General Moultrie 'as if the stars were tumbling down' demolished all the terrestrial resolve in the inhabitants (who the day before had pleaded with Lincoln not to evacuate). On May 12 the Continental troops marched out to the tune of the 'Turk's March' and laid down their arms. A relief force of 350 Virginia Continentals, which turned about on hearing news of the fall of Charleston, was not so lucky. Tarleton pursued them to the North Carolina border, overtook them and bayoneted them till (and long after) they cried for quarter; at the cost

of five men, he killed or mutilated more than 250 and extinguished any spark of loyalism in an entire province, in the space of fifteen minutes.

The consequences of this took rather longer to show. When Clinton left for New York, he handed over command in the South to Cornwallis together with the ambiguous discretionary kind of orders which had become a feature of the British command: he was to consolidate and defend; on the other hand he could also attack, as far north as Virginia if he liked. He chose, predictably, to attack and when he did so it was in the belief that the locals were 'most sincerely happy at returning to their union with Great Britain'. The Carolinians behind Sumter and Marion and Pickens were to prove him disastrously wrong.

To replace the captured Lincoln it had pleased Congress (but not Washington) to appoint Gates to command in the south. He determined to check Cornwallis's proposed northwards offensive by attacking the British garrison at Camden in South Carolina. For nearly three weeks he drove his men on through country which for food offered little more than green corn and unripe peaches. It was a bizarre decision, therefore, on the eve of attacking to issue to men who had marched so far on bilious stomachs a ration of beef, bread and molasses mixed with mush—which speciality according to the deputy adjutant-general 'operated so cathartically as to disorder very many of the men, who were breaking ranks all night'.

A far worse emetic turned out, the next morning (August 16), to be Lord Cornwallis who had arrived from nowhere and sallied forth to meet the Americans. So precipitous was the flight of the Virginia militia that it carried the commander with them, leaving Baron de Kalb and the Continentals to hold their ground as best they could. By the end of the day the patriot army was broken and scattered; it had lost 600 men including de Kalb and—so far as reputation went—Gates himself. He had exchanged the laurels of the north for the willows of the south, as Lee had sourly predicted he would.

Egged on by the American Secretary ('I make no doubt but your Lordship will by this time, have had

the honour to recover the province of North Carolina to his Majesty') Cornwallis plunged northwards, undeterred by setbacks. At King's Mountain on October 7 a precious corps of 1,200 loyalists under Major Patrick Ferguson was destroyed by patriot frontiersmen. Taking his position on the level summit of the mountain Ferguson had declared that 'God Almighty could not drive him from it'. But whatever deficiency he had detected in the Divine, he did not encounter it in the unorthodox tactics of these veteran Indian fighters. In the most decisive encounter of the war between purely partisan forces, bitterness ran high: at the critical point of the battle Ferguson himself rode about hacking down any white flags his men had dared to raise; the patriots for their part had to be restrained later from their 'disorderly manner of slaughtering and disturbing the prisoners'. That day, the tories who escaped to fight on for His Majesty were not worth counting.

On January 17 Tarleton was meted out some of his own punishment at the hands of Daniel Morgan's riflemen. The 'butcher' had been ordered west by Cornwallis to put an end to Morgan's favourite sport of flushing out Tories, and had set off in lightning pursuit. He tracked them down at the Cowpens in South Carolina where he met not only the deadly rifle-fire he had expected, but also the exuberance of Colonel Washington's dragoons. Tarleton himself escaped, but half his army was left behind on the battlefield and so was his ferocious reputation, dented irreparably.

The Thunderer. *Gillray: The flamboyant and reckless Captain Tarleton, still no more than twenty-eight when he returned to England from the American War (after which this print was published, August 1782) made a very fitting companion for the impressionable Prince of Wales—not yet twenty-one he had appalled his father by his staggering gambling and other debts (said to be nearly £30,000).*

THE ROAD TO YORKTOWN

By the spring of 1781 Lord Cornwallis had grown, he said, 'quite tired of marching about the country in search of adventure'. Even his victories were turning out to be as expensive as his defeats. Another victory such as that at Guilford Courthouse, as Fox remarked when shown the casualty lists, would ruin the British army. That confrontation on March 15 with the main Continental army in the south (though only one man in seven was a regular) was to have been the decisive hammer-blow which would crack Virginia like a nut. Indeed in one sense it was 'the compleat victory' Cornwallis claimed it to be. Had he not pitted his 2,000 veterans against more than twice their number under Nathanael Greene? And the enemy had withdrawn from the field. But they had not withdrawn far and Greene (as he was to demonstrate time and again over the next eighteen months) had the happy knack of being beaten, to his own advantage. 'We fight, get beat, rise, and fight again,' as he it put himself.

By the book, Cornwallis should have pursued Greene when he marched south to harass the British outposts in South Carolina. But he had not abandoned his designs on Virginia, where he knew there was already a small predatory force in action under Benedict Arnold and another grudgingly sent on its way there by Clinton. The commander-in-chief warned against an expedition into Virginia: 'there is no possibility of restoring Order in any rebellious Province on this Continent,' he wrote to Cornwallis, 'without the hearty Assistance of numerous Friends. These, my Lord, I think are not to be found in Virginia.' Even Cornwallis was beginning to grow aware that 'their friendship is only passive'—a conclusion borne out by the Tories who, after Guilford Courthouse, rode into the British camp to offer their congratulations and rode straight home again. But His Lordship marched on to Virginia and his nemesis.

In South Carolina, on the other hand, patriots were flocking to Greene in almost embarrassing numbers; he preferred to have horses for his regulars who ranged the province with devastating effect. True to form, Greene won no battles but in defeat watched the tide of war turn ineluctably in his favour. At Camden he was successfully opposed by Lord Rawdon; yet within the fortnight his army was marching triumphantly through the streets of the town, as the British prudently retreated to the coast. At the fort enigmatically called Ninety-Six he was obliged to curtail his siege operations once again by the timely intervention of Rawdon. But the British had marched 240 miles through 'the antechamber of hell', saw the fort could not hold out indefinitely and, to Greene's amazement, marched back again. Ninety-Six was his. At Eutaw Springs on September 8 he attacked a British army under Colonel Stuart on equal terms, and was forced to retire; but not before 800 redcoats had fallen or surrendered in the carnage. The Royal army had no alternative but to retrace its steps to Charleston—whence it was not to emerge again for the remainder of the war.

For the end of the war was getting nearer with every step Cornwallis took deeper into Virginia. It was true he had augmented his army to more than 7,000 men by absorbing Arnold's force and other reinforcements. It was also true he had had some successes; he'd captured a supply depot and a few tobacco warehouses, and even put the Virginia legislature to flight at Charlottesville. But he needed a base, against the Americans who were massing under the restless Lafayette. He decided upon Yorktown, where throughout August his men dug themselves in. And as they dug, the American rattlesnake began tightening his coils around them.

TOP RIGHT

The American Rattlesnake. *Gillray: This serpent is a very much more formidable reptile than the disjointed specimen which first appeared during the internal dissentions of the war with the French. It had already 'burgoyn'd' one British army, now looked like having done the same to another—and still had 'space to let'.*

BOTTOM FAR RIGHT

Le general Cornwallis a Yorck. *Anon: The parallel between Yorktown and Saratoga was too obvious for cartoonists to avoid. This French print is the sequel to one celebrating the surrender of Burgoyne (see page 101), both of them published after the British capitulation at Yorkstown.*

BOTTOM NEAR RIGHT

Le Lord Cornwallis. *Anon: Subtitled 'leaving Carolina having been kept there a long time' this French caricature (bearing not the slightest resemblance) is one of the very few prints in which Cornwallis makes an appearance. During his long service in America he is entirely absent from British cartoons—perhaps it was his misfortune (or good luck) to have been most active at a time when the vitriol of the cartoonists was being directed into more domestic channels.*

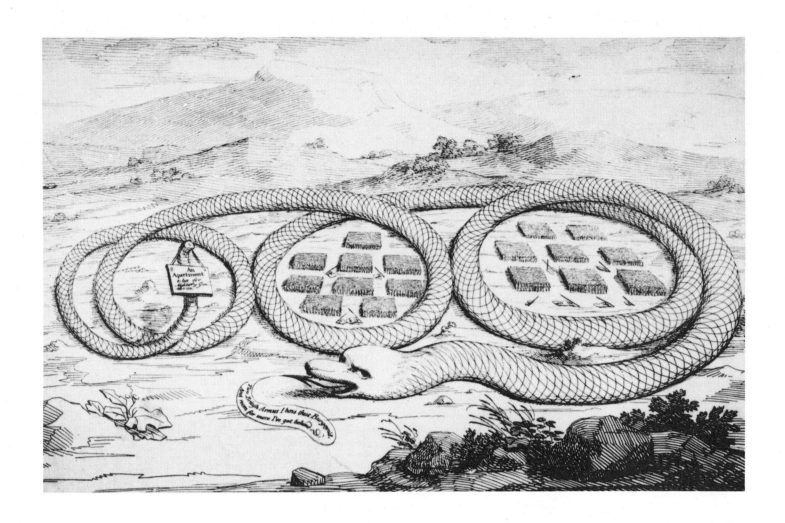

Le Lord Cornwallis
fortant des Carolines après y avoir
été Longtems Reisser.

YORKTOWN: THE LAST SURRENDER

The spring of this fateful year had found Washington and Rochambeau actively planning their first combined land operation of the war. The news that De Grasse's fleet had safely reached the West Indies and would be available to them by summer encouraged both generals to set their sights high: on the capture of New York, no less, without possession of which not even Lord George Germain would consider continuing the war. But as Cornwallis's predicament became hearteningly apparent—and when De Grasse announced he was bound, not for Newport, but for the Chesapeake—Rochambeau persuaded Washington to throw the whole weight of the alliance against Yorktown. A formidable weight it was to be, too, arrayed against Cornwallis's attenuated defences: 7,000 Frenchmen, 5,500 Continentals and 3,500 Virginia militia spoiling for a fight on their home ground.

August gave way to September and Cornwallis on his sandy outcrop over the York river and his 'few acres of unhealthy swamp' learnt of the inexorable build-up all around him. He learnt of the arrival of the French fleet at Chesapeake Bay, and of the reinforcements to Lafayette's army and correctly concluded he was trapped. To the north or south the only escape by land had always been through hundreds of miles of friendless country; his only hope was the sea. He wrote to Clinton: 'If you cannot relieve me very soon you must be prepared to hear the worst.' There were several reasons why Clinton had not yet come to his rescue nor entertained the imminent prospect of doing so. For one thing he firmly believed that Washington intended to attack New York (and had an intercepted letter from him to Lafayette to prove it). For another, the flower of the British fleet was hove to in New York harbour repairing itself after an inglorious skirmish with De Grasse on September 5. Sir Thomas Graves was a better admiral than Arbuthnot (whom he had replaced) but not sufficiently so to take on overwhelming odds. The sooner Cornwallis begged Clinton to come, the longer Clinton told him to hang on, for there was no option.

On October 9 the besieging artillery opened up a devastating fire which precluded virtually any retaliation. Sickness galloped through the throttled British lines. A brave sortie into the French trenches and a despairing expedition across the York river served only to demonstrate how futile their situation was. On October 17 Cornwallis raised the white flag, the very same day that Clinton and the fleet set sail from New York on their fruitless errand of mercy. Cornwallis asked for terms already familiar: that his men should be permitted to return to England under pledge never to serve again for the duration of the war. But Washington had in mind the realities of Charleston rather than the courtesies of Saratoga. It was to be complete surrender, with no misunderstandings this time.

TOP RIGHT

Yorktown. *Anon: A Dutch view of the British surrender. Beneath a blistering Virginia sun America (her shackles broken at her feet) receives the capitulation of Cornwallis (and Bute). Blindfolded Justice is there to see fair play—and so is a boatload of armed Frenchmen. An Indian puts the finishing touches to cargoes bound for Cadiz, Nantes and Marseilles— America's trade with Europe which can now flourish once more. On the near bank, the British coffer is empty; only the money-bags remain for the mice to nibble. This print has many features in common with an English satire of 1778 (see page 109) which had been copied and recopied many times in Holland—probably because it had been relatively kind to the Dutch. The English cow remains a symbol of her starved commerce; Spain, France and Holland continue to carry off her milk (in defence to his new allies, the Dutch artist has erected an altar to Spain's new-world conquests). The frock-coated Englishman no longer beats his breast in fury, however—he is now a supplicant, and the British lion has awoken from its slumbers only to beg and to wail. Even the magnificent British warship (The Eagle) has foundered.*

BOTTOM RIGHT

America Triumphant and Britannia in Distress. *Anon: This emblematic print appeared as the frontispiece to the Weatherwise Almanac of 1782. An accompanying key explains that America sporting the cap of liberty (1) is now firmly ensconced on her own quarter of the globe and, extending the olive branch, invites the shipping of all nations (5) to partake of her commerce. Fame (2) proclaims the joyful news to all the world, while Britannia (3) and her evil genius weep for her lost trade. Also to be noted is the British flag (4) toppled from her fortress, and (6) New York 'wherein is exhibited the Traitor Arnold, taken with remorse for selling his country and judas-like hanging himself'.*

AMERICA TRIUMPHANT and BRITANNIA in DISTRESS

THE REPERCUSSIONS OF YORKTOWN

'Oh God!' exclaimed Lord North when confirmation of Cornwallis's surrender reached him on November 25. 'It is all over!' Sure enough, in America the long agony *was* over. Tarleton and his troops at Gloucester had also laid down their arms; the garrisons at New York and Charleston made no further contribution to the war (except as bargaining counters). But in London North's final agony was only just beginning. In two days' time the new session of Parliament would open, giving no time for a re-assessment of policy. The one small grain of comfort was that the Opposition would also be unprepared to muster its forces. Individual opponents raised the first gusts of the gale that was to descend after Christmas: Fox was soon at full steam, wondering where the ministers intended to fix the blame this time. 'Anywhere but in the right place,' he concluded, 'but on their own weakness, obstinacy, inhumanity or treason.'

But the most immediate danger to the Ministry came, ironically, from the King and from within the ministerial ranks. The King obstinately and truculently refused to face the facts. 'I have no doubt,' he wrote to North on the 28th, 'when men are a little recovered of the shock felt by the bad news . . . they will then find the necessity of carrying on the war, though the mode of it may require alterations.' That was, as North knew only too well, a disastrous misjudgement of the temper of the House. Already there were once staunch and faithful colleagues talking of defection. Henry Dundas, the Lord Advocate (with a significant Scottish following) and Richard Rigby (himself not without influence among the old Bedford followers) were quite specific about the urgent need to recognize that Britain had been beaten in America; an opinion not very different from Lord North's own—though his loyalty to his King forbade him to articulate it. Dundas, however, was firmly of the view that the continuance of the ministry demanded 'a human sacrifice'.

Two candidates presented themselves: Lords Sandwich and Germain, the ministers whose fortunes were inextricably tied to the success or failure of British arms. In the event, the axe was to fall on Germain, for he alone, in splendid isolation on the government front benches, urged a prosecution of the war and took everything the Opposition could hurl at him. He would *not* resign nor would he ever be 'the minister to sign any instrument which gave independence to America'. But on January 22 Dundas and Rigby presented their ultimatum; they announced they would cease to attend Parliament so long as Germain remained in office—and walked out. By the end of the month the American Secretary was out, but the price of his resignation had been a peerage—and no common-or-garden peerage at that, but an elevation to Viscount. This suited the King who, having more regard for Lord George's policies than his person, did not wish his own position to be weakened by a humiliating dismissal of his only visible ally. It did not suit a good many members of the House of Lords, however, one of whom resented having 'the greatest criminal this country has ever known' in their midst. That the new Viscount took this on the chin instead of reaching for his duelling-pistols showed, perhaps, that even he in his heart was as weary of fighting as anyone else.

TOP RIGHT

John Bull's Alternative. *Anon: To some people at this critical moment, it must indeed have seemed that the only alternative to self-destruction would be to accept handouts from the French (right)—in this case a leek, a most insulting vegetable. This print is of further interest in that it contains the first unequivocal portrayal of an Englishman as John Bull, an archetype which was to increase in significance considerably during the Napoleonic Wars.*

BOTTOM RIGHT

State Cooks, or The Downfall of the Fish Kettle. *Anon: The chefs in question, The King (left) and Lord North, have spilled their kettle full of fish (by the defeat at Yorktown, news of which arrived a fortnight before this print was published). But the artist displays as much insight into the mood of Lord North as he does acquaintance with the geography of America. Far from wishing to 'cook them yet', North desired nothing more than to conclude the war at the earliest honourable moment. Thirteen colonies have tumbled out of the vessel, but they inexplicably (or ignorantly) include the Floridas, Quebec and Nova Scotia. The New England provinces have been lumped together and Delaware is missing entirely.*

L—or—d Am—hers—t on Duty.

If I had Power,
I'd kill 20 in an Hour.

CHAPTER

6

THE STRUGGLE
FOR PEACE

From Yorktown to the
Peace of Versailles

1781-1783

The war in America was over, but peace was a long time coming. The King still could not believe the colonists had won, but his puppet ministry was on the verge of collapse and without it there was no hope of continuing the war. Lord North soldiered on until March 1782, but on the 19th succumbed to the will of Parliament —or at least of the country gentlemen whose defection had left him in a minority. A Whig coalition took over (much to the King's disgust) bent on concluding as fast a peace as possible, even it seemed at the complete sacrifice of every principle for which the country had been at war for seven years. Yet the new ministry, too, was divided on the question: Fox wished to recognize the independence of the colonists before negotiating a treaty, Shelburne did not. Both men had negotiators at Paris but before much had been accomplished these dissentions were exposed by an unforeseen occurrence. In July the nominal head of the coalition, the Marquess of Rockingham, died. When Shelburne was asked to form an administration, Fox resigned in protest and by the end of the year was conspiring with, of all people, his old enemy North to return to power.

Meanwhile the negotiators in Paris were making heavy weather of the peace treaty. From the start it was clear that in peace the allies had by no means the same unanimity of purpose they had had in war. Indeed until April 1782, when Admiral Rodney resoundingly defeated the French fleet in the West Indies, the French continued hostilities; and until October, when Lord Howe came to its relief, the Spaniards continued to invest Gibraltar. Neither of the Bourbon monarchs wished to see their republican ally wax rich and strong across the Atlantic, Spain in particular who attempted to extend its territories in America to the detriment of the colonists. The American negotiators in Paris, Franklin, Adams and Jay, were not oblivious to all this and by no means inadequate to the subtleties of European diplomacy. They allowed—in contravention of the terms of the alliance—a separate treaty to be drawn up, which ultimately benefited both Britain and her ex-colonies. The Americans' independence was duly recognized and her boundaries to the west defined. Spain regained the Floridas and Minorca, but not what it really wanted, Gibraltar. France won back a few West Indian islands, but at a cost which six years later was to prove prohibitive.

All this diplomatic toing and froing, as well as the attendant ministerial ins and outs, were watched with rabid interest by the cartoonists. With the advent of the Rockingham coalition it had been predicted in the press that this would be the ruin of the print-sellers; there would be nothing to satirize. It proved otherwise. Rodney's victory at the Saints, and the Ministry's treatment of him, was manna from heaven for the cartoonists. Shelburne, inevitably, was castigated for the terms of the peace and Fox, unknown to him at the time, was about to be subjected to one of the most sustained barrages of personal abuse in the annals of graphic satire. Only Rockingham, safe in his nonentity, escaped attack as he always had. Indeed, far from showing any signs of degeneration, the cartoon profession entered into a new and glorious era which the tensions of the American war had done much to generate. By 1784 not only had Gillray entered the field, but so had Thomas Rowlandson, James Sayers and Isaac Cruikshank. When the next war came, against the formidable armies of Napoleon, the cartoonists were ready for it.

THE FALL OF LORD NORTH

If, by the jettisoning of Lord George Germain, the Ministry had appeased its most virulent critics within its own ranks, there still remained the full weight of the Opposition to contend with. In the first two months of the new session, no less than six major assaults on the government were made, the cumulative effect of which was to consolidate the Opposition and to erode the Ministry's majority to the point where all further resistance was useless. In the first half of February the target was the conduct in recent months of the Admiralty (since Germain's departure the most vulnerable link in the government's chain). Lord Sandwich prepared himself for almost anything, but not for Charles Fox who spiked the First Lord's guns immediately by concentrating only on the failure to prevent De Grasse from reaching the West Indies, the loss of the St. Eustatius convoy and the mismanagement of the war against the Dutch. Sandwich won the round by the skin of his teeth (236–217), and more by the energy with which he rounded up all possible support than by the virtues of his administration.

The results of the naval inquiry were a sombre warning to the Ministry of things to come. The next phase of the Opposition's campaign was an attack on the government's policy in general. Here the Ministry was most seriously handicapped by the King's intransigence which it dared not reflect too obviously and, on the other hand, by the necessity not to prejudice any possible peace negotiations by presenting too weak a front. On February 27 General Conway moved 'that it is the opinion of this House that the further prosecution of offensive warfare on the continent of North America . . . will be the means of weakening the efforts of this country against her European enemies . . . (and will) frustrate the earnest desire graciously expressed by His Majesty to restore the blessings of public tranquillity'. That this was by no means an accurate interpretation of His Majesty's earnest desire did not prevent the motion being carried by nineteen votes . . . it was a fair representation of the House's desire and

signalled the imminent collapse of Lord North's ministry.

The King had been toying for some time with the idea of abdication, but sheer defeat was the one thing guaranteed to snap him out of it. When he heard that North had given up the ghost he wrote: 'I am mortified Lord North thinks he cannot now remain in office; I hope I shall see him after the Drawing Room that I may explain my mind to him'. His explanation was that North should now sound out the Lords Gower and Weymouth, even Shelburne, to form a coalition and recover the lost votes. North agreed to try; but none of these ideas proved feasible and the Ministry stumbled on into March 'convinced that . . . it would not go on'. In fact, on the two motions of no confidence on March 8 and 15 it won marginal majorities, thanks to those country gentlemen who disapproved of the war but could not conceive of anyone better than Lord North. Yet the Ministry was unable to get a better majority than nine, and North appealing to the King by pointing out that 'his Royal predecessors were obliged to yield to it (Parliament) much against their wish in more instances than one' overcame his resistance to a change in government. Even so North contrived to make an honourable exit only by a matter of hours: on March 20 he rose in the House to offer his resignation. He was beaten to the standing position by the Earl of Surrey who was proposing to move for the removal of the ministers. Only by the blindness of the Speaker in one eye and after an hour's debate was North allowed to resign rather than be voted ignominiously out of office.

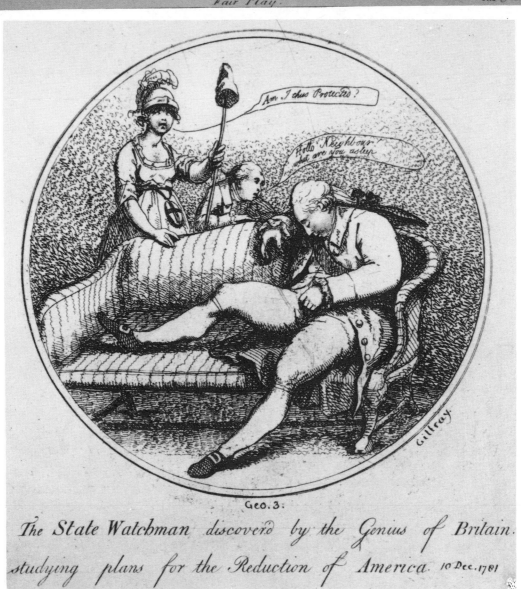

THE FALL OF LORD NORTH (continued)

TOP RIGHT

The Royal Hunt, or a Prospect of the Year 1782 after Townshend: This print (published February 16) was accorded a profound political influence by the Morning Herald, which alleged that it had been shown to the King by the Prince of Wales and had persuaded him to dismiss the Ministry. This inflated claim is not to be taken too seriously, but it nevertheless is a very concise summing-up of the state of the parties at the turn of the year. On the left Lord North and Sandwich are carousing in the company of wanton ladies. Immediately behind them stand their outraged supporters, Germain (now out of office), Amherst and Rigby. Four opposition members, Pitt, Richmond, Burke and Fox try to divert their attention to the tottering condition of Britain's Temple of Fame. The enemy are tugging away at Gibraltar, one of its last remaining props; Britannia weeps in despair. Inscribed on the temple are memorials to George II and Britain's conquests in his reign.

BOTTOM RIGHT

Anticipation; or the Contrast to the Royal Hunt after Townshend: This sequel of May 16 presents a much more hopeful (though very premature) picture of the Empire under the new Ministry. The King (left) has abandoned his hunting, his horses are up for sale, his eyes cleared of the film which had clouded them. The old ministers are reduced to harmless pursuits like washing (North, front left) and catch-singing (Sandwich centre). The Temple of Fame now occupied by Fox, Burke and Camden is being restored (the artist still seems to imagine that Rhode Island is in the West Indies). Rodney's ships thunder into action; Britain's enemies flee and Britannia graciously holds out the olive branch.

THIS PAGE

The Knave of Hearts. Anon: On the eve of his elevation to a ministry, this print provides a characteristic portrayal of Charles Fox, as a gambler (his faro bank at Brooks's Club was highly successful), as a radical by design (his cap and staff of liberty have bells on) and a despiser of sinecures by necessity.

THE KNAVE OF HEARTS.
Publish'd as the Act directs Feb.ʸ 1782. Price 6.ᴰ

THE OPPOSITION IN POWER

Up to the very last minute the King was adamant that what he called his 'sentiments of honour' would not permit him to treat personally with the leaders of the Opposition—by which he meant Fox and Lord Rockingham. He condescended to receive Shelburne, whose Chathamites would be essential to any new Ministry that was not based on the Court, and an arrangement was duly come to, unpalatable though it was. Rockingham was to move into the Treasury, Fox and Shelburne would be Secretaries of State, with the rest of the Coalition reading like a roll-call of American champions including Burke, Conway, Keppel, Camden, Richmond, Barré, Dunning, Grafton; the one exception was Thurlow who remained as Chancellor at the King's insistence. So when Lord North and his ex-ministers trooped into St. James's Palace on March 27 to hand over their Seals of Office, no one could have been in the least doubt that peace was round the corner.

Throughout the ministerial crisis the King's views on the war had not wavered an inch. He would have continued to wage it down to the last drop of British blood and the last pinch of gunpowder. But over these he no longer had any control; the thought plunged him into a fit of despair more reminiscent of his late Premier. 'His Majesty is convinced that the sudden change of sentiments of one branch of the legislature' (so ran a message of abdication he drafted that March but never made public) 'has totally incapacitated him from either conducting the war with effect, or from obtaining any peace but on conditions which would prove destructive to the commerce as well as the essential rights of the British nation.' Secretary Fox entertained no such inhibitions and immediately sent an emissary to Paris to bargain for peace on terms which were a little too impetuous for Secretary Shelburne's taste, who also sent a representative to negotiate. In America the war was all over bar the shouting; Clinton had been replaced by Carleton, whose orders were to do no more than defend himself if attacked. Even this proved unnecessary for before Washington was in a position to attack either New York or Charleston it had become clear that Britain had no wish to cling on to these two fragments of Empire.

With almost no resistance from Parliament the new Ministry proceeded to demolish the superstructure of sinecures which had sustained the former incumbents in office—though perhaps with not quite the conviction with which it had denounced them in Opposition. Mr. Burke's Bill for the Suppression of sundry Useless, Expensive and Inconvenient Offices, as well as one or two others, had time to get on the Statute book before tragedy struck. On July 1 Lord Rockingham died—not a consummate statesman in his own right, but the buffer in the Ministry between the divergent policies of Fox and Shelburne. At once the divisions within the brand-new ministry were exposed. The King offered the premiership to Shelburne, and five days later Fox resigned in high dudgeon taking with him one or two lesser ministers —but the vacuum was more than filled by the debut of William Pitt who, with all the experience of his twenty-two years, having declined a minor office under Rockingham, now submitted to accept the post of Chancellor of the Exchequer. The King was delighted to see the back of Fox, even when he heard that he was to put forward a motion for unconditional surrender. 'Common sense tells me that if unconditional independence is granted,' he informed Lord Shelburne, 'we cannot ever expect any understanding with America, for then we have given up the whole and have nothing to give.' Fox could do what he liked in Parliament, so long as he wasn't negotiating with the Americans.

TOP RIGHT
The Reconciliation between Britannia and her daugher America. *Anon: Fox, right (known generally as Mr. Fox rather than as plain Charles since his assumption of the responsibilities of office) has cast aside the cards and dice and applies himself to the efforts of Spain and France (left) to disengage America from her filial overtures to Britain. He calls on his First Lord of the Admiralty, Keppel (far right) to give 'that Frenchman and his cousin Don . . . a spank'. They were soon to get that spanking from Rodney (see page 172), though the* new ministry were to gain little credit from it. Holland phlegmatically smokes his pipe (far left) waiting to see who emerges from the 'negotiations' best.*

BOTTOM RIGHT
The Captive Prince—or—Liberty run Mad. *Anon: The unhappy King and his new Ministry: Fox and Cavendish shackle his feet; the other senior members are rather more absorbed in their own preoccupations. Left to right: Burke composes a laudatory address to his reluctant patron, Conway wallows in a conflict of loyalties, Keppel and Richmond glory in their new commands. Rockingham, having purloined the crown, is about to 'dispose of these jewels for the Public Use'. George III's comment on these dangerously democratic proceedings ('Oh, my misguided People!') underlines that for the first time in his reign, here was a government come to power through the spontaneous pressure of public opinion rather than through the choice of the sovereign.*

The RECONCILIATION between BRITANIA and her daughter AMERICA,

The CAPTIVE PRINCE — or — LIBERTY run MAD.

THE SAINTS: THE LAST VICTORY

If Yorktown had been the final act of the long drawn-out drama, the epilogue (fortunately for Britain) was still to come. When he had done all he could usefully do on the Chesapeake, De Grasse gathered every ship in American waters and returned to the West Indies to mop up. By the end of November St. Eustatius had fallen yet again. The tiny island of St. Kitts—in spite of Hood's timely arrival and smart manoeuvring—surrendered to sheer weight of numbers. Jamaica waited only on the arrival of De Guichen's reinforcements (which had received an expensive setback at the hands of Rear-Admiral Kempenfelt on December 12). While De Guichen was refitting his broken ships in Brest, British dockyards embarked on a last, intense war-effort in an attempt to win the race across the Atlantic.

By the middle of January 1782 there were twelve ships-of-the-line ready in Portsmouth to sail with Rodney (whose bladder, meanwhile, had also been pronounced ship-shape). He arrived at Barbados five weeks later, giving himself—and the largest British fleet seen in the West Indies for many years—three weeks to prepare a warm reception for De Guichen. In the event the French admiral eluded all observation and slipped into Martinique safely to join De Grasse. 'I have really fretted myself ill,' wrote Hood to Sandwich, but less out of chagrin at missing the French as pique at being relegated to second-in-command. But sooner or later the two mighty fleets were bound to come into collision and settle the disputed ownership once and for all.

They did so on the morning of April 12, near a group of otherwise undistinguished islands known as The Saints. If De Grasse was expecting a traditional, arms-length engagement ('piff-paff from one side to another' as one of his countrymen contemptuously put it) in which he could mutilate the British masts and slow down pursuit, he was in for a shock. Rodney sailed straight into the French line and cut it at three points. This tactic, far ahead of its time, so utterly demoralized the enemy that by nightfall they had surrendered five of their ships, including De Grasse's own flagship. That evening the French fleet lay at the mercy of the British, as Rodney's second-in-command was not slow to point out afterwards. But Sir George concluded enough of a victory had been won, and was later able to justify his decision by the almost total disintegration of the French presence in the Caribbean seas.

BELOW

Rodney introducing De Grasse. *Gillray: A print in the same series as the Gillray above. Rodney lays the French admiral's sword at the feet of the King. His new ministers, Fox (Secretary of State) and Keppel (First Lord of the Admiralty) stand on either side. It is an uncomfortable moment for them both: Keppel recalls as he reads of the capture of De Grasse's flagship that 'this is the very ship I ought to have taken on the 27th of July' (at Ushant); Fox mutters that 'this fellow fights too well for us and I have obligations to Pigot'. Pigot's enormous losses to Fox at the faro bank at their club, Brookes's, were the talk of the town. It was rumoured that the only way Fox could hope to obtain repayment was by appointing his debtor to a lucrative post and getting the money back in instalments.*

TOP RIGHT

St. George and the Dragon. *Gillray: Before St. George (Rodney) can make a final end to the French dragon, Fox runs up to him holding out a peerage and begging him to stop. The embarrassing fact was that before news of Rodney's victory reached England the Rockingham–Fox administration had come to power and had relieved the Admiral of his command in favour of one of their own protégés, Admiral Pigot. They were too late to stop Pigot sailing to take up his new command and gave Lord Sandwich the pleasure of writing in glee to Rodney: 'I believe those who have done it repent most heartily of the measure, but they know not how to retract'.*

BOTTOM RIGHT

Rodney's New Invented Turn About. *Anon: The little admiral's whipping of the French fleet certainly strengthened Britain's hand in the negotiations even then under way in Paris (this print was not published until July 1782). Trincomalee—see the comment beneath the Dutchman's feet—had been captured by Admiral Hughes in January.*

St GEORGE & the Dragon.

The Little Admiral giving the Enemy's of Great Britain
a Flagellation

May 1782

THE NEGOTIATIONS IN PARIS

From the moment he took office Lord Shelburne must have known he was on a hiding to nothing. Not only was he attempting to conclude on humiliating terms a war he had not begun, he was also having to do it without the support (indeed, as it turned out, in spite of) the two most powerful factions in Parliament, Lord North's army of courtiers and Fox's corps of radicals. Nevertheless the peace negotiations meandered on through the summer and into autumn, with only an occasional caustic reference from the King to the disastrous debate on February 27 and the urgency it had generated for a speedy settlement. Despite the loss of Minorca to the Spanish in February, Shelburne's hand at the table had been immeasurably strengthened by Rodney's efforts at The Saints and it was to be dealt a trump in October when Lord Howe succeeded in relieving the garrison which had been under siege at Gibraltar since June 1779. As the negotiations spun out, so Britain's fortunes against her European enemies seemed to improve—and the easier it became to drive a wedge between the Americans and their allies.

Congress's peace commissioners, Franklin, John Jay and John Adams, had been appointed in June 1781, and Franklin and Adams at least had been around the embassies of Europe long enough to be well versed in the ways of western diplomacy. They, too, appreciated the advantages of a separate treaty with Britain. It ran contrary to all their instructions from Congress, to confide at all times in the French Ministers and to arrange nothing without their consent, but their mistrust of Spain was well-founded. Charles III might have been an ally but he was no friend of the Americans, and now he was laying claim not just to the Floridas but to vast tracts in the interior of America as well, even to deny the Americans the use of the lower reaches of the Mississippi. When the commissioners rejected this ungrateful claim, he merely suggested another method of containing American expansion by giving Spain control over Indian territories as far north as the Cumberland River, and Britain con-

trol as far south as the Ohio. It was unthinkable—and all the more disturbing to find France reinforcing her Bourbon brother. Come to that, now that the fighting was over, even Vergennes didn't seem to have his old enthusiasm for the idea of independence.

So the Americans went their own conspiratorial way. When, in the middle of September they heard that Shelburne had persuaded his colleagues to recognize (if not to formally proclaim) the colonies' independence, they quickly conceded that Canada was to remain in the Empire and that the British would have access to the Mississippi, and that debts would be honoured. None the less they had their independence and their western boundaries recognized to the best of their satisfaction. A preliminary treaty was signed on November 30, one which however cynically they might have viewed its chances of success (and there were many who believed it only a matter of time before the Americans would lapse into anarchy) no British politician could reasonably complain of.

But complaints there were. Fox, insisting that independence should have been granted irrespective of a peace, used the terms as a lever to dislodge Shelburne. To Pitt, prevailed upon to conciliate, Fox intimated that 'nothing would induce him to work with Shelburne'. To which Pitt replied briefly and conclusively that 'he had not come to betray Shelburne'. Fox was driven to desperate measures; he wooed and won the support of the man who for the last decade had monopolized every ounce of his invective, Lord North himself. This marriage of outcasts shocked even some of their own supporters, but as a destructive influence it was unstoppable. Shelburne's majorities evaporated during February 1783 and on the 24th he threw in the towel, ten days after declaring that his country had officially ceased all hostilities.

TOP RIGHT
The Habeas Corpus, or The Wild Geese flying away with Fox to America. *Anon: Fox's defection from Shelburne's Ministry was accompanied by a torrent of abusive prints against him—surprisingly since the Ministry itself was far from popular. His constant and uncompromising*

support of virtually all the American claims is reflected in this example, where a flight of geese cart him off to 'his dear Independent Congress' observing that that is where he really belongs and speculating whether or not to dump him in the Atlantic en route.

BOTTOM RIGHT
The State Cooks making Peace ----- Porridge. *Anon: In this print the Ministry are eager to serve up generous helpings of peace, but their gruel appears not to be to the taste of the allies. America will have none of it 'without my friends like it' and Spain (far right) 'will not taste a drop till I have taken Gibraltar'—the major stumbling-block to progress at this time. Fox (with a fox's head) is the only one of the ministers readily identifiable, but he is probably handing the bowl to Conway (in military uniform). The general tenor of their remarks is towards offering their customers 'more pepper of Rodney' or a 'few forcemeat balls'.*

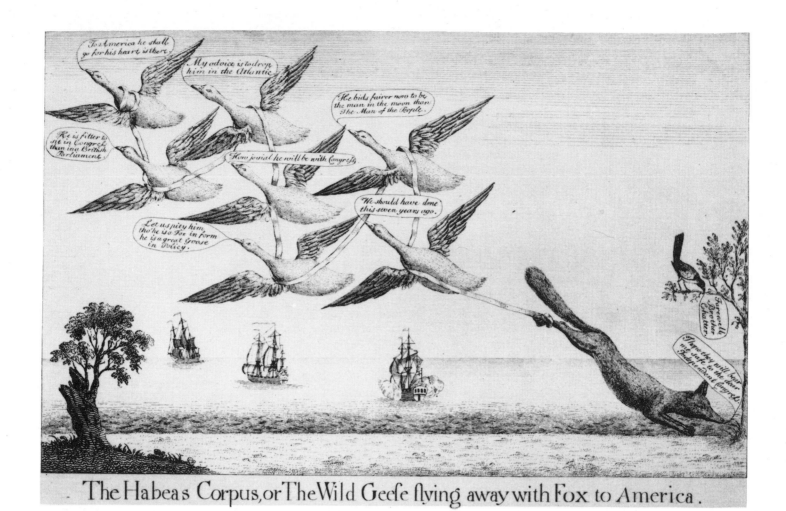

The Habeas Corpus, or The Wild Geese flying away with Fox to America.

THE STATE COOKS MAKING PEACE ———— PORRIDGE.

The State Cooks a making Peace ——Porridge are found   Ah! what can the Cooks do in such a hard case?
Which they hand to our different Enimies round.   If such folks will not eat tho' F_x has said grace.
But they all seem averse, and will not hear Reason   Why give them what obstinate Children deserve
And swear that it wants more Ingredients & Season.   Beat them well, & if they wont eat it then let em Starve.

Pub.d July 6.th 1782 by E. Hedges N.º g Cornhill.

THE NEGOTIATIONS IN PARIS (continued)

TOP RIGHT

The Belligerent Plenipos. *Colley: Published at the time of (or soon after) the signing of the preliminary peace treaty with America, this print depicts an American delighted with her new acquisition but the rest of her crippled allies bawling for their unrequited demands. The King (left) implies that he has granted independence also to various parts of his enemies' anatomies, which lie at his feet. In vain the King of France demands Canada and Grenada as compensation for his mutilated arm, a Dutchman 'insists on St. Eustatius and Ceylon for his leg', a Spaniard stamps his wooden leg in frustration for Gibraltar. The inclusion of a rather sub-angelic Ireland (top) is a reference to Henry Grattan's renewed demands for constitutional freedom for his country. In April he had published an Irish Declaration of Rights; the following month Fox had obliged by having the Ireland Act repealed and granting an independent legislature.*

BOTTOM RIGHT

The American Rattlesnake presenting Monsieur his Ally a Dish of Frogs. *Anon: In the now familiar guise of a snake (see page 157) America is seen fawningly offering a Frenchman a basket of frogs (grenouilles, frogs' legs were and still are a great French delicacy). This print was produced early in November 1782, when separate peace negotiations between Richard Oswald, the British representative, and the American commissioners were at a crucial stage. Deeply suspicious of French motives, Franklin neglected to inform Vergennes of the progress of the negotiations (though the French Minister could have been unaware of very little that was going on in his capital). Yet the Americans had pressing reasons not to alienate their ally; Congress and the vast majority of their countrymen were sincerely grateful to France —and anyway Franklin still hoped to borrow a large sum of money from her to help the new republic pay its way. Meanwhile the Ministry in England was doing all it could to disengage the allies and to exploit any differences of opinion—though not at the risk of reopening hostilities in America (as the accompanying verse heroically advocates).*

THIS PAGE

Blessed are the Peacemakers. *Anon: On the very day Shelburne resigned following a vote of censure on the peace preliminaries this print appeared in the shops (February 24); the final brick in the edifice of odium which had been growing for months against the First Minister. France and Spain lead the King in a halter to a church inscribed Inquisition. Shelburne, clutching the text of the peace preliminaries, is made out to be a complacent accomplice though no doubt spurred on by the flailing thongs of America (who in turn has a churlish Holland in tow). The royal insignia tumble from their already rickety platform. In reality the King was of the opinion that the activities of North and Fox in opposition presented a far greater threat to crown and country than any shortcomings in the peace treaty: 'I am sorry,' he wrote 'it has been my lot to reign in the most profligate age, and when the most unnatural coalition seems to have taken place, which can but add confusion and distraction among a too much divided nation'.*

Blessed are the PEACE MAKERS

THE LOYALISTS IN DEFEAT

Seven humiliating years of war had done little to justify the loyalty to King George of those stout Tories who had refused to be driven into exile by the persecutions of 1774. Those who had taken up arms in the royal cause had been hunted down and meted out harsh and summary punishment at the hands of the patriots. Those who had sought the protection of the King's army had been ingloriously hustled out of Boston, out of Newport and Philadelphia in ignominious evacuation. Even when their safety was temporarily assured, as in New York, their property and their dignity had been cruelly abused; in times of crisis it was *their* food and *their* timber which had been requisitioned first to fill British (and German) bellies and warm their feet. There were few who had not been ruined, quite literally, by the war. For them the conclusion of peace was not the end of the war. In some states it took many years for punitive laws to be erased from the statute books —and even longer for memories to be wiped as clean. It had been written into the peace treaty that Congress should make earnest efforts to persuade its component states not be exact vengeance on the loyalists, but only the most insensitive of them would not have realized that a piece of paper does not change men's hearts.

When Carleton and the last of his troops left New York 30,000 loyalists (at least, it is estimated) left with him. Some went to join other expatriates in Canada—and in doing so helped to neutralize French influence in that province and strengthen its links with Britain. Others fled to Britain to form themselves into that saddest of all social groupings—the emigré communities which exist at best on sufferance. For though official sympathy was ungrudgingly extended to the exiles—in the form of pensions amounting to several millions of pounds—the colonists found they had little in common with the country whose Empire they had struggled and suffered to preserve. Almost as if they had had to learn a new language, it took several generations for these families to be assimilated into the 'British way of life'. Those who eventually returned to their homeland, as some did, returned to a life very much less comfortable than the one they had known. The loyalists may be said to have been the real losers in the War of Independence; the patriots won their freedom; Britain turned to conquer a new Empire. The loyalists lost everything.

BELOW

Shelb--ns Sacrifice. *Anon: Britannia (right) is seen about to plunge her spear into the neck of a complaisant Lord Shelburne in this print published February 1783 on the eve of the official ending of hostilities. Her wrath is occasioned by the First Minister's presumed indifference to the fate of the loyalists left in America.* Whatever *the distress (or lack of it) felt in London for the Tories, their situation is clearly here being used as a convenient stick to beat the Premier— whose peace negotiations were inevitably going to become more unpopular with the passage of time. A real appeal to the emotions is made by the appearance of the Duke of Cumberland (centre, back), nicknamed 'the butcher' for his vicious reprisals on the Scottish clans after the battle of Culloden which brought the Jacobite rising of 1745 to an end.*

TOP RIGHT

The Tory's Day of Judgement. *Tisdale: This engraving, in fact, appeared as an illustration to Trumbull's poem 'M'Fingal' in 1795, but for sheer explicitness it deserves inclusion here. The term 'lynching' (which did not originally carry the connotation of an arbitrary execution) almost certainly derives from the punishment dealt out to Tories during the War of Independence. The originator of lynch law is traditionally assumed to be one Captain William Lynch of Pittsylvania, Virginia, in or around 1776.*

BOTTOM RIGHT

The Savages let loose, or the Cruel Fate of the Loyalists. *Anon: Like the previous example, pure propaganda. Far from 'recommending' such treatment to Congress, Shelburne had tried to prevent it. There is no evidence that such violent recriminations took place, nor that Indians were turned against their former allies, the Tories (unlikely in any event). It is, however, conceivable that this idea was inspired by the exaggerated talk of arriving exiles, who may quite genuinely have expected no less a fate.*

POSTSCRIPT

The Peace of Paris was finally signed on September 3 1783, and Britain began the sorry task of evacuating the remnants of her troops under Carleton out of the United States. Gracelessly the King signed the warrant for the Proclamation of Peace. 'I have no objection to that ceremony being performed on Tuesday,' he wrote to Lord North. 'Indeed I am glad it is on a day I am not in Town, as I think this completes the downfall of the lustre of this Empire . . . and feel I am innocent of the evils that have occurred, though deeply wounded that it should have happened during my reign.' He was equally wounded by North's apostasy to the infamous coalition with his arch-enemy, Fox. For the time being he tolerated it—there was no option—but he looked for any opportunity to contrive its downfall. His chance came in December when Fox's India Bill was defeated in the Lords; the following day he sacked the reprobate Ministry. In its place he found William Pitt, 24 years old and with almost no following in Parliament. Yet Pitt went on to win decisively in the general election in March, and except for one short interval remained in office for the rest of his life. His life's work was to lay the foundations of a new Empire for Britain.

The King was not alone in his bitterness against the ex-colonists, nor in his belief that in time they would return to the fold to escape the anarchy which was bound to prevail. Britain did not deign to send an ambassador to America until 1790, though Congress had sent no less a personage than John Adams to the Court of St. James. With the conspicuous exceptions of France and Holland few European nations were inclined to take the infant republic seriously. And indeed Congress proved inadequate to provide the strong central government which the thirteen individual states (with which the peace treaty had been signed) needed but none wanted. Under the Articles of Confederation (finally ratified in 1781) it occupied a decidedly inferior position. Without the consent of a majority of states it had no power to issue money, make war or alliances. Neither did it have the power to tax, and it was chronically short of money.

Severe depression followed on the heels of war. For want of money the embryo navy had to be disbanded. For lack of pay there had been growing restlessness in the Continental army; early in 1783 a delegation of officers had lobbied Congress and was put off. In March, but for the timely intervention of Washington himself, there might even have been a mutiny. Nor did peace bring instant prosperity to the nation's trade. Gone were the concessions and bounties for the planters of the south. In the West Indies all British ports were closed to American ships; in the Mediterranean Barbary pirates made every commercial venture almost an act of foolhardiness. Requisitions from individual states were frequently fulfilled only with reluctance, sometimes not at all. The 'firm league of friendship' for the states' mutual welfare (embodied in the Articles) did not always seem to embrace mutual tolerance on the questions of state frontiers or tariffs. Nor was there any way of persuading Britain to relinquish her fur posts until debts to British merchants were paid (some of them remained unpaid decades later).

There were formidable problems indeed. But other problems, of a different kind, had been formidable in 1775 and had been overcome by the same men who now faced these. Then they had been rebels faced with the choice between 'death or liberty'. Now they were, as Washington declared at the emotional ceremony at Annapolis, where he resigned his commission before Congress, free citizens faced with the 'opportunity of becoming a respectable nation'. How they overcame these problems is another—equally great—story.

RIGHT

Proclamation of Peace. *Anon: A month after the signing of the Paris Treaty (September 3) peace was officially proclaimed by heralds in the City, less ethereal no doubt than the lady in this print. America has thrown off its chains and exults with tomahawk and staff of liberty. France (second left) has his hand in Spain's and is attempting to console his ally with the glittering prospect of the tobacco trade with America. Spain for his part, having failed to regain Gibraltar, is only too ready to 'cry for peace'. Next to him, an Englishman is still engaged in a set-to with a Dutchman (right), gripping him by the throat and warning him that he would 'never know the taste of spice again' if he did not make peace too (hostilities were continuing in the East Indies; a separate peace with Holland was concluded in 1784). The last two lines of the verse caption reflect the widely-held view in Britain that eventually nemesis would fall upon the ex-colonists for their hubris in defying the mother-country.*

PROCLAMATION of PEACE

Peace! Peace! crys Monsieur, before Hood again calls:
Spain Welcomes the sound, dreading Eliotts hot Balls:
Return but my Gelt, Holland roars out in fear,
I too, will make peace: Indeed! will you Myneer?

Aye Sink me you shall, and for you, Misre
The time may yet come, to repent of your

POSTSCRIPT (continued)

BELOW

Original Air Balloon. *Anon; An unmistakable taste of sour grapes and cynicism pervades this print, one of the last of the revolutionary satires to appear in the print-shops (December 29). The balloon America has been cut loose from its mooring by a buccaneering Franklin (3), who at last has taken off his mask and revealed himself. Chained together by their family compact Spain and France (1 & 2), and Holland (4) watch the ascent covetously. The American soil on which they stand is now 'to be lett on Fighting Leases'—the implication being that it will once again become a battle-ground for imperial powers to win territory. Across the water the coalition of Fox (5) and North (7) dances to the music of the devil, while the soldiers of Howe, Clinton and Burgoyne are ground down beneath oppressive taxes. The passengers in the balloon are the most peculiar duo of George Washington (10) and Silas Deane (9) respectively under the baleful influence of Cromwell (11, brandishing reminders of what he did to the monarch) and John the Painter (12, clutching a gibbet). This last is a reference to an otherwise uncelebrated series of incidents in 1776–7. John the Painter (James Aitken) was a saboteur executed in March 1777. In December 1776 he had set fire to a building in Portsmouth dockyard and a warehouse in Bristol the following month. Intent, apparently, on destroying British trade he had put forward his plan to Silas Deane, then in Paris as one of Congress's commissioners, and had obtained a false French passport. This print was inspired (like so many others in the fall of 1783) by the ballooning experiments of the Montgolfier brothers during that year.*

TOP RIGHT

The Blessings of Peace. *Anon: Here, in April 1783, are many of the heroes and villains of the war gathered together in one glorious retrospective tableau. On the left, America is crowned by Franklin (1) as she sits on the laps of France and Spain. A puppy dog (probably Holland) meanwhile watches the recriminations of British politicians across the water. In the centre of it all stands the King (9) asking what he should do. From Fox (left, 4) he gets the answer 'Peace on any terms'. Next to him Richmond (5) who had been made Master of Ordnance in the new Ministry is priding himself on his petty economies. Shelburne (6) disclaims responsibility for the 'ruinous state' of the country. Burke (7) continues to advise the King to economize—but nearest to the King, Thurlow and Mansfield (8 & 10), are for once in disagreement: the first says, most strangely for him, 'follow the voice of the people', the other claims 'he can do no wrong'. Lord North (12) actually admits the error of his ways. Pitt (13) is conducting a private vendetta with Sheridan (11, a prominent Opposition member whom Pitt had accused of theatricality in a recent debate). Keppel (15) still broods on the battle of Ushant, and receives little comfort from his colleague Dunning (16). To Lord Amherst (17) has fallen the unpleasant duty of informing the war veterans that the government has 'no further use for you'. In the background a riot is in progress and a soldier fires on a fleeing man—a reference to the naval mutiny at Portsmouth in March 1783, which had been successfully put down by Lord Howe. England's imperial sun sets (for the first time), while a witch on her broomstick flies off with peace trailing from her petticoats.*

BOTTOM RIGHT

Mrs. General Washington Bestowing thirteen stripes on Britannia. *Anon: This peculiar design from the Ramblers Magazine of March 1783 has the dubious distinction of presenting Washington in an exceptionally hostile fashion. Its excuse, so the accompanying text explains, was a scurrilous report currently going the rounds that the Commander-in-Chief was in fact a woman.*

POSTSCRIPT (continued)

THIS PAGE
Britannia Roused, or the Coalition Monster destroyed. *Rowlandson: Fox (top) and North are hurled to the ground by an angry Britannia. Their coalition ministry (under the nominal leadership of the Duke of Portland) was dismissed by the King on December 17 1783 after (it is said) he had persuaded the House of Lords not to vote for Fox's India Bill. This personal intervention by the King into the affairs of Parliament caused an uproar, but as an act of political revenge it was entirely successful.*

TOP RIGHT
The Tea-tax-tempest, or Old Time with his Magick-Lanthern. *Anon: America (left) and a sombre Britannia are treated to a slide-show of the American Revolution. Father Time, reclining on a globe, gives a running commentary, pointing out all the momentous events of the past few years: the exploding tea-pot (the Boston Tea Party), the French Cock fanning the flames, the Stamped paper helping the pot to boil, redcoats on the run from the American army . . . and so on. The magic-lantern theme was a favourite with the more didactic cartoonists; this particular print is an up-dated version of a similar one which had appeared in 1778.*

BOTTOM RIGHT
The House that Jack built. *Anon: This retrospective parade of policies and politicians appeared (April 25 1785) a week after Pitt's motion for the reform of Parliament had been defeated. It recalls all the folly, bombast and corruption recent parliaments had exhibited over the Irish and American crises, and the consequent drain on the nation's resources (the house that Jack built). From right to left it illustrates a parody of the famous nursery rhyme: This is the cock that crowed in the morn (Burke), and waked the priest all shaven and shorn (Charles Jenkinson, former Minister of War) that married the man all tattered and torn (Shelburne) that kissed the maiden all forlorn (Ireland), that milked the cow with the crumpled horn (William Pitt) that tossed the dog (Charles Fox) that worried the cat (America) that killed the rat (Lord North) that ate the malt (The Treasury) that lay in the house that Jack built.*

BRITTANNIA ROUSED, OR THE COALITION MONSTERS DESTROYED

The TEA-TAX-TEMPEST. or OLD TIME with his MAGICK=LANTHERN.

Pub.ᵈ March 12 1783. by W. Humphrey, N.º 227 Strand.

12. Mar. 1783

Veluti in Speculum. *Anon: And in the end, the reckoning. The devil invites the British commanders to examine themselves (and their conduct) in a mirror. To the front stands Lord Amherst, who had filled the role of chief military adviser to the Ministry during the latest stages of the war. Behind him is probably General Murray who had surrendered Minorca to the Spanish in February 1782 (as the map of Fort St. Philip on the wall emphasizes). He had been charged with misconduct, but acquitted on almost all counts. Behind him, in profile, is General Howe. The diminutive officer with the riding crop is probably Tarleton, but who the others are is pure speculation (Dorothy George suggests they might be Cornwallis, Clinton and Howe—and why not?).*

Selected Bibliography

For published sources (of which there are very few) specifically on the graphic satire of the period, I have gone to Clarence Brigham's *Complete Engravings of Paul Revere*, R. T. H. Halsey's *The Boston Port Bill As Pictured By A Contemporary London Cartoonist*, and his exhibition catalogue for the New York Public Library *Impolitical Prints*, to the first volume of M. Dorothy George's *English Political Caricature* and her invaluable catalogue of Prints in the British Museum, and to the first volume of William Murrell's *American Graphic Humor*.

For the general background to the Revolution I have relied heavily on John R. Alden's *The American Revolution*, L. H. Gipson's *The Coming of the American Revolution*, Bernhard Knollenberg's *Origin of the American Revolution*, and all six volumes of G. O. Trevelyan's *American Revolution*. Of the more detailed studies of particular aspects of the revolution, I ought to single out Arthur M. Schlesinger's *Prelude to Independence*, Ian R. Christie's *The End of North's Ministry*, Sir Lewis Namier's *England in the Age of the American Revolution*, Bernard Donaghue's *British Politics and the American Revolution* and John Brooke's *The Chatham Administration*.

For eyewitness and contemporary accounts Hugh Rankin's *The American Revolution* and the book he edited with George F. Scheer, *Rebels and Redcoats*, have proved invaluable. So have the two volumes of *Horace Walpole's Last Journals*, S. E. Morison's *Sources and Documents illustrating the American Revolution*, Bonamy Dobree's edition of *The letters of King George III*, and the loyalist account *Peter Oliver's Origin and Progress of the American Revolution* edited by Douglas Adair and John A. Schutz.

I greatly appreciated two general discussions of the Revolution: Esmond Wright's *Fabric of Freedom* and Ian R. Christie's *Crisis of Empire*. Studies of individual participants are too numerous to mention, but can all be found in the excellent bibliography in J. R. Alden's *The American Revolution*.

Index